I0124675

Teaching After Witnessing a School Shooting

This book is part of the Peter Lang Education list.
Every volume is peer reviewed and meets
the highest quality standards for content and production.

PETER LANG
New York • Bern • Berlin
Brussels • Vienna • Oxford • Warsaw

Edward Mooney, Jr.

Teaching After Witnessing a School Shooting

Echoes of Gunfire

PETER LANG

New York • Bern • Berlin

Brussels • Vienna • Oxford • Warsaw

Library of Congress Cataloging-in-Publication Data

Names: Mooney, Edward, Jr. author.
Title: Teaching after witnessing a school shooting: echoes of gunfire /
Edward Mooney, Jr.
Description: New York: Peter Lang, 2021.
Includes bibliographical references and index.
Identifiers: LCCN 2020054197 (print) | LCCN 2020054198 (ebook)
ISBN 978-1-4331-8506-9 (paperback) | ISBN 978-1-4331-8507-6 (ebook pdf)
ISBN 978-1-4331-8508-3 (epub) | ISBN 978-1-4331-8509-0 (mobi)
Subjects: LCSH: School shootings—Psychological aspects. |
Teachers—Psychology. | Teaching—Psychological aspects.
Classification: LCC LB3013.3 .M665 2021 (print) | LCC LB3013.3 (ebook) |
DDC 370.15—dc23
LC record available at https://lccn.loc.gov/2020054197
LC ebook record available at https://lccn.loc.gov/2020054198
DOI 10.3726/b17954

Bibliographic information published by **Die Deutsche Nationalbibliothek**.
Die Deutsche Nationalbibliothek lists this publication in the
"DeutscheNationalbibliografie"; detailed bibliographic data are available
on the Internet at http://dnb.d-nb.de/.

© 2021 Peter Lang Publishing, Inc., New York
80 Broad Street, 5th floor, New York, NY 10004
www.peterlang.com

All rights reserved.
Reprint or reproduction, even partially, in all forms such as microfilm,
xerography, microfiche, microcard, and offset strictly prohibited.

For Saugus High School, Saugus, California
November 14, 2019

Dedicated to my grandson
Adam Eichensher, SHS Class of 2022

"To reach a mind, first reach a heart."

—Edward Mooney, Jr.

CONTENTS

LIST OF FIGURES

AUTHOR'S NOTE

So, why did I write this book? Some readers may wonder about that – and guess at my motivations. So, right up front, I'll spell it out. My hope is that everyone who reads this will be prepared to assist future teachers who will witness a school shooting, even if that means only to understand and empathize. It is my hope that this will not be necessary – that society will find a solution to this bane on our way of life – but I want us to be prepared in case that time is in the distant future.

The source material serving as the foundation of this book comes from my dissertation, which earned me, along with the requisite coursework, the degree of Doctor of Education from Northeastern University in Boston. As you'll discover, I spoke to a number of teachers who had to experience a shooting. I realized that the general public needs to understand what they deal with – for years after the incident.

I was asked to re-work that paper, creating a book for the general public outlining the effects of teachers witnessing a school shooting. I was immediately confronted with the difficult task of "translating" an academic paper into a readable "story," if you will. I struggled for some time to find a system that would allow the story to "flow."

One day, as I was wrestling with yet another framework, I received a phone call asking about some aspect of school shootings. I've handled quite a number of those over the years. After answering, and as I hung up, an idea came to mind. I saw that conversation as an entryway that would allow me to craft the narrative – I would be having a conversation with the reader, as I had just done over the phone. So, as you read, imagine that you and I are having a discussion about this topic – and I'm answering your questions.

Janice is a composite of a number of people I've spoken with over the years, and not a real person. She serves a valuable purpose as a guide to understanding this research. As I worked through the manuscript, I found myself recalling quite a number of phone calls and email messages – on all aspects of my research, from a variety of sources. I made the decision, for clarity, to combine many of these messages and calls into one conversation. So, while the material in this book is based on research, the frame around it, that of a conversation with one person, is a construct designed to move the reader between sections of the work.

Beyond the effects of witnessing a school shooting, it's also my hope that the reader can gain some insight into how a dissertation is prepared, and the work behind the final document. How this research came to be was, in itself, quite a story.

PREFACE: HOW TO READ THIS BOOK

While this work has been designed to read straight through, with a back-ground narrative – a plot, if you will – the book has also been designed to serve as a reference, of sorts. Each chapter, or "question," can serve as a source of material for discussion or further research. At the end of the main text, there is a listing of suggested readings, taken form the dissertation.

In addition, it was the intention of the author to maintain a feeling of a dissertation in this work, in order for those who teach research methodologies to connect the methodology to the realities of the research journey. In a way, Janice's questions were also the questions the author dealt with while teaching such a course. It's hoped that this "interweaving" of a story-like dialog with actual text from a research project will allow those on their own projects to elate to the struggle behind accomplishing this sort of thing.

ACKNOWLEDGEMENTS

I believe it is important that the reader knows that there were many emotionally challenging days as I completed the research that serves as the foundation of this book. The overwhelming struggles that the teachers I interviewed wrestled with reverberated within me. As difficult as it was for me to hear their painful stories, as I struggled with a lesser trauma, I came to realize that these professionals are carrying a burden far more difficult. I acknowledge all teachers who are forced to witness a school shooting. I wrote this book because I believe your stories need to be heard. I acknowledge how much your sharing was difficult, yet you felt the sharing was worth it, if it could help others.

Working with me, through those difficult days, were a number of people who encouraged, believed, and assisted in so many ways. I want to acknowledge my committee members and professors at Northeastern University in Boston: Doctors Krystal Clemons, Lynda Beltz, Ray McCarthy, Jennifer O'Connor, Karen Reiss Medwed, Margaret Dougherty, Claire Jackson, and, from the University of Portland, Jacqueline Waggoner. One person in particular provided great emotional encouragement – and editing: Caroline Houtz Mooney. She was there for me through it all.

The threads of all of the insight, encouragement and support from these people are woven into the lines and pages of this book. Thank you.

ABOUT THE AUTHOR

After more than a quarter of a century of service as a high school teacher, Edward Mooney, Ed.D., moved to working as a professor of teacher education. His specialties include educational psychology, instructional methods, research methods and online teaching; in addition, he has supervised a number of student teachers in his newest role. As of this writing, he teaches online at Chadron State College, in Chadron, Nebraska.

As the reader will discover, Edward grew up as an "at-risk" student. Over the years of his childhood, his father descended into the depths of alcoholism, and became abusive, physically and emotionally. A few teachers in high school gave him direction and support, well beyond the curriculum, and awakened him to the power of teachers to change lives.

As he went through college, at Montana State University (B.S.), and the University of California, Riverside (M.A.), he found himself with a number of opportunities to teach a seminar or a class. After those years, he worked as a teacher of computers for Digital Equipment Corporation, where he truly realized how much teaching meant to him. He signed up for night classes and earned his teaching licenses (secondary science and social studies, and multiple subjects) at Chapman University.

Edward has an assortment of outside interests, including vexillology (the study of flags), creative writing, gardening, collecting maps, and camping. He enjoys world cultures, languages, and the study of geology. One of his greatest joys is his family – he's very proud of his five children and six grandchildren.

INTRODUCTION

For the last two years, I've been searching for an old friend – her name is Melissa. I tried every method possible, short of hiring a private detective. I made numerous phone calls, and sent dozens of email messages. I searched online. I even pulled out my old research notes, and found the list of people that I had worked with during my project. I sent messages via social media, such as Facebook – but I got no responses. It didn't seem possible that I couldn't find anyone who knew how to contact her. I was perplexed.

In despair, I closed the research folder on my computer. I felt like I was at a dead end. The phone range as I was staring at the papers outlining a book on witnessing school shootings.

I felt some hope when I heard the name of my caller – she was a teacher who had been at the school where Michelle taught – on that fateful day. I had spoken to her once. Janice sounded the same. I told her I wanted to re-connect with Melissa, as I knew a difficult anniversary was coming – it had been ten years since she witnessed the shooting at her school. I wanted to see how she was doing.

Janice informed me that she didn't know where she was, but she'd try to get a message to her, with my contact information. After a pause, I had to ask the question.

"You don't know where she is? I remember you two were pretty close."

"I'm sorry, but I don't," she replied. There was another moment of silence.

"Oh . . ." I was at a loss for words.

"Things changed a lot since you did your research, and not for the better for her," she continued.

"I'm really sorry to hear that . . ." I trailed off as I struggled with a strong sense of sadness. An uncomfortable silence followed as I looked up at the top of the wall and tried to think of something to say. Fortunately, Janice spoke up.

"Here, I have a pen and some paper. Why don't you give me your email address and phone number? Well, I have your number."

I gave her my contact information, and was thanking her as I lowered the phone to the receiver. I heard a muffled sound from the phone, and brought it back to my ear.

"Janice?" I asked quietly.

"Yeah . . . I uh . . . well . . ." Her voiced faded.

"Are you okay?" Concern welled up inside.

"I guess. I don't know."

"What's going on? I'm listening."

"Talking with you voice brought back memories." Janice's voice seemed to have more emotion in it.

"I'm sorry. I didn't want that. I don't . . ." I felt a bit low.

"No, no. Really, it's okay. Maybe it's a good thing that I called. So much has changed since that day years ago. It isn't good." Janice interrupted me.

"I'm sorry to hear that." I bit my lower lip – I was using the word "sorry" too much.

"As you may know, she's divorced now." Janice paused.

"No, I didn't know. That must have been hard." I broke the silence.

"Uh-huh, it was rough. The family is still trying to dig out from under the mess."

"What about her kids? Does her husband get to see them much? Have they worked that out?"

"He sees them all the time. He has full custody. She rarely sees them – last I heard." A long silence filled the air.

"Oh . . . I see . . ." I wasn't sure what to say. I squirmed in my seat, feeling uncomfortable. I took a deep breath.

"Yeah," Janice answered in a quiet voice. More silence followed.

"I appreciate you letting me know. At least I have a bigger picture of where she is now."

"It's just, well, it's hard to talk about. The emotions are still raw, even for me. Some days are better than others."

"Oh, I understand . . ." I started. I was taking a stab at conversation, not sure which way to go.

"Do you?" Janice asked. She sounded a bit testy.

"A little bit. I know it's easy to say one understands, but I was shot at when I was a high school teacher, a long time ago."

"Oh, I guess you would understand."

"Well, not totally, but a bit. No one died or was hit where I was, and that's a huge difference." I took another deep breath,

"I can imagine," Janice answered.

"Sorry, but this is really hard for me to wrap my mind around, Janice. The kids are so important to her. That would be hard on her."

"I'm sure it still is. But the judge thought it was best for the kids. I was in court that day. That was not easy to sit through," Janice answered. I heard her sigh.

I felt concern. I had to come to know Melissa's family a little. While it was his wife's experience that I studied, her husband and kids were always there for her the whole time I was doing my work.

"It seems like yesterday that she and I were sitting in a restaurant going over what happened at her school. To be honest, I was worried about how this would affect her family, and people like you. It wasn't a part of my study, but I wondered."

"Yeah, it affected me. It's been like riding an emotional roller coaster with no seat belt, to be honest."

"Trauma does that to people," I answered.

"Yeah, I've heard that word a lot over the last ten years. Seen definitions."

"It's one thing to read about trauma, and another thing to cope with it, day-to-day, Janice. That's an animal of a different color."

"It's an animal that doesn't seem to want to leave my house, Ed."

"I worried about that. You didn't actually see the shooting, but you feel affected – still. Have you found a therapist?"

"Yeah, but I felt it was going nowhere."

"I understand that. It takes time."

"I feel like I got caught up in something I never saw coming. I feel like I'm still trying to find 'which way is up'."

"Recovering from trauma feels like that." I tried to assure her.

"But I keep coming back to one question."

"What's that?" I asked.

"How in the hell did this happen? I mean, none of us there that day had a perfect life, but I felt like a storm roared in and swept a bunch of us out to sea."

"In a way, that's exactly what happened, Janice. There was no warning, and then came gale force winds, and rain, and everything you thought would protect you fell apart."

"That's a good way of putting it. You said you went through a school shooting Did the shooting cause all of this mess Melissa and I are choking on?"

"Well, first of all, what I went through wasn't as rough as what Melissa saw. And I had different issues in my life back then. It's not as simple as that, even though I wish it was. But the shooting is definitely a huge factor – a big variable."

"Oh, like a math formula."

"Sort of, yes," I replied. "Lots of variables, like family, and our own life history. There's more."

"I get it. I think."

"My formula changed recently. It's one of the reasons I called, looking for Melissa."

"What do you mean?" Janice asked.

"My grandson was at a school shooting," I answered in a quiet voice.

"Oh, God, no . . . was he . . ."

"Oh, no, he wasn't hurt."

"But were there . . ." Janice's voice trailed off.

"Yes, a couple of kids died."

"How horrible. Ten years after what we went through, this still goes on."

"I agree. This shooting at Saugus High School was, in some ways, worse for me."

"Because your grandson was there, I guess?"

"Yes. I felt so helpless. I heard my daughter, his mother, crying on the phone, and there was nothing I could say or do."

"Wow. Even though you've been researching school shootings, you still felt this way."

"It's one thing to read about, write about it, and talk about it – and it's another thing to go through it. Trauma is like that." I responded.

"Like what?"

"Trauma leaves you feeling helpless in the face of terrible pain and danger. I felt helpless."

"Care to talk about it, Doc? I'm a school counselor." Janice asked, with a bit of teasing in her voice.

"Hah! Thanks."

"It sounds like you've been studying school shootings for a decade, but these feelings are pretty fresh."

"They are."

"I can say that a phone call while sitting in a medical waiting room changed my perspective forever. It was November 14th, 2019, and my cell phone rang. I heard my daughter, Lisa, pushing back against strong emotions, tell me that there had just been a shooting, with deaths, at Saugus High School. That's near Los Angeles, California."

"I've been to Saugus. North of San Fernando."

"Yes, that's it. I could see, in my mind's eye, Jacob and Nathan's graduation, from the school the year before. They're twins. That memory turned painful, as I realized that my other grandson, Adam, was still a student there. I struggled to speak."

"I can understand why! The fear!"

"All I could say was, 'Adam?'"

"And . . .?"

"Lisa took a deep breath and told me she had heard he was unhurt."

"Then you were able to breathe again . . ." Janice seemed to understand.

"Yes. But from that moment on I gained an unwanted new perspective on school shootings. I had seen one as a teacher; now I experienced the pain of a family touched by horror. It was in that moment that I realized I had to do what little I could to push back against the horrors of school shootings."

"So that's why you're trying to find Melissa?"

"Yes, and no. Coincidentally, I had planned on touching base with her all these years later, maybe to do another study, a follow-up. But, for some reason, my daughter's voice reminded me of the trembling, and the same dammed-up emotion behind it, that Melissa had. I needed to know how Melissa has worked through what happened – maybe that way I could help my daughter, going forward. Maybe it doesn't make any sense." I shook my head.

"It does, to me. We've all been searching for ways to heal, to move forward, since that shooting. You understand what our journey has been like all these years," Janice said quietly.

"It keeps coming back to haunt me – the specter of school shootings." I responded.

"It haunts me, too."

"In this way, our lives are intertwined. We can understand how the other one feels."

"I've noticed – many who haven't been through this sort of thing can't quite comprehend," Janice commented.

"And that is why I'm working on a book, based on my dissertation. I need to find a way to get anyone willing to listen to understand that after the news media stops covering a school shooting, it lingers with those who had to witness it, those who felt the terror. People need to know what it's like for those who survived." I looked up and noticed a photograph of my grandson. I took a deep breath.

"Please let me know how I can help. I agree completely."

"I really want to talk to Melissa. Please help me find her, Janice."

"I'll do what I can, and get her in touch with you. Hold the last chapter for her . . ."

"I will; you can count on it."

· 1 ·

A QUESTION ABOUT PERSONAL EXPERIENCE

"Being a researcher, I know you're the one who usually asks the questions, but could I ask you a few? You know, about school shootings?" Janice asked.

"Sure, and I'll see if I can answer them," I replied.

"I hope so!"

"So, what's your first question?"

"Tell me about you. Have you ever taught school?"

"Good question. I think I know why you're asking that."

"Maybe you do. I left teaching because I got tired of people who don't know anything about teaching kids telling me how I should do my job."

"I understand that, and I mean it. I understand because of personal experience. Yes, I taught high school for many years."

"You understand?"

"Yes, I do. I started my life after college as a computer programmer, and I had kids in school. I was an 'outsider,' so to speak, before I became a teacher."

"Okay, I'll give you that. You've been on both sides – a parent and a teacher. But here's a follow-up question. Do you know what it's like to be in a shooting?"

"Let me answer that with the back-story of me becoming a teacher . . ."

An Answer

So, I made a decision, in 1987, to change my profession from computer programming to teaching. After finishing my credential work, my wife and I moved our family from an urban area to a rural community about 200 miles away. With the ink on the teaching license still wet, I began service as a high school teacher.

It was a turbulent start. Early on, I questioned whether or not I had made the right choice when I changed careers, but everything seemed to smooth out, over time. I finally felt that I could connect to teens. I felt good hanging around other teachers. I had a good rapport with my principal. I got used to going to the bathroom within narrow slices of time. I went from questioning why I had disrupted my family's life to a sense of satisfaction, that we had made the right choice for our family. I felt we could settle down, and give our kids a few years in one place.

In my second year of teaching, which is right about when a teacher starts to feel comfortable with his or her role, an event during lunch changed my life, and it almost finished it. The bell ending fourth period rang, and I grabbed my sandwich, cookies and a drink, and headed out to a planter outside of my classroom. I enjoyed sitting under the large trees, in the shade, and relaxing with my students.

Of all the lunches I consumed over my decades of teaching, that one is forever etched into my memory. I remember the sandwich – cheese, lettuce, mustard and relish on wheat bread. The cookies were chocolate chip, and the drink was flavored sparkling water. The sandwich itself, as much as I appreciated my wife making it, was not what made it memorable. It was what happened as I bit into it that seared it into my brain.

A boy was sitting on my right, a girl was on my left. We were talking about the random assortment of the things that teens like to talk about when they're out of the classroom. It was not unlike the many days that I remember from my years at Foothill High School in Tustin, California. It was pleasant, and I always enjoy the taste of mustard . . .

BLAM! CRACK! I jumped, almost instinctively. Terrible noises interrupted our eating and talking. I dropped my sandwich. I can still see it falling, in slow-motion, to the lawn below. Something rained down on my head from above. Pieces of the tree behind me splattered all over my hat, pants and shirt. For some reason, I looked out toward the street, from the direction I heard the loud bang. Someone was leaning out of a pickup truck, pointing something in my direction. I saw the muzzle flash and knew it was a gun.

As soon as I realized we were being shot at, I grabbed at my students; I threw one of them behind the planter we were sitting on, and I pushed the other one to the ground. A second later, I was grabbing the tree and falling behind it myself. The bangs and cracks of the gun and the bullets hitting the tree finished just after I had hit the ground.

I carefully looked out from my shelter and got a description of the vehicle. Every teacher back then had a pen in his or her pocket; I scribbled words and part of a license plate number on my lunch bag. I then turned to my students. Both were safe – no one had been injured.

Other students ran over. The security officer ran and helped me get off of the ground. Another teacher ran toward the office.

The rest of the day became a blur. The memories are like a patchwork – bits and pieces of colors and shapes, here and there. So many things are lost to me. I know people spoke to me, but I can't remember who they were. I remember, at times, finding it hard to breathe. I don't know who brought me a diet soda.

But I do remember sitting in the conference room with a police officer. I remember hearing that the two students were unhurt. I remember being afraid of calling my wife, to tell her about it. I remember my principal, Larry Yeghoian, urging me, in his wonderfully calming voice, to do just that. He led me into his office and shut the door – so I could have some privacy. I remember fighting back tears as I explained to my wife what had happened – and how her cheese sandwich had been ruined.

It was difficult for me to feel safe after that. They did catch the shooter and the driver, and they found their way to jail, but I felt vulnerable from that day on.

I tried talking to people about it. They mostly shrugged and told me to "shake it off." I hadn't been hit – it was "just" a drive-by shooting, they'd say. I started having nightmares, and found myself startled by otherwise innocent sounds, such as when a neighbor dropped a heavy tool on the concrete in his garage while I was trimming some hedges about 15 feet away. I dropped to the ground quickly and was embarrassed as I lifted myself from the lawn. As I brushed myself off, I worked on an excuse I could give someone if they had seen me fall. I settled on "slipped on the wet grass" since I noticed the remains of the morning's sprinkler run. Thankfully, no one had noticed, so I didn't need the excuse.

As I look back now, that day changed many of the habits I had become comfortable with in my job. I started eating lunch inside. I felt nervous whenever I saw kids sitting on the planter where I was sitting when it happened. My wife wondered if I should transfer to another school – or move back to Orange County. We started wondering what to do – I could not feel safe.

One morning a week or two later, while driving to school along a lonely stretch of road, I began to think of the school ahead. I felt a bit of panic, so I stopped the car and got out. There, in the middle of farm fields and orchards, I looked back toward my subdivision, off in the distance. I turned around and looked at the line of trees that led toward my classroom. I got back into the car, and started it, but had a rough time deciding to go north, toward school, or south, toward home. Another car approached, from the south, slowed down, stopped and rolled down his passenger-side window. He asked if I was having trouble.

I couldn't answer him. He asked again. I cleared my throat and thanked him for stopping to ask, but I was okay. He looked at me for the longest time, then drove off. As I turned to face forward, I looked in the rear-view mirror and noticed streaks of tears on my face.

Later that day, one of our counselors came by, just to see how I was doing. She was an incredibly kind and compassionate woman, but I had a tough time admitting that the struggle within was hard on me. I told her I was "doing okay," but she stayed in front of me, staring. She asked if I was sure, and I nodded.

Since then, I've come to see that I wrestled with the same issue that many men confront – we shouldn't feel anxiety. Growing up, I was a sensitive kid, and my father always criticized me for having strong emotions. His criticism didn't change how I felt; what I actually learned from my childhood was how to mask my real feelings. Decades later, I discovered, with my wife's help, that anxiety on the inside looks like anger on the outside.

But back then, I decided that what a lot of my friends were saying was the way to go – I'd "just get over it" after a period of time. My wife was doubtful.

I taught there for three more years. By then, our daughters had grown into teens, and presented the requisite problems with that phase of life. Shortly after the birth of our son, I felt compelled to make a change. Looking back, I now see that my cup was full. Our house was too small, we were dealing with the typical problems with teens, money was tight and, to cap it all off, I felt afraid to go to school.

I left that high school, which I still love, and it took many years for me to see that needing to feel safe was a strong reason why. No, time did not allow me to simply "get over it." The desire to fit into my father's image of what a man should be – not feeling fear – pushed the feelings about the shooting deeper into the recesses of my mind. The decades since then have shown me that the trauma of the gunfire from that "simple" school shooting long ago echoes in my life today.

It wasn't long before the first "echo" happened. Almost a decade later, on Monday, April 20, 1999, two teenagers with powerful firearms invaded the halls of Columbine High School, killing 15 (including the shooters) and injuring 24 people. That is burned into my memory. I returned to the horror I had seen, albeit at a much smaller scale, and had a difficult night. All the emotions of my own experience crashed back into my present. I could hear the screams of the students from a decade before, and imagined how much more intense they must have been at Columbine.

The next day, a Tuesday, I found it very difficult to go to school. I spent most of the night tossing and turning, mostly awake, arguing with myself about calling in sick or going in. There were two arguing for me to go to school – the voice of my father, and thoughts of the students who would come to school looking for assurance. There was one emotion arguing for calling in sick – the voice of the man who was tired of being afraid at work.

Once again, my wife and I had a long talk, and I decided I had to go to school – even if little academic work would be accomplished. It was that night that I confronted the fear that had taken root while eating lunch over a decade before. I did it not only for myself, but for the young people looking to teachers for leadership. I knew that they needed someone who understood how it felt to come to school after a school shooting. I also knew there would be teachers there trying to gloss over what had happened at Columbine, and kids would feel more isolated because of them. I felt I might be able to make a difference.

I chose leadership, not fear and retreat. Leadership is shown by actions, not through words, and not through a denial of feelings that some adults might offer. My going to school was, I hoped, a sign to them. It was also a sign to myself, that it was okay to confront anxiety and that I could still be a man in spite of it. It was a chance to confront the voice my father left behind form my childhood.

As I opened my classroom door that morning, I was stunned by how few students attended on April 21st, but I understood why. I saw fewer than half of my students that day, and just a few more on the following day, April 22nd. We could accomplish little that week. I could see and hear the fear that my students wrestled with, and their pain echoed in my own heart. Once again, I could only imagine the level of horror that was affecting the students, teachers, parents, administrators, support staff, law enforcement and medical personnel at Columbine High School.

These experiences, emotions and internal struggles are the seeds of this work. Columbine made me realize how much the earlier shooting had affected me – my teaching, my relationships, and my sense of security. Columbine made me want to reach out to teachers who had also witnessed such brutality.

More than two years later, on September 11, 2001, the trauma of "Nine Eleven" invaded our schools. The looks of shock and fear on the faces of my students that week, again, remain with me. Since then, I've developed a growing awareness of the effects of trauma on students, teachers, and learning – and it's not good (just like general society). I've also come to be aware of how childhood abuse and neglect affect our ability to cope with trauma as adults.

In the decades since the shooting I lived through, I have come to see how the kindness of my principal made a huge difference for me. I've also, through research, come to understand how school leaders, families, and society handle a school shooting can make or break the lives of all of those involved.

It's my hope that my work will bring a spotlight on to the plight of teachers who have had to witness something that is not on any job description – a school shooting. It's also my hope that these stories will give us insight into how to respond to the needs of these teachers after a shooting. My greatest hope remains that we can find a solution to school shootings. I know, from my own experience, that the echoes of gunfire haunt witnesses for years.

· 2 ·

A QUESTION ABOUT BECOMING A TEACHER

"Okay, you were a teacher who was shot at."

"Yes," I replied.

"Another question pops up. Is that what made you go back and get a doctor's degree?"

"Well, not really. That had more to do with events in my earlier life."

"What kind of events?" Janice asked.

"It may seem strange, but the journey started while I was growing up with an abusive alcoholic father, and then being deserted by my first wife," I replied.

"Oh, wow. That's rough. I have to know more. How do those experiences connect to school shootings, and you getting a doctor's degree?"

"Well, let's rewind a little . . .," I started.

An Answer

Long before my work in the Doctor of Education program at Northeastern University, I was a man with a freshly issued Master of Arts diploma, earned two years after receiving a Bachelor of Science degree. While working as a computer programmer, my career goal remained one of becoming a college professor. Sadly, as a single parent, necessity forced me to shelve any further graduate work. After re-marrying, I became a high school teacher.

I chose that direction because I saw great power and meaning in teaching high school. I had grown up with an abusive alcoholic father, and school became my haven.

During the passage of a quarter of a century a clear pattern presented itself; it was apparent that relationships matter heavily in the classroom, both in terms of academic success and classroom management. Teachers who develop two-way avenues of respect, compassion and openness build large groups of followers. They are the embodiment of motivation. They inspire many to continue learning, to continue caring, and to continue building relationships built on trust, openness, and a passion for understanding. A fire was lit deep inside of me. Since my high school years, I have held on to the idea that I am able to find success because of the caring of a few teachers who reached out to me in my darkest days.

As I saw students in the dawn of a new light, from behind the lectern, I came to better understand that the struggles of my own adolescent years had been aided by those committed teachers – Lowell Schroeder, Wendell Ward and Coach Bill Snyder. I came to see that I could do the same for the generations that rose up after mine. This became my quest – to inspire another generation, and by doing so, giving hope to those who were like me, at risk of giving up on any constructive direction in life. For most of my career I have worked in schools with struggling children, from broken and hurting families. I have seen how people have been mistreated; I see the need for these young people to have an ethical, open and caring teacher walk with them as learning unfolded – sometimes to be their only model of an ethical life. They were terribly jaded; they found little to believe in. I knew I had to present myself, as best as I can, as someone they could believe in. We all need models of behavior; we all need leadership.

The years passed. My children were raised, and grandchildren have been welcomed into the family, but one unfinished task still sat unfinished. No matter what, I felt compelled to complete my academic goal, a doctorate. I saw this every time I stood before my class, urging all of my young charges to dream dreams and not be afraid to work hard to make them come true. As someone who believes in leadership, I knew I had to expect the same of myself. One day a student asked me about my dreams, and I mentioned this very pursuit. She challenged me to follow my dream, as I had been challenging her.

While the prospect of returning to college in my mid-50s was, frankly, terrifying, I could not drop that proverbial gauntlet. I started looking for a college. Northeastern University opened the door for me in 2010. One larger problem remained – why should I embark on this journey? Would it help my career? I decided I may not know the answer to that, but perhaps it would appear as I progressed. Martin Luther King once wrote, "Faith is taking the first step even when you don't see the whole staircase." That became my mantra.

One of the tasks I had to accomplish as a newly admitted doctoral student was to choose a first course. One stood out – Ethical Decision Making for Educators. For me, having worked for decades to be a teacher that children from broken homes could believe in, I knew I had to start with that class. The subject matter compelled me.

In an assignment in that class we were asked to analyze a case study, one in which a middle school boy shot and killed another student in his class; the teacher watched in horror as the shots were fired. This story sounded familiar. I searched online and discovered the incident had occurred near where I lived. I felt a need to express my compassion to the woman who had faced that day of horror, that teacher, and I sent a brief message via Facebook. She responded with a phone call. I listened – and said very little – as she told of the difficulties she had struggled with since the murder. I was shaken.

I felt something inside resonate with how she felt. She expressed many of the same emotions I had wrestled with. After listening to that teacher for hours, I went online and scoured the Northeastern library to find any literature on what a teacher goes through after witnessing a murder in a classroom. I was stunned to find nothing. No teacher's side of such a story had been told. A few articles came tantalizingly close, with one actually calling for a review of how teachers handle the trauma of school shootings. But there were no first-hand narratives as of that date.

It was then that I saw a purpose for my work – to start a conversation about how witnessing severe school violence (which seems so prevalent nowadays) affects a teacher. Physical abuse affected me as a teen, and I had just spent decades watching as a myriad of social issues affected young people in their walk toward adulthood. There is a great deal of literature about these impediments to growth and building a future, but there is nothing about how the horror of murder in her own classroom can affect a teacher.

If relationships do, indeed, matter in a classroom, then we must look long and hard at how severe violence, such as murder, impedes all forms of relationships, and thus growth of any kind. This story of these teachers, hopefully, will shed some light on how witnessing severe school violence affects professional educators.

Violence, of all kinds, seems to be a part of the tapestry of modern school culture, and I recalled something that a professor of mine said while I was working on my teaching license. Dr. Barbara Tye said that schools were a mirror of society, not an isolated outlier. What we see in schools reflect values, fears, choices and attitudes of the general society around us.

Indeed, I discovered through my research journey that there was an intertwining between societal values, how I was raised, and the ability of teachers to cope with trauma. To illustrate, two of my experiences with violence could be compared. These were two traumatic experiences that ended quite differently for me. I noticed the response from people around me to the traumas affected how I was able to move forward emotionally.

The first experience was one of the first acts of violence I witnessed as a teacher. I was heading to the school office at the end of lunch, concerned about turning in a report requested by the school. I heard a loud commotion as I scanned the papers. Looking up, I saw two boys throwing punches at each other and a crowd forming around them. I stopped, unsure about what to do.

As a survivor of childhood physical abuse, I had to confront my own "demons" – including aversion to physical violence of any kind. As I saw blood splatter on the wall near the boys, I decided I had to intervene. I stepped between the combatants; they were glaring at each other. I had to use physical strength and a loud voice to break up the fight. A moment of shock hit me as I saw blood and a tooth hanging loose in the mouth of one of the boys.

It was over as quickly as it had started. I was shaking as our school security guard led the boys off. Someone grabbed me on the shoulder and I flinched; it was my principal. He asked if I was okay; I nodded. He asked me to come into the office with him. I figured I had to write out some sort of report.

After I scribbled down some observations about what I had just witnessed, my principal surprised me by asking me to sit down. I replied that I had to get to fifth period. His response was, "No, you don't. I have a sub in there for you. You need a breather."

I will never forget that moment of kindness. He asked how I felt about what I had seen – he told me he knew how tough a new teacher's "first fight" was. He offered to allow me to take the last two periods off and go home. He also offered the services of our counselors, if I needed to talk. Looking back, he created a safe space for me, one in which I felt it was acceptable to feel one's emotions.

I've always cared about my first principal, long after we went our separate ways; maybe it's because he first cared about me. I see that my own exposure to violence as a teen impacted how I processed violence. I also see how my first principal's compassion made a difference over the years to come. He softened the blow to my emotions.

The second example of violence was very different. Fast-forward to a day when I had two decades of teaching experience. While I was preparing my classroom after break, a student ran in screaming, "Mr. Mooney, Jimmy's 'ground pounding' Alex!" I had no idea what "ground pounding" was, but I could tell by the student's demeanor that it was not good.

As I ran out of my classroom, I noticed, on the grass nearby, a husky boy pinning a medium-sized boy to the ground – and another burly teen, Jimmy, slamming his fist into Alex's face and head. The amount of blood flying about was horrible. Gashes exposed bone and teeth.

I yelled and tried to push Jimmy off of the boy on the ground, with no effect. I almost tackled the boy pinning Alex, and knocked him off. He tumbled away and ran. I heard a ruckus behind me and noticed two athletic-looking security guards running in our direction.

The two guards, using tremendous force, were able to break the other boy's concentration. As they tore him away, I was appalled at the physical damage to Alex's head. I ran into my classroom and grabbed some paper towels. I returned to give whatever first aid I could as I yelled for someone to call an ambulance.

I stayed with Jimmy until a vice principal arrived. She tapped me on the arm and instructed me to "get back to my classroom." I replied by saying that I was worried about Alex. She admonished me. In a stern voice she said I was not thinking right; I needed to supervise my class.

From my classroom window I watched the ambulance crew wheel Alex away. Like years before, I was shaking. For some reason that first fight, over two decades before, flashed back. I remembered how my first principal was concerned about me, and then I considered how I had just been given a verbal reprimand about how I should be doing my job.

After the second incident, no one offered to watch my class. No one offered to let me go home. My arm had a small cut on it. No one offered to care for my wound, even if it was minor. I felt bitter, and alone. I wondered why that newest fight seemed to emotionally hit me harder than the first one.

I know that I will never truly "get used to" violence. My own demons affect my perceptions. Maybe the way my administrators handled fights throughout my career mattered. Maybe human beings can't really accept violence as a normal part of life. Maybe the emotional wounds heal slowly. Maybe it's all of these things.

References

Dr. Martin Luther King Quotes. (2012). Retrieved from http://www.drmartinlutherking.net/martin-luther-king-quotes.php

· 3 ·

A QUESTION ABOUT THE HISTORY
OF SCHOOL SHOOTINGS

"Does that answer your question?" I asked Janice.

"Yes, thanks. You were abused, and a couple of teachers changed your life. You saw how important teaching is in the lives of kids."

"Exactly. I still feel that way. I still hear from former students who tell me that I had a positive effect in their lives. I believe that now more than ever. There are teachers all over this country who don't realize how much of a difference they've made in the lives of kids."

"I agree. I had teachers change my life, too. But I didn't have to deal with the violence and abuse that you experienced," Janice softly said.

"I'm glad to hear that. Each of us has had to walk on our own paths. Not all childhoods are alike."

"I can see that. And you having a history of having to deal with violence would make you empathetic to people who've witnessed school shootings."

"Sadly, I believe that's true," I responded. "I experienced violence at home, and at school. I saw too many fights, and too much blood."

"That's discouraging. It makes me think. This didn't start when you were a kid. I wonder how many teachers have had to deal with fights, and shootings. When did these shootings start?"

"Believe it or not, we have to go way back in American history. And, sadly, there's not much written about that."

"So, Melissa is kind of one in a long chain of teachers who had to watch a school shooting?" Janice asked.

"Unfortunately, yes."

An Answer

Primer: A History of American School Violence

A teacher witnessing the murder of one student by another in the early years of the twenty-first century is not an incident that stands alone in space or time. Unfortunately, what Melissa experienced is but one link in a long chain of episodes of violence in American schools. The topic of this project, the incident of violence, was not a surprise event disconnected from anything else. A short review of a history of the milestones of school shootings and violence may shed some light on this idea.

In 2002, Watson and Watson issued a seminal piece of literature on this topic entitled "School as a Safe Haven." In this work they address not only school violence, but the wider factors of school safety such as mechanical failures, school bus problems, and decrepit facilities, among others. Beyond their work, little has been done to chronicle the rise of violence in American schools. Indeed, they offer that there has been "very little historical perspective developed or written on the safety of the American school" (Watson & Watson, 2002, p. x). The preparation for this doctoral project strongly supports this claim – especially in the realm of severe school violence.

The Earliest Years of American History

While schoolyard fights and confrontations between parents, teachers and students spring from the earliest days of the American republic, there is no documentation of serious confrontations between the school and the community it served. There are no records available, at this point, of any serious consequences of these confrontations other than perhaps a black eye or a broken window. In fact, this research indicates that there is an opportunity for a study of a history of school violence prior to 1945.

After World War II: The 1940s and 1950s

Watson and Watson refer to the years right after World War II as an "age of innocence" (Watson & Watson, 2002, p. xi). They stipulate that "concern on the part of educators and support staff for the safety of children while they were in school, but not a heightened awareness of threats and dangers to safety" (Watson & Watson, 2002, p. xii). Indeed, through the 1940s and 1950s there were only three major incidents widely reported.

Earliest Violence: Knives

As the war in Europe was on the threshold of victory, the first modern incident involving weapons occurred – but the confrontation did not involve a gun. In early 1945,

> A 15-year-old junior high school student was in the basement leaving the school swimming pool when the two boys attempted to rob him at knifepoint. One of the would-be robbers stabbed the swimmer in the chest with a knife, so he grabbed a knife from the other robber and began slashing the would-be thieves, stabbing one of them in the chest. (Watson & Watson, 2002, p. 148)

No one was killed in this very early violent act. The authors of the study point out that this was not seen as highly unusual as "it was not unusual in that time for boys to carry knives all of the time" (Watson & Watson, 2002, p. 148). In contrast, the carrying of a knife on campus nowadays typically requires heavy penalties.

The Advent of Guns

Moving forward two years, guns came on to the school violence stage. In March of 1947, a 15-year-old student "took out a gun at school in Newark, New Jersey, and approached his carpentry teacher in the classroom shop where he took two shots at the teacher from a distance of ten feet. He missed both times." (Watson & Watson, 2002, p. 148). One could argue that this was the beginning of modern gun violence in schools in the United States. At the time, as surprising as it may sound nowadays, the boy was caught, yet his "clear intention to kill the teacher went unrealized" (Watson & Watson, 2002, p. 148). As the incident covered in this doctoral project happened in California, it is pertinent to note that modern gun violence is not confined to the West Coast.

Knife violence escalated to gun violence, all within the decade of the 1940s. Another dimension of school violence appeared in the early 1950s – an outsider coming onto campus with weapons. Once again, this initial incident did not involve a gun; the weapon was actually a minor piece of furniture. A group of girls in a high school physical education class was listening to their health teacher in the gym when a man came into the room. He threatened the teacher with a vase. A student slipped out of the room and found a policeman outside of the school. The policeman chased the man, and "shot the assailant after the man threw the vase at the officer" (Watson & Watson, 2002, p. 35). It is interesting to note in this incident that a police officer was close by; this happened in an urban school back in the days when there were police officers "on the beat" patrolling on foot.

The 1950s saw a rise in the concept of rigidity in schools; discipline was heavily stressed, and movies such as "The Blackboard Jungle" brought attention to unruly children. Watson and Watson stipulate that "incidents of delinquent behavior against schools on the part of junior and senior high school boys either increased or were given more attention by the media during the fifties" (Watson & Watson, 2002, p. 35).

The 1960s and 1970s: School Violence Spreads

While we consider the Civil Rights Movement to be an issue from the 1960s, the seeds of that trend were sown in the decade before. In fact, that movement provided the foundation for one of the earliest acts of mass violence on a school campus. The 1954 Supreme Court decision of Brown vs. The Board of Education produced a widespread anger in the Deep South. Shortly after the issuance of that ruling, on October 1st of that year, an angry crowd of 800 white adults and students attacked 4 black pupils in front of a Baltimore high school (Watson & Watson, 2002, p. 90). The local school board decided to keep the schools open despite the fighting and protesting.

Multiple Murders on Campus

In the 1960s, one major campus shooting stood out – involving Charles Whitman shooting from the tower at the University of Texas in Austin, Texas. Seventeen people were killed and 31 more were wounded with a high-powered rifle before two police officers were able to break through and kill him. Many consider this to be the first of the modern school mass-murders; episodes that seemed to happen from time to time over the last half a century.

Private Schools and Guns

As America moved into the 1970s, private schools found themselves dealing with severe violence. One hundred twenty-one children at St. Cecilia's Catholic School (Peoria, Illinois) were confronted by three men with high-powered rifles and pistols. They took 26 people hostage, including 2 teachers. Police, for the first time, were forced to shoot one of the kidnappers as he came out with a child and a gun, screaming, "Kill me, kill me, kill me!" (Watson & Watson, 2002, p. 150). As the child ran off the gunman was shot and killed. None of the hostages were hurt that day.

Planned School Shootings

In January of 1975, in New York, a 17-year-old high school senior brought gun cases to school. He set a small fire and then pulled a fire alarm. As emergency responders arrived he began shooting at them (Watson & Watson, 2002, p. 151). In 1975 there were a handful of other incidents similar to this; the idea of copy-cat shootings was born.

A Focus on the Witnesses

The idea of psychological well-being of witnesses did not come into the consciousness of American society until November of 1976. In that month a gunman barged into an elementary classroom in Detroit and shot and killed the teacher. Police later arrested her husband. There were so many children who witnessed the crime that, for the first time, post-traumatic stress symptoms were reported throughout the class. Parents reported that their children were experiencing bed wetting, nightmares, and terror at the thought of going to school. Counseling was provided, but several months later, therapists found "that the psychological damage done to the children had not been repaired" (Watson & Watson, 2002, p. 154). As no teacher or staff member had directly witnessed the shooting, there was no discussion of psychological support for those members of the school community.

The 1980s and 1990s: Schools React to the Violence

Semi-automatic Weapons on Campuses

In the mid-1980s school personnel first confronted students with semi-automatic weapons, and were forced to deal with a grim situation in which they could not defend themselves. In January of 1985, a 14 year-old boy brought a semi-automatic rifle and a .357 magnum handgun to school in Los Angeles. The principal "reproached him about the weapons" (Watson & Watson, 2002, p. 154). Because of this the boy opened fire, killing the school administrator. A teacher standing nearby was wounded. This incident forced districts to look into and hire professionally trained security guards.

Shootings Affect School Management

A few months later a shooting incident profoundly changed how schools were operated. In Los Angeles, in September of 1986, a college student returning to visit his high school teacher at Fairfax High School got into an argument with two then-current high school students. One of them pulled a gun and shot the college student. Because of this the school saw a major decline in enrollment, and forced the school district to reassign teachers to other schools. Parents withdrew their children as they had decided "the school was not safe" (Watson & Watson, 2002, p. 164). Because of the Fairfax incident, school security was heavily beefed up, including the carrying of weapons on campus. This was the beginning of a trend that continues into this century. Fences grew around schools, and a fortress mentality was born.

Sadly, another school mentality was born in this time frame as well – the tradition of denial. Just before Christmas in 1987, in Arkansas, four high school students were among fourteen people killed as the gunman (a grandfather and father) slaughtered his own family. The shootings "were a shock to the high school, and needless to say were very traumatic for the young people who knew the dead students" (Watson & Watson 2002, p. 174). When the high school opened its doors again after vacation, the principal reported that the students were adapting "just fine" (Watson & Watson, 2002, p. 174). He believed that they did not need any psychological assistance.

The Media and School Shootings

Of course, no history of school violence would be complete without a mention of the massacre in Littleton, Colorado. On April 20th, 1999, two students at Columbine High School murdered a total of 12 students and 1 teacher. Twenty-one other students, as well as three adults, were wounded while trying to escape. Shootings, by this point in American history, were not unheard of. While very disturbing, the number of people killed was not exceptional. The event was considered one of note because the shooters, two of them, committed suicide; but the biggest change, in terms of society, was that media coverage was widespread via television, cell phones and the internet. Details were available to anyone, nationally and internationally, within minutes.

The Twenty-First Century: 2000 to 2020

Severe school violence continues into the twenty-first century. As the new millennium unfolds, schools across the country scramble to find ways not to become the next evening news item. Indeed, the media seems to have perfected a school shooting coverage system. It's now unheard of to have a school shooting occur without a rush of journalists arriving at the school involved within minutes.

More and more schools are creating barrier doors at front entrances, placing metal detectors at entry points, adding door locks and entry blocks in classrooms, and requiring see-through backpacks. Some companies began to market supposedly bullet-proof backpacks. There is a growing number of schools who have contracted with law enforcement agencies to position officers on school campuses. In addition, a number of states and districts are arguing over and implementing the idea that school employees should carry weapons.

While school shootings, in some years happening almost once a week since 2010, are numerous, and could be described in a book on its own, there have been a number of unusual shootings. There are a few shootings that have changed the look of this phenomenon.

One of the most horrific shootings during the first twenty years of the new millennium happened in Newtown, Connecticut, at Sandy Hook Elementary School, on December 14, 2012. This incident brought the horror of shooting deaths to the lowest grade possible, kindergarten. Since late 2012, there are now school shooting victims of every age, from kindergarten through college. Sandy Hook Elementary School represented the second highest number of victims in a school shooting, with 28 deaths. Sadly, most of the top ten school shootings, in terms of the number of deaths, have happened in the new century.

That shooting ignited a firestorm of debate on gun control, the mentally ill, and the role of the media in shootings. A new phenomenon splashed into the courts and the media – lawsuits against people claiming the shooting never happened. As of 2020, some of these lawsuits continue to work their ways through the courts.

On October 24, 2014, at Marysville Pilchuck High School in Marysville, Washington, the shooter lured his victims to his lunch table, and then opened fire. Researchers believe this was the first example of luring people to be shot.

On August 25, 2015, at Hornsby Elementary School in Augusta, Georgia, a student was playing with a loaded pistol inside of his desk when it went off. The number of students caught bringing weapons to school, not to shoot, but just to have on his or her person, increased significantly since the year 2000. This is one reason why clear backpacks have been required by many schools in the United States.

While many of the shootings involved shooters dealing with difficult family issues, or were bullied, a relatively new phenomenon arrived in this realm on April 10, 2017. Three people died at an elementary school in San Bernardino, California, when an estranged husband brought a gun to his wife's classroom – and opened fire. She was instantly killed, and a student in her class later died of his wounds. The husband committed suicide on the spot. The idea of murder-suicide over a broken relationship entered the discussion on school shootings.

Another shooting made the list of most casualties the following year – on February 14, 2018. A gunman opened fire with a semi-automatic rifle at Marjory Stoneman Douglas High School in Parkland, Florida, killing seventeen people. This represented the third highest number of victims in a school shooting. This came only a bit over five years after the second highest casualty count, Sandy Hook Elementary School, in 2012. The Stoneman Douglas shooting inspired a political uprising by high school students. That movement could be chronicled, again in another book, as it has mushroomed in the twenty-first century.

But 2018 was not done. Indeed, that is the year that has the record for the number of school shootings. The fourth highest number of deaths from a school shooting was recorded on May 18th, 2018, at Santa Fe High School in Santa Fe, Texas, in the Houston metropolitan area. Ten people died.

The school shooting of November 14, 2019, at Saugus High School, in Saugus, California, where two students died, was notable for all of the media coverage surrounding the event. Los Angeles area news helicopters, vans and on-the-street interviews documented the event, and this response is now common. The one unique aspect of this is that the author of this book was able to watched his own daughter and grandson being interviewed on live television news. Some time later, the Los Angeles Dodgers baseball team visited the school to show solidarity with the community.

While the year 2020 was marked by the closures and struggles of the COVID-19 pandemic, school shootings happened almost up to the date when most schools shut down for health reasons. On January 11, 2020 a 15-year-old was arrested after two people were wounded by gunfire during a high school basketball game in the Dallas, Texas, area. Guns are now being brought to athletic events – and being used. A student was badly wounded, and a Dallas police officer was grazed by a bullet. The student later died from his injuries.

Looking Beyond 2020

Since the COVID-19 pandemic, school shootings are dramatically down, for obvious reasons, but this does not mean the problem has been resolved. With schools re-opening, and after months of domestic strife, economic uncertainty and anxiety of every type, some are concerned that another round of shootings may erupt.

Concern has been expressed about the psychological and social effects of the COVID-19 pandemic. What effect will the social isolation from the pandemic have on families and individuals? Could these conditions serve as a seedbed of future school shootings? While this is impossible to predict, one needs to consider the reasons young people turn to gun violence.

In an American Psychiatric Association publication, *Gun violence and mental illness,* the authors describe the factors that lead to a young person choosing to use a gun. After reviewing a number of sources, including interviews with surviving gunmen, they concluded that "From an etiological standpoint, the factors contributing to mass murder are broad, and therefore analysis of any single incident should be approached using a model that addresses individual biological, social, and psychological factors" (Gold & Simon, 2016, p. 86).

They describe the biological factors as including "... possible brain pathology, as well as psychiatric illnesses such as depression and psychosis" (Gold & Simon, 2016, p. 86). On the psychological side, factors include "... a negative or fragile self-image, paranoid dynamics, and retreat into violent and omnipotent revenge fantasies" (Gold & Simon, 2016, p. 86).

The more troubling factors, related to the pandemic of 2020, are social factors. These shooters often struggle with "... isolation, possible ostracism by peers, and an absence of prosocial supports" (Gold & Simon, 2016, p. 86). A number of teens may be struggling with these issues as we come out of the pandemic. Educators and parents should be aware of this as we move into the third decade of the century.

Conclusion

Severe violence – what started out innocuously (compared to modern campus battles) as a knife fight between boys in the final days of World War II has mushroomed. In this section the evolution of this phenomenon has been explored – the milestones, so to speak, along the way, have been highlighted, illustrating the path to the incident in which one woman, in California, witnessed one of her students shoot and kill another right in front of her. What Melissa and Mike experienced did not happen in a vacuum of non-violence.

The violence now includes confrontations involving automatic weapons, victims who are children of all ages, dead and wounded staff members, members of law enforcement having to deal with the carnage, administrative changes of all types, and people of all ages struggling with Post-Traumatic Stress Disorder. Schools have changed the way the facilities are designed and built. Now many political figures are calling for armed teachers on campus. American schools have a history of violence and, unfortunately, may have more ahead.

Finally, Watson and Watson speculate about the root of this pattern. They point out that,

> In the time from the end of World War II to the end of the century, adolescence itself changed greatly. In 1955, 60 percent of U.S. households consisted of a working father, a housewife mother, and two or more children. By 1980, that number had decreased to 11 percent, and by 1985 only seven percent of families were so characterized. Additionally, by the turn of the century, children reached puberty earlier and were confronted with issues far beyond those concerns considered "normal" in the 1950s. (Watson & Watson, 2002, p. 20)

Robert L. Maginnis speculated that "the school violence epidemic is rooted in larger societal problems" (Watson & Watson, 2002, p. 206). History seems to support this assertion.

References

Butin, D. (2010). *The education dissertation: A guide for practitioner scholars.* Thousand Oaks, CA: Corwin.

Gold, L. H., & Simon, R. I. (2016). *Gun violence and mental illness*. Arlington, VA: American Psychiatric Association Publishing.

Maginnis, R. L. (2000). *Violence in the schoolhouse: A ten year update*. Washington, D.C.: Family Research Council. Retrieved from http://www.frc.org/insight/is94e5cr.html

Watson, R. J., & Watson, R. S. (2002). *School as a safe haven*. Westport, CT: Greenwood Press.

· 4 ·

A QUESTION ABOUT SEVERITY

"Oh, my! That's overwhelming. It's not just about how long this has gone on, but how it's rooted in a wider societal problem," Janice exclaimed.

"The more I read, dug into it and thought about it, the more I saw that we have to place school shootings in a context, in the system of our society. This is not happening just out of magical thin air," I responded.

"I think I can see that. As a teacher, I've seen kids coming to school from broken homes, homes with no medical care, homes, with alcoholic parents."

"Every year that I taught Id' thought I'd seen or heard of it all. The next year the last 'biggest family nightmare' would get topped, or so it seemed to me."

"That's what my experience tells me, too," Janice said enthusiastically.

"I remember kids who lived in their friend's garage, sleeping in the back seat of unused cars."

"I had a little girl tell me once that her family was living in a backyard shed on a property her uncle owned," Janice sighed.

"And I once watched a physical education teacher walk a high school boy through how to take a shower."

"No way!"

"Yes. I'll bet if we tried, we could spend a couple of hours trying to top each other's stories," I said as I shook my head.

"I've done that with teachers I've worked with," Janice drew a deep breath. "Who hasn't?"

"Is it like this with school shootings? How bad is this, overall?"

"It's not good, I can tell you that," I responded.

"I started teaching in the 90's. I remember Columbine. What has the trend been?"

An Answer

Statement of the Problem

Shootings on American school campuses are a growing problem. A recent study reported that in the period between 1996 and 2006, "207 student homicides occurred in U.S. schools, an average of 21 deaths per year" (Borum, Cornell, Modzeleski, & Jimerson, 2010, p. 27). This same work noted that the annual rate of these school murders has nearly doubled since 2000.

Many teachers who witness school shootings are not offered job modifications plans to assist them in returning to duty. A number of these teachers leave the profession because of the trauma, suffering for the rest of their lives. There is an absence of literature addressing this problem.

Psychologists report that the more out of control a person feels in a stressful event the more traumatic it will prove to be in the long term (Seligman, 1972). Individuals with a strong emotional and professional support system survive stressful situations much better than those without such networks. Someone without support struggles for a lifetime, and never returns to a sense of security (Seligman, 1972, p. 76). Extreme conditions produce premature deaths (Seligman, 1972, p. 88).

This is an ethics problem as well. Freire wrote that the "trust of the people in the leaders reflects the confidence of the leaders in the people" (Freire, The Pedagogy of the Oppressed, p. 42). Indeed, "The reward of a trusting environment is immeasurable, yet the price of lack of trust is dear" (Blasé & Blasé, 2001, p. 23). Can teachers feel that they will be supported when they witness severe violence if they see there was no support in a prior incident?

The focus of this doctoral research project is to address the question of, "What are the psychological and professional effects on a teacher witnessing an episode of severe school violence?" To date there are no studies and no documentation on what effects witnessing a severe incident of school violence has on a teacher's career.

An understanding of how a teacher is affected by school violence could assist in the development of a teacher trauma incident management system – and, perhaps, an institute to serve as a central resource for teachers and schools struggling with school violence in the future. These would be opportunities for further research. An additional question, thus another study, beckons, one of, "What professional support system(s), including job modifications and working condition alterations, could assist the re-entry of teachers who were post-traumatic Stress victims of severe school violence?"

Significance of the Problem

Teacher turnover in California schools is severe. In 2002, the National Commission on Teaching and America's Future estimated that teacher attrition is at a point where "almost half leave after five years" (The National Commission on Teaching and America's Future [NCTAF], 2002, p. 3). "The fact is, an alarming and unsustainable number of teachers are leaving" (NCTAF, 2002, p. 3). The loss of skilled educators could prove debilitating for the profession of teaching.

Van der Kolk (1993) described how trauma changes a person psychologically and physiologically. Left untreated, the changes become permanent. Victims degrade into rigid thinking, paranoia, defensiveness, over-reactivity and health problems (Van der Kolk, 1993, p. 231). Job modifications can restore victims to a productive life with fewer health issues.

The impacts of school gunplay are at the top of the list of severity of campus issues. A University of California, Los Angeles, study listed the most traumatic as "... community violence, catastrophic school violence after a sniper attack, a school shooting" (Steinberg, Brymer, Decker, & Pynoos, 2004, p. 99). Teachers leave the field for such reasons.

In one of our two stories, a young teacher, with the pseudonym Melissa, witnessed first hand a fatal shooting in her classroom. A student pulled out a loaded gun and shot the student sitting in front of him. The teacher is now on permanent disability as a result of this trauma and perhaps as a result of a lack of re-entry support mechanisms for educators in her district. She paid for this experience emotionally and professionally. The children and the profession of education lost an outstanding teacher. With school shootings on the rise, more teachers will be following this teacher's path out of the profession, further impacting the problem with teacher retention.

On the other hand, another teacher, with the pseudonym Mike, watched as a lone gunman walked onto his campus and opened fire on students. Because of his quick actions, the gunman was stopped, and no one was killed. While one boy struggled with a major gunshot wound, he survived. The teacher's career, too, survived the incident; he felt he had a great deal of support from his district and his community.

One teacher left the profession while the other teacher was able to stay in his classroom. Understanding what made the difference in these two cases could allow the profession to assist in the rehabilitation of the witnesses of school shootings.

References

Blasé, J., & Blasé, J. (2001). *Empowering teachers: What successful principals do* (2nd ed.). Thousand Oaks, CA: Corwin Press.

Borum, R., Cornell, D., Modzeleski, W., & Jimerson, S. (2010). What can be done about school Shootings? A review of the evidence. *Educational Researcher, 39*(1), 27–37. doi:10.3102/0013189X09357620

Freire, P. (2000). *The pedagogy of the oppressed.* New York: Continuum International Publishing.

Seligman, M. (1972). *Helplessness: On depression, development and death.* San Francisco: Freeman and Company.

Steinberg, A., Brymer, M., Decker, K., & Pynoos, R. (2004). The University of California at Los Angeles post-traumatic stress disorder reaction index. *Current Psychiatry Reports, 6,* 96–100.

The National Commission on Teaching and America's Future. (2002, August 20–22). Unraveling the "Teacher Shortage" problem: Teacher retention is the key. *NCTAF Symposium* (pp. 1–16). Washington, D.C.: The National Commission on Teaching and America's Future.

Van der Kolk, B. (1993). Biological considerations about emotions, trauma, memory and the brain. In S. Ablon, D. Brown, & J. Mack (Eds.), *Human feelings: Explorations in affect development and meaning.* New York: Routledge.

· 5 ·

A QUESTION ABOUT DESIGNING THE STUDY

"That's kind of overwhelming. It seems like there are so many different factors in school shootings. It seems to me that it would be really hard to study all of this," Janice commented.

"In many ways, yes. In some ways, no. There are commonalities, and there is a framework of knowledge to draw upon," I replied.

"What do you mean?"

"Well, you look for a framework to build inside of, sort of like the frame of a house, where you'll put pipes, wires, and wallboard."

"A framework. That makes sense. Maybe . . ."

"Look at it this way, in terms of how a school shooting affects a teacher, we have to understand a little about how trauma affects people," I explained.

"That seems logical."

"And we need what are called 'constructs.'"

"Constructs? I'm not following you . . ."

"Yes. Think about how we're talking right now. You understand my sentences because we have a framework in our language. We agree on what are verbs and what are nouns."

"I get that."

"In my study, to connect with language, I came up with nouns and verbs, so to speak, so the effects could be measured and described."

"Okay, I'm following you . . . go on . . .," Janice said.

"Well, my nouns and verbs were Post Traumatic Stress Disorder and Organizational Climate."

"Oh, PTSD! I know a little about that. But 'Organizational Climate?'"

"Think of it like this – PTSD is a description of something painful, and Organizational Climate is a description of the system in which you are living and working. So, what hurts you, and how much, and how society works with, or against, you as you deal with the pain."

"Now I'm tracking with you," Janice said.

"Let me step back a minute, just to give you a bigger picture," I began.

An Answer

Theoretical Framework

Within the nature of a framework, theories have two critical components: (a) the theory describes specific behavior(s), and (b) the theory must make predictions about future behaviors. In this study, certain psychological theories would serve to explain and, indeed, predict the behavior of a teacher who witnessed an act of severe classroom violence. Dr. David Szabla described constructs as mechanisms that allow "the researcher to effectively examine and describe" (Szabla, 2006, p. 18). In this study, two constructs contributed to the disability of the teacher in question: Post Traumatic Stress Disorder and Organizational Climate. The second teacher was affected by Post Traumatic Stress Disorder, to a different degree, and, of course, different factors involving Organizational Climate.

Post Traumatic Stress Disorder

This study is designed to explore why one teacher decides to leave the profession, while another does not, and understand what effects that witnessing a severe act of school violence had on their decisions. As an act of violence (referred to as a traumatic incident) is the central issue, the most profound construct would be that of the psychological issue of *Post Traumatic Stress Disorder* (PTSD).

It should be understood that in this study the investigator is not viewing Post-Traumatic Stress Disorder from a licensed psychologist's perspective. The investigator is not a psychologist; as such, the discussion in this work should not be seen as diagnostic or clinical in nature, but academic. The research was undertaken from the view of a scholar working to understand the various connections and ramifications affecting a teacher dealing with trauma.

The American Psychological Association defines PTSD as "an anxiety problem that develops in some people after extremely traumatic events ..." The definition continues to say that "People with PTSD may relive the event via intrusive memories, flashbacks and nightmares; avoid anything that reminds them of the trauma; and have anxious feelings they didn't have before that are so intense their lives are disrupted" (Kazdin, 2000, p.251).

Recent models of dealing with PTSD suggest that,

> ... adjustment to trauma is a dynamic process influenced by pre-trauma factors (low socioeconomic status, family instability, early trauma history), resilience-recovery variables (personality, coping strategies, social support and additional stressful life events) and traumatic event characteristics (intensity and duration of exposure, perceived threat, exposure to atrocities or abusive behavior, injury). (Lawrence & Fauerbach, 2003, p. 63)

In dealing with the trauma there are a number of steps that witnesses must go through. Dr. Randy Hartman described the steps to full PTSD as starting with an activating event (Hartman, 2011). This is followed, if proper treatment is not applied, with emotional or physical pain, memory confusion, guilt, shame, a sense of worthlessness, anxiety, fear, anger (fight-or-flight response), resentment (distrust), depression and, eventually, long-term acute anxiety.

Personality and Post-traumatic Stress Disorder

A number of studies have shown that the variables of personality have a major impact on how a traumatic event is processed in the weeks, months, and years after. Agaibi and Wilson write that "theoretical models of traumatic stress syndromes and the literature on PTSD have established that there is a wide range of outcomes in how persons cope with traumatic experiences" (Agaibi & Wilson, 2005, p. 195). Indeed, "Post-traumatic resilience is a form of behavioral adaptation to situational stress and a style of personality functioning" (Agaibi & Wilson, 2005, p. 196).

The Participants and Post-traumatic Stress Disorder

While the researcher is not making a diagnosis, Hartman's Steps were observed in the two participants. In the case of one of the participants, Melissa, all of the steps described by Hartman are observed. Interviews show that she moved from one step to another, back and forth, which is typical of severe PTSD cases. No accommodations or modifications were offered by her district, further exacerbating her symptoms. Her sense of "not being heard" contributed to a deep-seated sense of resentment and anger (step 10) during a time when she needed her school district's compassion.

In the case of the other participant, Mike, most of the steps in Hartman's steps were observed, again from a non-diagnostic perspective. Like Melissa, he went back and forth from one step to another, but was able to function at a high level. His district offered psychological support, job modifications, and continual counseling access. Mike was able to work through his trauma and continue teaching.

Organizational Climate

A second construct that allows this study to analyze the experiences of this teacher effectively is one of organizational climate. In 1978 George Litwin began work on what would later be called the Burke-Litwin Model – what is described as an organizational model "with climate as the centerpiece" (Burke, 2010, p. 210). They defined organizational climate as "a set of psychological priorities of a given . . . environment that are based on the collective perceptions of the people" (Burke, 2010, p. 210).

Burke and Litwin identified 12 areas of consideration they considered to be primary for "organizational understanding and analysis" (Burke, 2010, p. 214). These include external environment, mission and strategy, leadership, organization culture, structure, management practices, systems (policies and procedures), work unit climate, task requirements and individual skills, motivation, individual needs and values and, finally, individual and organizational performance.

The Transactional Factors

In the Burke-Litwin Model, six transactional factors are outlined. A transactional factor can be seen as one which is concerned with "more of the day-to-day operations (transactions) of the organization" (Burke, 2010, p. 217). These factors include management practices, structure, policies and procedures, work unit climate, motivation, individual needs and values, task requirements and individual skills, and individual and organizational performance. The model describes all of these factors as being intertwined, with changes (negative or positive) in one area affecting the others.

Management Practices

The Burke-Litwin model describes this as a "particular set of specific behaviors" (Burke, 2010, p. 221) utilized by management personnel. For example, one manager may challenge employees and confront them while another uses praise and positive feedback to elicit better results from employees.

A pertinent question for this study that arises from this factor could be, "How does the manager treat the employee after a trauma in the workplace?"

Structure

In this model, structure is defined as,

> ... the arrangement of organizational functions (e.g. accounting, manufacturing, human resource management) and operational units (e.g., the western region, customer service for product group x, Goddard Space Flight Center within NASA) that signify levels of responsibility, decision making authority, and lines of communications. (Burke, 2010, p. 221)

In many ways, this could be compared with an old fashioned organizational chart, showing relationships between parts of the larger organization.

A meaningful question for this study that arises from this factor would be, "Who is responsible for dealing with an employee following a trauma in the workplace?"

Policies and Procedures

Burke refers to policies and procedures as "helpful mechanisms" (Burke, 2010, p. 221) with such subcategories as management information systems, the organization's reward system, performance appraisal systems, the setting of goals and processes, the budget process, and human resource allocation. Burke describes this category as covering "a lot of territory."

A relevant question for this study that arises from this factor might be, "What human resource procedures would be used to deal with an employee who witnessed a trauma in the workplace?"

Work Unit Climate

Simply put, work unit climate addresses the collective perceptions of members of the same work unit. Burke tells us that these employees have opinions on, among other things, how well they are managed, how clear the expectations are, how they feel their performance is recognized, how much support they feel they receive from other unit members, and whether or not their management is fair.

An appropriate question for this study that arises from this factor might be, "How fairly do management representatives treat employees affected by workplace trauma?"

Motivation

Burke tells us that this area includes the individual's need to achieve, to affiliate with others, and to have some degree of power. Employees need to feel they are being directed toward "goals that, when reached, will help to satisfy our needs" (Burke, 2010, p. 223).

This concern raises the questions of, "How do the actions of management after a trauma affect the motivations of employees?" and "Does management look after our needs during times of trauma in the workplace?"

Individual Needs and Values

Simply put, this concerns the extent to which one's needs are met on the job. The Burke-Litwin model specifically lists security, achievement, and the congruence between what the employees feels is important in life and what the organization stands for in terms of "purpose, values and how people (in and out of the organization, including customers) are treated" (Burke, 2010, p. 222).

Two questions in the light of this study arise from this category. One would be, "Does the employee feel safe while on the job after a trauma?" and, "Does the organization treat people fairly after a workplace trauma?"

Task Requirements and Individual Skills

The clearest way to explain this is, "Does the employee have the emotional, physical and intellectual skills to perform the tasks at hand?" In this study, one might add the idea of "after a trauma."

Individual and Organizational Performance

In a simple sense, this is the relationship between the performance of the individual and the organization, and vice-versa – what the organization does can influence the performance of the individual. In this study a relevant question might be, "Do the actions of the organization after a workplace trauma affect the performance of the individual?"

Conclusion

This construct, organizational climate, played a heavy role in the career decisions of Melissa and Mike after witnessing school shootings. The intersection of conditions in the organizational climate and the effects of Post-Traumatic Stress Disorder proved to be difficult to cope with for one, and not as difficult for the other.

Melissa and Organizational Climate

Melissa's story demonstrates that the organizational climate of her school district fostered distrust. Her district, through their decisions and handling of Melissa's needs (including ignoring psychological recommendations for job modifications) perpetuated a system of protecting of the district without regard to the needs of the individual. Melissa's development of Post-Traumatic Stress Disorder made her more and more suspicious of the intentions of her employer. None of this was dealt with by the school district.

Mike and Organizational Climate

Mike's story illustrates that the organizational climate of his school district fostered a sense of support and trust. His district, through its concern for Mike's needs (including regular psychological checks) reinforced a system of support. Mike's successful working through Post-Traumatic Stress Disorder made him more trusting of the intentions of his employer, and gave him resiliency that allowed him to continue in his responsibilities.

The Relationship between the Constructs

The interplay between the two major issues created the scenario of a teacher's psychological disability. There are teachers who continue in their profession after an experience with violence on a school campus; for example, Post-Traumatic Stress Disorder does not stand alone as a cause of Melissa's disability. Mike's case is a good example of this concept.

As illustrated in Figure 1, teachers seeking help after trauma, but struggling with a poor organizational climate could continue in their profession for

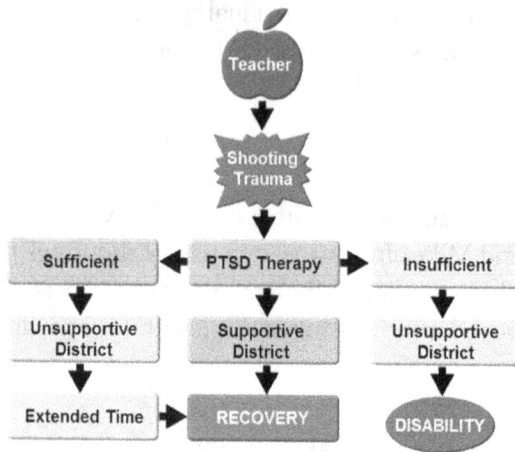

Figure 1: The relationship between the constructs.

years. The recovery may take an extended period of time, but there remains a distinct possibility of continuing in the profession. In an ideal situation, proper therapeutic treatment combined with a supportive and flexible school system can facilitate a more rapid return to professional responsibilities.

In the case of Melissa, struggling heavily with developing PTSD, the unsupportive organizational climate of her school district nurtured the growing fight-or-flight response, the fear, and the distrust that builds lowered self-esteem and the panic attacks that describe severe PTSD. This led to her permanent disability. In Mike's case, the supportive climate of his school district contributed to calming his fight-or-flight response. Of course, the traumas themselves were not equal, and the individual psychological issues prior to the incidents were not either.

Research Questions

The Central Question

The primary focus of this research project is to address the question, "What are the psychological and professional effects on a teacher who witnessed an episode of severe school violence?" A narrative methodology, focusing on two participants who observed school shootings, was used to explore this question.

Questions from the Constructs

While reviewing the constructs of this study a number of questions arose. Post-Traumatic Stress Disorder and organizational climate contributed to Melissa's struggles. These factors contributed to Mike's successful working-through of his issues.

Post-traumatic Stress Disorder

Reviewing Hartman's 12 steps of PTSD, again from an academic and not clinical perspective, which of the 12 factors affected Melissa and Mike in the weeks and months following the school shootings? These factors include the activating event, pain, confusion, guilt, shame, self-worth dissipation, anxiety, fear, anger, resentment, depression and acute anxiety.

Organizational Climate

The six transactional factors put forth by the Burke-Litwin Model allow a framework on which Melissa's and Mike's experiences could be analyzed. Rephrasing the questions put forth in this construct in light of this shooting incident, the following issues are presented:

How did the way Melissa's and Mike's administrators dealt with them after the classroom trauma affect their ability to function? Did their actions somehow contribute to Melissa's post-trauma issues, and Mike's successful recovery?

How did human resource procedures used by their school districts affect Melissa's and Mike's ability to function? Did the process itself somehow feed into Melissa's problems?

Did Melissa and Mike believe they were fairly dealt with by administration after the school shootings? Did Melissa ever feel there was a hidden agenda, or an agenda that was not to her benefit, going on behind the scenes? Did Mike?

How did the actions of Melissa's and Mike's administrators after the trauma affect their motivation? As she struggled after the classroom shooting, did Melissa struggle with motivation because of anything her superiors did or said? Did Mike?

Did Melissa and Mike believe that their administrations looked after their needs after the school shootings? Did they feel that the schools were behind them, or did they feel that there was a chasm between them? Was there unity after the shooting?

Did Melissa and Mike feel safe while in their schools after the shooting traumas? Did the school districts take actions to work with their psychological needs in order to allow them to return to work and feel safe?

Do Melissa and Mike believe that their school districts treat people fairly after a workplace trauma? Did the actions and events after the school shooting make them feel that fairness was at work in the process, or something else?

Did Melissa and Mike have the emotional, physical and intellectual skills to perform the tasks within their jobs after the shooting? Were there any difficult psychological or physical issues that prevented them from being successful in their classrooms?

Did the actions of the school officials after the school shootings affect Melissa's or Mike's performance? Did their administrators' decisions, actions and behaviors allow Melissa and Mike to continue in their prior success, or did those actions hinder their performance? What actions and decisions contributed to the final disposition of their situations?

These questions emanate from the constructs of Post-Traumatic Stress Disorder and Organizational Climate. They will shed light on the factors that contributed to the struggles of Melissa and Mike after witnessing classroom shootings.

References

Agaibi, C., & Wilson, J. (2005, July). Trauma, PTSD, and resilience: A review of the literature. *Trauma Violence Abuse, 6,* 195–216. doi:10.1177/1524838005277438

Burke, W. W. (2010). *Organization change: Theory and practice* (3rd ed.). Thousand Oaks, CA: Sage.

Hartman, R. J. (2011). *The twelve steps to the formation of PTSD.* Retrieved from http://aaph.org/rjhartman/articles/twelve_steps_to_PTSD

Kazdin, A. (Ed.). (2000). *Encyclopedia of psychology.* New York: Oxford University Press (USA).

Lawrence, J., & Fauerbach, J. (2003, January/February). Personality, coping, chronic stress, social support and PTSD symptoms among adult burn survivors: A path analysis. *Journal of Burn Care & Rehabilitation, 24*(1), 63–72.

Szabla, D. (2006). *A multidimensional view of resistance: Exploring cognitive, emotional, and intentional responses to planned organizational change across different perceived change strategies.* (Doctoral dissertation, George Washington University).

· 6 ·

A QUESTION ABOUT PEOPLE

"That gives me an idea how the study worked. You have this framework of topics in which you pose questions, about two people, Mike and Melissa. And Melissa is my friend." Janice said.

"That's right! You're catching on!" I replied.

"I taught with Melissa, but I don't know Mike. Maybe I'm unclear. Did he teach at another school? I don't remember a 'Mike' at our school," Janice asked.

"You're right – he taught in another state. Since Melissa was the only teacher who witnessed that school shooting, it would be difficult to compare her experience with someone there. Besides, I also wanted different systems, hoping that would help me understand how the responses helped or hindered the recoveries."

"So, there would be similarities and differences. Like different towns and schools."

"Yes, there were. I found there were enough similarities to make a comparison worthwhile, and the differences could shed some light into why things worked out differently as well."

"So, tell me about the cities and the people . . ." Janice suggested.

An Answer

Introducing the Communities

Both communities discussed in this study are suburban bedroom cities, feeding workers into a larger metropolitan area. The area around Ash Tree Middle School, Melissa's place of employment, is heavily represented by minorities and blue-collar employment. Mike's Pine Ridge Middle School serves a larger number of white families and white collar professions.

Introducing the Schools

Both schools involved, assigned the pseudonyms Ash Tree Middle School and Pine Ridge Middle School, served students in grades six through eight. While they served a similar number of students, Ash Tree represented a more diverse ethnic population, with Pine Ridge having more of a monoculture. Ash Tree Middle School, in many measures, ranked lower on the socioeconomic scale.

Ash Tree was an older school, in terms of the physical plant, than Pine Ridge. Pine Ridge had numerous technological advantages, security-wise, such as automatic door locking mechanisms.

Introducing the Participants: Melissa

Melissa McCarthy was a teacher in her 30s when the shooting occurred at her school. She had been in the teaching profession for a decade and had received stellar evaluations throughout her career. Melissa holds Bachelor's and Master's degrees, and is married.

Her teaching philosophy was centered on building relationships with her students, and her classroom was well organized. Melissa prided herself on her attention to detail and her compassion for her students.

Her husband is an active professional in another field; they have known each other since childhood. Melissa is the mother of three children, ranging from, at the time of the murder, an infant up to a teen. Her youngest daughter was born shortly before the shooting.

Melissa had just returned to her classroom duties from maternity leave shortly before the shooting. She had been dealing with issues surrounding post-partum depression, and was under the supervision of her physician at the time.

Introducing the Participants: Mike

Mike was a teacher in his 50s at the time of the shooting at his school. He had taught at the high school and middle school levels for over 30 years and had always received outstanding evaluations. Mike holds advanced degrees and was married at the time of the incident. He is the father of two children.

Like Melissa, Mike's teaching philosophy was centered on building relationships and keeping communications open with his students. He had few classroom discipline issues.

· 7 ·

A QUESTION ABOUT VIOLENCE AFFECTING TEACHERS

"Oh, wow . . ." Janice started. The line grew quiet.

"Wow? Are you okay?"

"Yeah. I'd forgotten that Melissa had just come back from maternity leave. What a horrible thing to come back to!" Janice exclaimed.

"I agree. When she told me about the pregnancy, I had to stop her for a moment. I just didn't see that coming. Hearing her voice, seeing her expression, brought on a surge of emotions for me. For some reason, I remembered how my wife, right after having a baby, was up and down emotionally. All I could imagine was how seeing a shooting while she was going through that would have affected her." I responded, then took a deep breath.

"I had hard post-partum problems, too. I can tell you, that would have hit me like a freight train, emotionally."

"I was troubled by how her school didn't really work with her, about that, or seemingly little else, when she tried to come back. They didn't assign her to a different classroom – or even replace the bloodied carpet."

"I know. Some of us offered to switch rooms, to help her out, but administration wouldn't listen." Janice sighed.

"I just wished they could have been flexible," I offered.

"It seems like the right thing to do, in my opinion. You know, like doing the ethical or moral thing – doing the right thing."

"That was an important aspect of my study, Janice. How should we deal with teachers who witness a school shooting?"

"So, how did you start, going back to the idea of a framework, to figure that out?" Janice asked.

"Well, I started with a literature review . . ."

An Answer

Helping Teachers: Ethical Considerations

With 21 shooting deaths a year in American schools (Borum, Cornell, Modzeleski, & Jimerson, 2010) this particular subset of school violence has become more of a focus of educators over the last two decades. Sadly, as the Borum, Cornell, Modzeleski and Jimerson, study points out, this number has been rising since the beginning of the century. In many of these shootings, one or more teachers are affected, psychologically and professionally. One of the foundational questions of this study is, "How should society deal with the teachers emotionally and professionally affected by these shootings?"

Since the early days of the American Republic, educational leaders have recognized that schools are more than a place to disseminate learning. Horace Mann believed that we are not living isolated lives but are deeply affected by our relationships. He states that an "attachment to our fellow-beings, which binds men together in fraternal associations, is so strong, and is universally recognized as so natural, that we look upon hermits and solitaries as creatures half-mad or half-monstrous" (Mann, 1855, p. 127). Indeed, other early philosophers have noted this same concept. John Dewey wrote "Education, in its broadest sense, is the means of this social continuity of life" (Boydston, 1991, p.5). Teachers are a part of the fabric, the continuity, of this society. Not caring for a teacher emotionally wounded by witnessing a shooting unwinds and frays the fabric of our society a bit more; this affects the children, and the "social continuity of life" of which Dewey speaks.

Consider the question of the ethics of assisting a teacher stressed by such a shooting. If one defines ethics as Albert Schweitzer did, as a "sense of duty toward others," (Hansen, 2007, p. 158), then society must reach out and assist.

The Dalai Lama opined that when we neglect the well-being of others, ". . . and ignore the universal dimension of our actions, it is inevitable that we will come to see our interests as separate from theirs" (Lama, 1999, p. 163). To extrapolate from his thoughts, if we do not reach out to such victims, we create a "society of separateness." He continues by noting ". . . we find that if a person lives a very selfish life, without concern for others' welfare, they tend to become quite lonely and miserable" (Lama, 1999, p. 89). This does not describe the "social continuity" Dewey wrote about a century earlier. The fabric of society, once again, unravels a bit more.

Being social creatures, we cannot long or easily live apart from other members of our society. Horace Mann also wrote, "Doing nothing for others is the undoing of ourselves" (Harris, 1958, p. 83). Mann is correct; investigating possible actions to assist these teachers is not only desirable but necessary. As one member of our society is wounded, all are exposed to this pain. Reaching out to assist teachers affected by school shootings, therefore, is the ethical course, and one that binds and protects the social fabric and the continuity of life. If this continuity, as Dewey points out, is a primary duty of the schools, then we are defeating our purposes by not helping teachers who are witnesses to school violence.

By reaching out to wounded teachers, society opens a dialogue, one of, as Paulo Freire wrote, ". . . a horizontal relationship of which mutual trust between the dialoguers is a logical consequence." (Freire, The Pedagogy of the Oppressed, p. 71). This trust tightens the weave of the fabric called society. Freire continues this discourse about trust by stressing that, "The trust of the people in the leaders reflects the confidence of the leaders in the people" (Freire, The Pedagogy of the Oppressed, p. 42). Reaching out in such a way builds trust.

The Effects of School Violence on Teachers

How, then, do school shootings affect teachers? The psychological trauma of witnessing a school shooting includes ". . . both immediate and long-term consequences. Immediate reactions to this sort of trauma include physical, behavioral, emotional, and cognitive responses" (Daniels, Bradley, & Hays, 2007, p. 653).

These responses affect all aspects of the teacher's life. In the classroom, Elliott, Hamburg, and Williams (1998) reported that fear and heightened levels of stress lead to burnout and less effective work. Newman, Fox, Harding, Mehta, and Roth (2004) reported that teachers who are worried about their safety are more likely to leave the teaching profession.

The emotional shock wave of trauma spreads to those beyond the school affected by a shooting. There exists a pervasive fear among teachers and employees at other schools following a shooting. This fear is compounded by the ever-present thought that "our school could be the next one on the evening news and that our own students could be the ones running for their lives" (Daniels et al., 2007, p. 133). Daniels continues by mentioning that all in the profession watch to see how they deal with the trauma.

After a school shooting, multiple measures are taken to provide assistance for students. Daniels (2007) documented services provided for students, including critical incident stress debriefing and dealing with symptoms of PTSD that may develop over time. These and other services are frequently provided by school psychologists or local mental health professionals.

While there are many services offered to the children who witness school shootings, teachers seem cast aside when it comes to assistance. One explanation, Daniels (2007) cites, comes from a study of school shootings in the Paducah and Jonesboro districts. Newman et al. (2004) found that school administrators felt a need to get their schools back in session as soon as possible (Daniels, 2007, p. 654). Teachers, for some reason, are urged to return to "normal" as quickly as possible as a model for the children.

Yet, while they are being asked to return to "normal," Roberts (2007) describes a shooting as a "period of psychological disequilibria, experienced as a result of a hazardous event or situation that contributes a significant problem that cannot be remedied by using familiar coping strategies" (Roberts, 2007, p. 7). The disequilibrium has to be acknowledged and dealt with, Roberts urges.

School administrators urging a return to normal does not return a school to "equilibrium." One study of armed incidents in schools revealed that teachers do not feel safe or supported following lethal situations (Daniels, 2007). Kondrasuk et al. (2005) reported that 60% of their respondents did not voluntarily seek counseling, and 75% of school districts did not require counseling for teacher victims following an act of school violence.

The Psychological and Professional Toll

The most widespread toll of school violence on teachers comes from the psychological concept of Post-Traumatic Stress Disorder (PTSD). Again, this discussion focuses on an academic inquiry, not the diagnosis of a psychologist.

Ardis (2004) described PTSD as having four clusters of symptoms following exposure to trauma.

The first cluster involves intense fear combined with a sense of helplessness and horror. This stage occurs right after the trauma and can last for a few days. In many situations, Ardis continues, this proves to be debilitating – teachers are almost unable to function shortly after a shooting.

The next set of symptoms involves a re-experiencing of the events through "flashbacks." The teacher witnessing a school shooting would re-live, over and over again, the emotions of the event; this can be quite crippling.

The third set of symptoms includes avoidance – staying away from anything that reminds the victim of the trauma. The horror of the initial trauma, and the resultant flashbacks, drain the victim tremendously. In the case of teachers, any exposure to the classroom or area where the violence took place could trigger recurring flashbacks, and a renewal of the intense emotions felt as the trauma was happening. Daniels (2007) describes how, in the third stage, teacher absenteeism increases as these traumatized individuals seek to escape the cycle of emotional "re-injury."

Finally, Daniels describes the fourth stage as one in which individuals with PTSD experience increased sleep disturbances, irritability, difficulty concentrating, hyper-vigilance, or being easily startled. These symptoms "often arise within 3 months of the event (acute reaction) and may persist for longer than 3 months (chronic reaction). Symptoms of PTSD may be delayed in their onset, sometimes not surfacing until 6 months or more after the violence at school" (Daniels, 2007, p. 654). What is disturbing about this stage is that administrators, in a rush to "return to normalcy," do not recognize that these issues can linger for months, or perhaps years, after the incident.

The scale of this Post-Traumatic Stress Disorder may be staggering. Daniels (2007) estimates that each year 234,000 teachers in the United States are victims of school-related violence. While most of these are not shooting related, it does point to a huge need in the profession as a whole.

Indeed, the investigators in the Daniels study (2007) felt so compelled that they wrote, "We strongly recommend that in their efforts to provide assistance to the student body, psychologists not overlook opportunities to provide aid to teachers and other school staff who have been traumatized" (Daniels, 2007, p. 657). In this very important article there are numerous mentions of a lack of support for school staff experiencing the trauma of violence.

They noted "Although school districts make efforts to provide students with mental health services, it has also been shown that teachers and other school personnel may not receive the support they need following mass trauma" (Daniels, 2007, p. 657).

A catastrophic school shooting is a time of crisis, which has been described as "a period of psychological disequilibria, experienced as a result of a hazardous event or situation that contributes a significant problem that cannot be remedied by using familiar coping strategies" (Roberts, 2007, p. 7). A catastrophic shooting calls for remedies outside of the typical response to lower-level crises.

References

Ardis, C. (2004). School violence from the classroom teacher's perspective. In W. L. Turk (Ed.), *School crime and policing* (pp. 131–150). Upper Saddle River, NJ: Pearson Education.

Borum, R., Cornell, D., Modzeleski, W., & Jimerson, S. (2010). What can be done about school Shootings? A review of the evidence. *Educational Researcher, 39*(1), 27–37. doi:10.3102/0013189X09357620

Boydston, J. (Ed.) (1991). *The collected works of John Dewey.* Carbondale, IL: Southern Illinois University Press.

Daniels, J., Bradley, M., & Hays, M. (2007, December). The impact of school violence on school personnel: Implications for psychologists. *Professional Psychology: Research and Practice, 38*(6), 652–659.

Elliot, D., Hamburg, B., & Williams, K. (1998). *Violence in American schools: A new perspective.* Cambridge: Cambridge University Press.

Freire, P. (2000) *The pedagogy of the oppressed.* New York: Continuum International Publishing.

Hansen, D. T. (Ed.) (2007). *Ethical visions of education: Philosophies in practice.* New York City: Teachers College Press.

Harris, W. T. (1958). *Public schools and moral education: The influence of Horace Mann.* New York, NY: Columbia University Press.

Kondrasuk, J. N., Greene, T., Waggoner, J., Edwards, K., & Nayak-Rhodes, A. (2005). Violence affecting school employees. *Education, 125,* 638–647.

Lama, D. (1999). *Ethics for the new millennium.* New York City: Riverhead Books.

Mann, H. (1855). *Lectures on education.* Boston: L.N. Ide.

Newman, K., Fox, C., Roth, W., & Mehta, J. (2004). *Rampage: The social roots of school shootings.* New York, NY: Basic Books.

Roberts, A. R. (2007). *Crisis intervention handbook: Assessment, treatment and research* (2nd ed.). New York: Oxford University Press.

· 8 ·

A QUESTION ABOUT SUPPORTING TEACHERS

"That's an interesting word – 'disequilibria.' That describes what Melissa seemed like after the shooting. Everything in her life seemed out of balance," Janice commented.

"And that is typical for someone who goes through a trauma. What Melissa experienced was trauma. I have had to tell people that repeatedly," I responded.

"I think it's because we believe trauma only happens to soldiers in wars, not in a classroom with kids around."

"A lot of people I've talked to tell me that, Janice."

"It was hard on those of us around her. We seemed to be wandering around, not sure what to do. We wanted to help, but we didn't know how to help."

"I can imagine. I asked myself what I would have done, if I had been there that day, and I came up empty-handed."

"You've done research – what does your work tell you could be done?" Janice asked.

An Answer

The Foundations of a Possible Teacher Support System

The Daniels (2007) study points out that the ability of a teacher struggling with the effects of Post-Traumatic Stress Disorder to function is seriously affected after the teacher witnesses a shooting on campus. In a study completed in 2003, Jordan described the recovery stages for shooting victims and their families. While not describing a recovery model, the work provides a framework upon which programs modifications and support can be based.

Stage 1, which Jordan refers to as the "Traumatic Disaster Event," can be described as the time "... when the school shooting occurs. It can last from a few minutes to hours" (Jordan, 2003, p. 410). In these few minutes or hours after the trauma, basic physical and emotional crisis survival is the greatest need. The programs and support in these minutes and hours are best served by law enforcement and crisis management specialists.

Stage 2, which Jordan calls "Displacement and Separation," begins almost as soon as the crisis has receded as the shooting has completely stopped, and the situation is more under control as law enforcement and outside assistance has arrived and secured the area affected. Teachers in this phase immediately feel a strong need to re-connect with their loved ones and close friends. Once again, law enforcement and related authority figures on hand can be instrumental in alleviating fears that arise during this stage.

Stage 3A (the "A" represents an option, depending on the outcome of the shootings) deals mainly with the families after a teacher or other school employee has been killed on campus. This stage was named "Loss of Loved Ones" by Jordan. During this time, school and law authorities work to notify and counsel the families of the employees who lost their lives in the shooting. Stage 3B represents the needs of teachers being re-unified with their families, if the death of a teacher did not occur.

In Stage 4, which Jordan calls "Recovery," sub-components are identified. Teachers affected by a school shooting need behavioral, cognitive, and psychological responses. The theme through all of this is psychological intervention to prevent long-term Post-Traumatic Stress Disorder from arising, or minimizing it. In this phase, psychologists dedicate weeks and months to counseling and related intervention.

It is also in this fourth stage that job modifications could be considered and designed for these teachers – yet there is little mention of this concept.

In fact, Jordan writes "For a catastrophic school shooting, there has thus far not been a trauma and recovery model that provides insight for mental health professionals on how victims and their families experience the trauma and recovery process" (Jordan, 2003, p. 408). The stages have been described, but no job modification-based re-entry model has yet to be described.

Jordan hints at the need for such modifications and re-entry adaptations when he wrote about teachers who have no support system after a shooting. They are, over time, "unable to maintain 'normal behavior' on this superficial level" (Jordan, 2003, p. 405). Simply put, most teachers who do not work through a re-entry modification plan (almost all do not) and are unable to continue in their work after only a short period of time.

A system to deal with workplace shootings (and other severe trauma incidents) for non-education industries has been designed by the International Critical Incident Stress Foundation. While their work has not been adapted for the world of schools, and some adaptation would have to be made considering the differences in employment characteristics, much can be gleaned from their experiences over the last decade.

They note that when no Critical Incident Stress Management System ("Primer on Critical Incident Stress," 1997) was implemented, "long-term post-traumatic stress disorder, dysfunctional lives and serious health issues arise over time" ("Primer on Critical Incident Stress," 1997). As Daniels (2008) pointed out, there are few long-term resources or tools available to teachers after a shooting incident. According to the assertion of the International Critical Incident Stress Foundation, this leads to long-term post-traumatic stress, dysfunction and serious health and employment issues for those teachers so affected.

In the CISM model, the following Seven Core Components ("Primer on Critical Incident Stress," 1997) of a process are outlined:

1. Pre-crisis preparation. This includes stress management education, stress resistance, and crisis mitigation training for both individuals and organizations.
2. Disaster or large-scale incident, as well as school and community support programs including demobilizations, informational briefings, "town meetings" and staff advisement.
3. Defusing. This is a 3-phase, structured small group discussion provided within hours of a crisis for purposes of assessment, triaging, and acute symptom mitigation.

4. Critical Incident Stress Debriefing (CISD) refers to the "Mitchell model" (Mitchell & Everly, 1996) 7-phase, structured group discussion, usually provided 1–10 days post-crisis, and designed to mitigate acute symptoms, assess the need for follow-up, and if possible provide a sense of post-crisis psychological closure.
5. One-on-one crisis intervention/counseling or psychological support throughout the full range of the crisis spectrum.
6. Family crisis intervention, as well as organizational consultation.
7. Follow-up and referral mechanisms for assessment and treatment, if necessary. (All seven components are from "Primer on Critical Incident Stress," 1997)

Jordan (2003) and the International Critical Incident Stress Foundation have designed useful principles for how a re-entry job modifications model for teachers might be constructed. These concepts could prove to be worthwhile starting points for such a teacher re-entry system.

Literature Review Questions

Among a number of possible topics, literature questions include an ethical component, "Should we care for teachers affected by violence?" psychological elements, "How does school violence affect teachers?" and "What are the foundations of Post Traumatic Stress Disorder?" a trend component, "What is the trend of school violence?" and a practical (applied) element, "What job modifications are used in other professions because of psychological traumas?"

References

Daniels, J., Bradley, M., & Hays, M. (2007, December). The impact of school violence on school personnel: Implications for psychologists. *Professional Psychology: Research and Practice, 38*(6), 652–659.

Jordan, K. (2003). A trauma and recovery model for victims and their families after a catastrophic school shooting: Focusing on behavioral, cognitive, and psychological effects and needs. *Brief Treatment and Crisis Intervention, 3*(4), 397–411.

Mitchell, J., & Everly, G. (2001). *Critical incident stress management: Basic group crisis interventions.* Ellicott City, MD: International Critical Incident Stress Foundation.

Primer on Critical Incident Stress Management (CISM). (1997). Retrieved from http://www.icisf.org/

· 9 ·

A QUESTION ABOUT THE STUDY'S FOCUS

"Do people actually question whether or not we should help teachers who had to watch a school shooting?" Janice asked.

"I'm not sure, but I would guess there are people who think it's not their problem . . ." I started, and Janice interrupted.

"When I think about what happened back then, and how they wouldn't make changes in her job, or in her classroom, I get really angry. Why wouldn't they change her room, or transfer her, or . . . or . . . just about anything?"

"Those are great questions, Janice . . . and I . . ."

"It was like they were totally unaware of what she was going through. Her friends could see she was struggling. Why couldn't others?"

"I agree, Janice, and . . ." I started again.

"I'm sorry. I keep interrupting you. I just get so upset just thinking how it could have been done differently."

"Don't worry. I completely understand. I think chatting with Melissa, the first time we sat down and talked about her experience, before I started the study, made me realize I had to do this work. I saw how important this is – to get the word out."

"So, you heard her story before you did the research?"

"Yes. I was just interested, at first, in doing a paper for my ethics class, nothing more. My professor said I could look into this if I first did a litera-ture review, to see what had been done about teachers and school shootings before."

"What did you find?"

"Almost nothing was done at that point. In fact, I found an article men-tioning that someone should do that kind of a study."

"Wow."

"That's what I said! I told my professor and she suggested that I should speak to another professor, who specialized in case study-type research, and see what he thought."

"I guess he thought it was a good idea to pursue this . . ." Janice asked.

"Oh, yes. But he gave me an assignment first."

"An assignment? Were you in his class?"

"No, but they way I was taught, we saw a dissertation as being a class, or a few classes, on its own. Remember, to finish a doctorate, you need to write a paper. So I decided I'd follow through. Maybe this could work out."

"What did you have to do?" Janice asked.

"He said I need a problem statement – a question framing what I'm trying to understand or discover – a paradigm, which is kind of a viewpoint or frame-work, and I had to decide what research tradition I would use, like qualitative or quantitative, and a bunch of other stuff."

"I get that part – using numbers or . . .?"

". . . or looking for patterns in language, experiences and perceptions, so to speak."

"I get it."

"It took me a few months to dig up and write about everything he had given me – it was like a checklist."

"I can imagine. Those professors sure like throwing work at people!" Janice chuckled. I smiled.

"Well, yeah, but I also saw that he wanted me to be successful. I have to frame everything for other scholars to be able to understand my results."

"That makes sense. So, what did you come up with?"

"Well, let me give you kind of an overview of research – how this was put together . . ."

An Answer

Problem Statement

The central question of this research is, "What are the psychological and professional effects on a teacher witnessing an episode of severe school violence?" Worded differently, one could ask, "How does witnessing an episode of severe school violence affect a teacher's career?" The answers to this question were answered through a qualitative narrative process utilizing interviews with two teachers. One watched as one boy shot and killed another in her classroom, another witnessed a stranger as he fired on students in front of his school.

Teachers who witness severe school violence struggle with Post-Traumatic Stress Disorder. Roberts (2007) described a shooting as a "period of psychological disequilibria, experienced as a result of a hazardous event or situation that contributes a significant problem that cannot be remedied by using familiar coping strategies" (Roberts, 2007, p. 7). There is a large gap in knowledge about the psychological and professional experiences of these teachers (Daniels, et al. 2007). This study will contribute to the dialogue and take a step toward filling that gap in knowledge; it is not the purpose of this study to clinically diagnose the disorder.

The Paradigm

The underlying paradigm in this research would be social constructivism. Creswell describes this as a "worldview," one in which "individuals seek understanding of the world in which they live and work" (Creswell, 2012, p. 20). The goal of this form of research, again as described by Creswell, is "to rely as much as possible on the participants' view of the situation" (Creswell, 2012, p. 20).

When using social constructivism, the questions posed to the participants "become broad and general so that the participants can construct the meaning of a situation, a meaning typically forged in discussions of interactions with other persons" (Creswell, 2012, p. 21). The writer continues by stating that the "more open-ended the questioning, the better, as the researcher listens carefully to what people say or do in their life setting" (Creswell, 2012, p. 21). Finally, the researcher's intent is to "make sense (or interpret) the meanings others have about the world" (Creswell, 2012, p. 21).

Therefore, this research was conducted utilizing open-ended, broad questions in an interview format. The researcher interpreted the meanings that the participants have attributed to the incident and its aftermath.

Research Design

The most appropriate research design, therefore, that fits this paradigm, social constructivism, would be a qualitative project. The description and analysis of interviews with two teachers struggling with personal and professional issues after a school shooting would be best served using qualitative narrative analysis.

Research Tradition

Qualitative Research

This study fits well under the general characteristics of qualitative research (Creswell, 2012, p. 16). It will explore a problem and develop a detailed understanding of central phenomena. The study will have the literature review play a minor role but justify the problem. The purpose and research question will be stated in a general and broad way as to the participants' experiences. Data were collected based on words from a small number of individuals so that the participants' views are obtained. The data were analyzed for descriptions and themes using text analysis and interpreting the larger meaning of the findings. Finally, this report was written using flexible, emerging structures and evaluative criteria, and including the researcher's subjective reflexivity and bias.

Narrative Research

More specifically, this study fits well into the purpose of a narrative form of qualitative research. Kohler-Riessman describes the necessary ingredients in a narrative as "a speaker connects events into a sequence that is consequential for later action and for the meanings that the speaker wants listeners to take away from the story" (Kohler-Riessman, 2008, p. 3). In this project, an understanding of Melissa's and Mike's experiences could prove to be consequential for later action, that is, for teachers experiencing similar situations in the future, and the meanings could affect how we treat teachers who witness such events.

Beyond the speaker, Kohler-Riessman (2008) proposes that the interviewer, in the narrative methodology, is a "facilitator who asks questions" and a "vessel-like 'respondent' who gives answers." She describes a situation with two "active participants" (Kohler-Reissman, 2008, p. 23) jointly constructing narrative and meaning. The goal of the interviewer is one of "generating detailed accounts rather than general statements" (Kohler-Reissman, 2008, p. 23). Broad-based, open-ended questions, with inquiries building on cues from previous responses, would create this sort of detailed account.

In addition, this study fits well into the characteristics of the narrative form of qualitative research (Creswell, 2012, p. 78). He calls for a narrative as needing focus. In this situation, the researcher will be exploring the life of an individual. Melissa and Mike are individuals with powerful stories that need to be told. Creswell also tells us that that the most suitable type of problem for this format is the need to tell stories of individual experiences. Narrative fits this proposed project. He also tells us that one must use a humanities background, including psychology and sociology. This project will use PTSD and trauma theory as constructs, thus there will be a large tie-in to psychology.

Creswell defines the unit of analysis in the narrative methodology as studying one or more individuals. Two individuals are studied in this project, with the pseudonyms of Melissa and Mike. The data collection procedures centered on interviews and documents; that describes the data in this study.

The data analysis in this project used restorying, and the development of themes. Patterns in the lives of Melissa and Mike were explored, patterns that indicate PTSD caused by the trauma of seeing a shooting at their school. The restorying attempts to show the impact this episode of violence had on their professional careers and personal lives. Creswell describes restorying as "the process in which the researcher gathers stories, analyzes them for key elements of the story (e.g., time, place, plot and scene), and then rewrites the story to place it in a chronological sequence" (Creswell, 2012, p. 509).

This resultant written report is centered on a narrative about the story of these two people's lives. The stories of Melissa and Mike were compared and contrasted. The general structure of the study consists of an introduction, a description of research procedures, a report of stories, a description of how the individual theorizes about his or her life, with narrative segments identified, which allowed recognition of patterns of meaning. The study concludes with a summary. The result, or report, of this research is a restorying of Melissa's and Mike's experiences; therefore, this research project will be conducted utilizing a narrative qualitative methodology.

Key Theorists

The narrative concept is ancient – one of the oldest methods of investigation in existence. According to Kohler-Riesman, the narrative form began "with Aristotle's examination of the Greek tragedy" (Kohler-Riesman, 2008, p. 4). The theory developed, Kohler-Riesman continues, through "French structuralism, Russian formalism, poststructuralism, cultural analysis and postmodernism" (Kohler-Riesman, 2008, p. 4).

Anthropologists and ethnographers adopted the methodology in the nineteenth century; tape recordings of interviews entered the field in the twentieth century. Modern coding and data analysis arose in the middle of the twentieth century. Some of the early seminal articles and books on the topic, in modern times, include the following, in chronological order.

1950s: Sociological Narratives

The 1950s saw the rise of sociological narratives. Burke, in1952, published a book entitled "Rhetoric of motives." A search for reasons, or motives, through the use of interviews was used. This was followed by Mills, in 1959, with "The sociological imagination."

1960s: The Rise of Ethnic Narratives

The transcribing of oral histories and traditions, through the use of interviews, arose in the turbulent decade of the 1960s. Coles, in 1967, released "Children of crisis." This was followed, almost immediately, by Devereux's "From anxiety to method in behavioral sciences." In this work, one of the first attempts to deal with the amorphic structure of interview analysis, a defined structure was proposed. Goffman, in 1969, offered, "The presentation of self in everyday life."

1970s: Formal Organization and Structuring

Following Berger's publication of "Ways of seeing" in 1972, Goffman offered a fundamental outline of organizing the narrative, entitled "Frame analysis: An essay on the organization of experience" (1974). Hymes immediately followed that, in the same year, with "Foundations in sociolinguistics: An ethnographic approach."

1980s: Narrative Structure, Validation and Non-verbal Forms of Communication

In 1981, Bekhtin opened the decade with a discussion of "The dialogic imagination: Four essays." He offered a discussion of how the dialogue can be viewed in narrative studies. In that same year, Scollon and Scollon offered "Narrative, literacy, and face in interethnic communication." This opened up the concept of inter-ethnic validation and perspectives. White (1981) argued for "The value of narrativity in the representation of reality." The following year Spence attempted to connect the world of psychology with the narrative research form, with "Narrative truth and historical truth: Meaning and interpretation in psychoanalysis." In 1983 Heath connected the profession of this researcher, education, to the narrative form with "Ways with words: Language, life and work in communities and classrooms."

2000s: Recent Trends in Narrative Research

Since the turn of the century, more and more pieces of literature are being released regarding the organization, validation and structuring of narrative research. In addition, more researchers have been designing systems for applying this form of investigation to wider fields of endeavor; for example, in 2001 Boje published "Narrative methods for organizational and communication research." Andrews, Squire and Tamboukou used a systemic approach to describe "Doing narrative research in the social sciences." This was followed with what is now seen as an authoritative source on the narrative, Kohler-Riessman's "Narrative Methods of the Human Sciences."

At the same time, serious work has been done in cataloguing the various dimensions of this growing avenue of research. In 2005 Herman, Jahn and Ryan released the "Routledge encyclopedia of narrative theory" which has since proven to be a central resource for a large number of narrative researchers. In that same year Chase published a work entitled "Narrative inquiry: multiple lenses, approaches, voices," one in which the breadth of this field was explored.

Statement of Positionality

In narrative research, the biases and opinions of the researcher can bleed into the work. It's important, therefore, to reveal the background of the researcher. My perspective on the participants and the interviews investigated here comes from my 25 years of service as a public high school teacher in California. I've also worked as a technology coordinator on campus and as a football coach. I have not served as an administrator, or as a person in a classified, support, position. I do not have credentials as a school psychologist, or as a general clinical psychologist.

In terms of violence, I have been directly (an attack on me) and indirectly (an attack nearby) exposed to a large number of acts of violence. If I had to estimate a number, I would guess at about 15–20 a year for the entire time – perhaps 400–500 in total. It is worth mentioning my experiences with, and views on, school violence.

School Background

For most of my career I have not taught in schools containing a large number of upper-middle class families. My schools could be described as having a diverse mix of children from struggling families, and many of these young people have been involved in gangs and crime. I have always taught in schools with high percentages of minorities. These schools also have a great diversity of minorities – and many of these groups have been in conflict with the others from time to time.

In many ways, my schools were very similar to the school in which my participant in this study, Melissa, taught. Hers was one of a large number of Hispanic and Black students, and most of the families came from a blue-collar working class background.

Direct Attacks

I have had five direct attacks on me during my tenure as a teacher. I have had my tires slashed and been confronted by a gang member with a switch-blade. I have had combatants turn and take swings at me as I tried to break up fights. One student, who knew about a severe allergy I have, sprayed a chemical as she screamed; "I hope he dies!" I must admit to some bias because of that incident – the girl was not arrested or prosecuted for what I consider to be a premeditated assault on a school employee. The administration, despite numerous witness statements, declined to ask for law enforcement involvement. My position does include the idea that administration should do more to defend against violence on school campuses and should prosecute violent students as much as possible.

Indirect Attacks

Indirect incidents include a large number of fist fights, a few gang brawls, two or three "ground poundings" (a fight in which one student is held down on the ground by one or more other students and then "pounded" by another combatant), a large number of attacks of thrown food, two knife fights, one mass attack by students on an adult, and one incident of gun usage. I have seen violence in my classroom, in the school commons areas, in parking lots on campus, and in the main office.

Fortunately, I have only seen a handful, perhaps six or seven, gang brawls, involving numerous participants on either side, during that time. Ground poundings, while I have only seen two or three, have affected me dramatically. There is a sense of helplessness as one sees a young person held down as others inflict severe violence on him. In two of the incidents the victim was sent to a nearby hospital with severe injuries even though I was able to break the fight up within a minute or two. That is an indication of how violent these types of fights can be.

Food fights, often changing into fist fights, happen quite often. These often start as a non-hostile throwing of food, perhaps toward a trash can or in jest at a friend, that goes awry. Many times the food thrown misses its mark – ending up on a complete stranger. The stranger gets angry and decides to retaliate.

The two knife fights I have watched mostly involved screaming and threats. Fortunately, in both incidents a security guard was nearby and intervened. In one of these incidents one student received a minor gash on his forearm, but no one was seriously injured or killed.

In what was, perhaps, the worst single incident of violence I have witnessed, I had just left the school parking lot and noticed a large crowd of teenage girls surrounding someone next to a car, beside the road. I was stunned as I realized three girls were holding an adult as a number of others came over, screaming, wanting to add their own attack. I stopped my car in the middle of the road, noticed a large stick nearby, picked it up and ran yelling at the crowd at the top of my lungs. I got the reaction I wanted. They were stunned and took off running in all directions. The woman who had been attacked slumped to the ground, bloody, with her clothes torn. I helped her up and back into her car. I called the police who arrived shortly thereafter. A number of the teens were identified and arrested.

The most dramatic episode of violence I have experienced in school was one that shadowed the experience of my participant. While on the edge of campus eating my lunch with students, I heard a popping sound. I noticed a piece of the tree flying off. I realize what was going on and pushed the three students who were sitting with me behind a low wall. I heard two more "pops." I looked up and noticed a pickup truck driving by. Two young men, with red bandanas, were firing out of the windows. It was over in a matter of seconds as they entered the nearby freeway. No one was hurt, but I was shaken.

References

Andrews, M., Squire, C., & Tamboukou, M. (Eds.) (2009). *Doing narrative research in the social sciences.* London: Sage.

Bekhtin, M. (1981). *The dialogic imagination: Four essays. (C. Emerson, M. Holquist, Translators).* Austin: University of Texas Press.

Berger, J. (1972). *Ways of seeing.* London: Penguin Books.

Boje, D. M. (2001). *Narrative methods for organizational and communication research.* London: Sage.

Burke, K. (1952). *Rhetoric of motives.* New York: Prentice Hall.

Chase, S. E. (2005). Narrative inquiry: Multiple lenses, approaches, voices. In N. K. Denzin & Y. S. Lincoln (Eds.), *Handbook of qualitative research* (pp. 651–679). Thousand Oaks: Sage Publications.

Coles, R. (1967). *Children of crisis.* Boston: Little, Brown.

Creswell, J. (2012). *Qualitative inquiry and research design: Choosing among the five approaches* (3rd ed.). Thousand Oaks, CA: Sage Publications.

Daniels, J., Bradley, M., & Hays, M. (2007, December). The impact of school violence on school personnel: Implications for psychologists. *Professional Psychology: Research and Practice, 38*(6), 652–659.

Devereux, G. (1967). *From anxiety to method in behavioral sciences.* The Hague: The Netherlands Mouton.

Goffman, E. (1969). *The presentation of self in everyday life.* New York: Penguin.

Goffman, E. (1974). *Frame analysis: An essay on the organization of experience.* Cambridge, MA: Harvard University Press.

Heath, S. B. (1983). *Ways with words: Language, life and work in communities and classrooms.* New York: Cambridge University Press.

Herman, D., Jahn, M., & Ryan, M. (Eds.) (2005). *Routledge encyclopedia of narrative theory.* London & New York: Routledge.

Hymes, D. (1974). *Foundations in sociolinguistics: An ethnographic approach.* Philadelphia: University of Pennsylvania Press.

Kohler-Riessman, C. (2008). *Narrative methods for the human sciences* (2nd ed.). Thousand Oaks: Sage Publications.

Mills, C. W. (1959). *The sociological imagination.* New York: Oxford University Press.

Roberts, A. R. (2007). *Crisis intervention handbook: Assessment, treatment and research* (2nd ed.). New York: Oxford University Press.

Scollon, R., & Scollon, S. B. (1981). *Narrative, literacy, and face in interethnic communication.* Norwood, NJ: Ablex.

Spence, D. F. (1982). *Narrative truth and historical truth: Meaning and interpretation in psychoanalysis.* New York & London: Norton.

White, H. (1981). The value of narrativity in the representation of reality. In M. J. Mitchell (Ed.), *On narrative* (pp. 1–23). Chicago: University of Chicago Press.

· 1 0 ·

A QUESTION ABOUT THE TEACHERS STUDIED

"I'm a bit confused. Is it required that you have to put some of your own experience into this paper?" Janice asked.

"It's very important. You see, we all have biases, and a good researcher make sure he or she acknowledges them, and takes them into account during the work in progress. It's a bit easier with qualitative work, you know, working with numbers, but it should be done in all research."

"I didn't know . . ."

"Interestingly enough, I now look for biases in all research – not if it is there, but how it is acknowledged. It is impossible, I believe, to not have bias. It's the human condition."

"That sounds important in any study."

"Yes. We also have to know our limitations, and about the context of whatever experience or situation we're analyzing. I got a feeling for Melissa's pain, but I still had to also see her as someone who is living in a bigger context in life, like as a mom, and a wife. Every factor affected her, as every factor affects you and me in our daily lives."

"Wow. Thinking of all of the teachers who have witnessed school shootings, there must be a lot of factors to consider," Janice said.

"Oh, yeah. It was rough honing everything down, because each story had so many unique components to it," I responded.

"I'll bet. I want to ask about your two main participants, but that brought up another question – lots of factors from lots of teachers. How many teachers did you talk to?"

"Depends on how you 'count' them. I really didn't keep track of the total I contacted initially. I started with a number of them, just asking if they'd be willing to talk about their experience."

"And some didn't want to talk about it?"

"There were quite a few that didn't want to talk about it. There were some who wanted to talk with me about over the phone, but didn't want to go any further. That was frustrating, because I heard some powerful stories. But I can respect their choice. It's not easy . . ."

"I can imagine that. I'm not sure I would want to."

"So, let's say there were around forty people I spoke to . . . initially . . ."

"FORTY? How in the world did you find forty teachers who witnessed school shootings?" Janice asked, with a surprised tone.

"Well, as I said, forty is an estimate. It wasn't easy. I started with a list of schools that had shootings, then started making phone calls and sending email messages. One person would connect me with another person, that sort of thing."

"That must have taken some time!"

"Oh, yeah. I had to follow up a few times, you know, like sending an email after a phone call."

"So, out of the 'around' forty, how many were willing to discuss their experience?" Janice asked.

"I would say about half declined. Most people were polite, and I could tell they felt bad for turning me down. But I understood. As you said, I'm not sure how much I would want to talk about it."

"Some of them were rude?"

"Only one or two. One person hung up on me. Again, I realized it's rough. I was poking at someone's raw wound. I never felt angry at anyone who declined."

"So, about twenty . . ."

"Around there, yes."

"And with that group, how many were willing to really sit down and talk to you?"

"Strangely, maybe about half of those."

"I see why you had to start with a larger number."

"Well, I actually wanted to do a broader study, with more teachers, but the more I talked to people, the more I wanted to go deeper. I started noticing the powerful emotions that the ten expressed, both men and women."

"I see."

"I was thinking of doing a sort of questionnaire sort of study, where I just got their responses, like 'on a scale of one to ten.' That sort of thing."

"Yeah, like rating a product online."

"Sort of, yes, but the more I listened, and the more I heard the power of their emotions, the more I knew a narrative study, delving deeper, was better."

"Why is that?"

"In narrative research, we ask open-ended questions, and allow the participant to direct the conversation. The choice of topics, in itself, is telling about how the participant feels. I really didn't foresee how draining that would be, emotionally, for me."

"I get it, but then you needed to find people willing to go deeper."

"Right, and that became the goal. Of the ten that really talked about their experiences, four of them dug deeply into their experiences. At that point, I had come up with the idea of comparing the experiences of two teachers, as I noticed a pattern – the responses of the schools and administration shaped how teachers responded to the trauma."

"So, as you were chatting with people, you were strategizing how your study could develop?" Janice asked.

"Well, I had a strategy in mind, but my advisors encouraged me to see where the dialog took me, and to make modifications. Any good study will re-assess throughout the process."

"Okay. How did you pick the two you went with?"

"First, I noticed similarities in their stories – both taught in middle school. Both worked in communities that could be described as suburban. And I noticed one big difference."

"What was that?"

"One was able to continue his career, and the other one was not," I responded

"I see where you're going. Maybe you could ask why one was able to continue, and the other was not able to."

"Exactly. I saw an opportunity to find the reasons. This study was about documenting what they experienced, but I also wanted to try and see if we could understand how what happens around them before and after the shooting affects teachers."

"That makes sense. Nothing happens in a vacuum."

"You're right." I paused. A memory from years ago returned. I remembered a voice over the phone, then I heard Janice's voice.

"Ed? Are you okay?"

"Huh? What?"

"You seem kind of distracted." Janice said.

"Oh, sorry. A memory form when I was making those calls kind of crept back into my mind, unexpectedly."

"Oh? Care to talk about it? I'll listen . . ."

"Hah! Now I'm in the place where some of my participants were. Yeah, I'll share it."

"So, it was on a phone call?"

"Yes. A teacher had been in a classroom with another teacher. The shooting was going on. He dove behind a desk, as he noticed the other teacher was lying there." I paused.

"And . . .?"

"Sorry, I can feel the emotion in his voice as he told me the shooter left the room and he nudged the teacher next to him, who did not respond. Then he noticed blood on the floor." I sighed.

"Oh, no. What a nightmare! Was the other teacher . . . dead?"

"You know what, I think so. I kind of felt numb as I heard him recount the scene. I believe he said the other teacher had died."

"I cannot imagine . . ." Janice's voice trailed off.

"Yeah, so you can see why some people didn't wasn't to talk about it."

"Oh, absolutely! I can tell his voice left an imprint in you!"

"Yeah, I guess so. I think that was about eight years ago, and I can still hear his voice shaking."

"So, did he decide to participate?"

"No, I believe he offered to, but I could tell that the short talk we had was rough on him. Besides, that added a new dimension to the study, one I was not sure I wanted to clip on."

"Oh?"

"Yeah. You see, a lot of dissertations struggle because they don't keep their focus narrow. I wrestled with that a lot – so many different destinations I wanted to travel toward. A teacher seeing a colleague, a co-worker, a friend, shot would be another story."

"Oh, I have that problem with regular day to day chores! I get distracted."

"Don't we all!" I replied.

"So, do you have other memories like that one, teachers describing things that happened, that you can't forget?"

"Oh, my, yes. Another one that comes to mind is a teacher I spoke with who heard gunfire in the hall, then shepherded his student into hiding. He paused, deciding what to do next . . ." I took a breath.

"Oh, no. Another tough one?"

"Yeah. This man is an amazing hero, in my book. His bravery that day was worthy of some war stories I've read. If he had done what he did, and it was during World War II, for example, he would have won some sort of medal – I believe it."

"Really? What did he do?"

"He was shaking a little, but something inside compelled him to go out into the hallway. He saw a teenage boy walking down the hall, looking around, like for targets."

"And?"

"The boy saw him, turned and point his gun at the teacher."

"Oh, no!" Janice exclaimed.

"At that moment, the teacher recognized the boy as a kid he had coached in football. I think it was football." I paused again.

"Some sport . . ." Janice assisted.

"Yeah, it doesn't matter which sport. Anyway, they stared at each other, and he didn't know what to say for a moment."

"You are kidding me! It must have been shock. What happened?"

"He saw the boy's expression soften. The kid took a breath. I think the boy didn't expect to run into his coach."

"Then . . .?"

"The teacher gently said, 'Jimmy, put the gun down.'"

"And?"

"The boy raised it, taking aim at the teacher."

"Oh . . . my . . ."

"Uh-huh. That's how I felt. The teacher kept talking. He said things like, 'You don't want to do this, son.'"

"The boy lowered the gun?"

"After what must have seemed like hours, yes. It was probably only a few minutes, but the teacher told me it felt like hours."

"What happened next?"

"The boy kept pointing the gun in the teacher's direction, but not at him. The teacher noticed law enforcement outside of a window. They were watching him, taking their cues from the teacher. He kept talking, in a soft tone as he noticed the officers pointing their weapons at the boy."

"Oh, my lord . . ."

"That's what I said about this point in the story. The teacher, during their calm talk, seemed to have connected with the boy emotionally, and the boy started sobbing. The teacher slowly walked over, and the boy handed him the gun. The law enforcement people rushed in and arrested the boy."

"That teacher saved lives!"

"That's what I mean – he deserves some kind of medal, if this was in the military. The teacher is a kind man, and I know he didn't do it for recognition, but he deserves it."

"You aren't kidding! Now I know what you meant by not foreseeing how emotionally draining this would be on you."

"Yeah. And I could go on, but I think you can get a flavor of what I went through, talking to these teachers. I have a number of side stories like these from this long journey. Yes, I never saw the idea that I'd be riding an emotional roller coaster while doing my research."

"No one could have foreseen that!" Janice replied.

"I think that represents a foundation of my study – we have no idea what it's like for teachers when there is a school shooting."

"I'm getting that idea. So, tell me about Melissa and, was it, Mike?" Janice asked.

"Yes, I gave him the pseudonym 'Mike.' "

An Answer

The First Participant: Melissa

One of the participants in this study, Melissa, is a former teacher who, just after returning from maternity leave, witnessed the classroom shooting murder of one boy by another. She was only a few feet from the incident. In combination with her post-partum depression, Melissa suffered severe emotional trauma because of that day. She was offered no job modifications or psychological support by her employer, a public school district.

Because she was pressured to return to her classroom, and assume normal duties as if nothing had happened, after a very short leave, she found herself dealing with severe Post-Traumatic Stress Disorder (PTSD). Nightmares, degraded personal relationships and anxiety attacks made it impossible for her to continue. She is now retired on medical disability. One of Creswell's characteristics of a narrative study is drawing upon a research tradition found in psychology or sociology, among others (Creswell, 2007, p. 78). Creswell and Riessman also describe interviewing and document analysis as the appropriate data sampling activities.

The Second Participant: Mike

The other participant in the study, Mike, is a teacher who watched as a stranger came on to his campus after school as he was on bus duty. His quick thinking and actions stopped the gunman, perhaps saving many lives. Mike was offered counseling, administrative support, and much more. He was still teaching as of the writing of this report.

Limitations of the Study

Because this study is an in-depth restorying of the experiences of two people during and after the witnessing of severe episodes of school violence, it will be a challenge to extrapolate the themes and messages gleaned from the interviews to other witnesses of such violence. Each situation of violence has a great number of incident details and personality variables.

Aspects of these experiences that could be compared to other stories, of other teacher witnesses to school shootings, could include (among other factors) the number of people shot, whether or not the teacher witness was wounded, the personality of the teacher witness, the psychological issues affecting the teacher at the time of the incident, the teacher's gender, the grade level (ages of students) involved in the shooting, the response of the school administration after the trauma, the teacher witnesses' family and friends support structure, and variability in local and state laws regarding investigations, job re-assignments and rehabilitation.

One can imagine the coping of a witness to trauma as an interaction of many parts. As studies tell us, "Resilient coping to extreme stress and trauma is a multifaceted phenomena characterized as a complex repertoire of behavioral tendencies" (Agaibi & Wilson, 2005, p. 195).

The Traumas Themselves

No two traumas are identical. The number of variables while the incident is happening is considerable. One objective of this study is to identify variables, perspectives and issues that could be called "transportable" – that ideas common to all witnesses to school shootings could be identified and measured by other cases not covered within. Some variables may not be applicable to other shooting situations. Three groups of factors must be considered.

First, there is the incident itself. Varying numbers of people, both shooters and victims, will be involved. Weapons may vary. The relationships between the individuals will vary. In Melissa's case, for example, she knew the shooter and the victim. In Mike's situation, he only knew the victim, who did not die.

Second (from a trauma viewpoint), traumas "are not equal in their impact to the psyche and vary greatly in their stressor dimensions" (Agaibi & Wilson, 2005, p. 210). Different types of traumas will affect people differently.

Finally (from a psychological perspective), the personality of the witness is a strong factor separating one event from another. Issues such as the witness's view of himself can contribute to the impact. One teacher with self-confidence may experience a different impact than one with poor self-confidence. Studies have shown that "self-esteem and self-confidence function as personality moderators of traumatic experiences and serve as protective factors" (Agaibi & Wilson, 2005, p. 201)

Number of People Shot

In both of these studies, one person was seriously shot (in Mike's case one additional student received a more superficial wound). In Melissa's incident, after the shooter fired, he dropped his weapon and immediately left the school grounds. The abandonment of the weapon could be construed as an end to the shooting incident. In Mike's case, his tackling of the shooter ended the incident. In other school shootings, shooters might go from room to room, continuing to fire.

The Teacher Witness: Wounded or Not

In these cases, the teacher witnesses were not wounded, and did not feel a sense that they would be shot. In other cases, teachers have been wounded or killed. A threat to personal security such as that could impact the onset and severity of Post-Traumatic Stress Disorder immensely. Long-term medical needs, such as surgeries and physical therapy, can affect the recuperation of a teacher.

The Teacher's Personality

Post-Traumatic Stress Disorder is a common result of witnessing such a trauma event such as a shooting and murder, and is often diagnosed by clinical professionals after shootings. Lauterbach and Vrana have observed "personality variables and trauma intensity were significant predictors of PTSD severity" (Lauterbach & Vrana, 2001, p. 29).

Research indicates "post-traumatic symptoms were higher for people experiencing more traumatic events" (Lauterbach & Vrana, 2001, p. 40). In Melissa's case, she was dealing with a degree of post-partum depression following the birth of her latest baby. This made her emotionally vulnerable to a deeper impact of witnessing a school shooting. Mike did not have an equivalent challenge at the time of the incident in which he was involved. Other teachers, in other situations, could be impacted by the psychological issues in their own lives, and in varying ways. Some might have scars remaining from their own personal experiences, such as war experiences or past abuse, triggering a deeper crisis.

Future studies focusing on teachers witnessing severe school violence would have to account for "clearly identifiable vulnerability factors to the psychiatric sequelae of PTSD that include genetics, individual risk factors (e.g., family background), personality (e.g., types of ego defense, extraversion), biological factors (e.g., alterations in brain function), cognitive style, and information processing" (Agaibi & Wilson, 2005, p. 203).

Biology and Trauma

There are biological underpinnings to coping with severe trauma. Lauterbach and Vrana describe how "gender also modified how various personality traits predicted trauma exposure and trauma responsivity" (Lauterbach & Vrana, 2001, p. 42). In addition, there is "some evidence for a genetic loading for trauma exposure" (Lauterbach & Vrana, 2001, p. 41).

Melissa was strongly influenced by her dealing with post-partum depression. Mike, as a male, would not have to cope with such biological turmoil as post-pregnancy hormones.

The Grade Level of the Students

One of the facts that triggered horror across the United States (and indeed the world) in the Newtown, Connecticut, school shootings (Sandy Hook Elementary School) was the realization that most of the people killed were kindergarteners, generally aged five and six years. While no shooting is "easy to accept," younger children being involved could evoke a deeper horror.

References

Agaibi, C., & Wilson, J. (2005, July). Trauma, PTSD, and resilience: A review of the literature. *Trauma Violence Abuse, 6*, 195–216. doi:10.1177/1524838005277438

Creswell, J. (2012). *Qualitative inquiry and research design: Choosing among the five approaches* (3rd ed.). Thousand Oaks, CA: Sage Publications.

Lauterbach, D., & Vrana, S. (2001, January). The relationship among personality variables, exposure to traumatic events, and severity of posttraumatic stress symptoms. *Journal of Traumatic Stress, 14*(1), 29–45.

· 1 1 ·

A QUESTION ABOUT THE SCHOOLS STUDIED

"You looked at the teachers, but did you do the same thing with the schools?" Janice asked.

"Of course. The schools, as organizations, play a big role in how things are handled."

An Answer

The Response of the Administration

The Burke-Litwin Model suggests that organizational climate plays a major role in how a crisis affects members of an organization, and the organization itself. That model specifically lists security and fairness in terms of "purpose, values and how people (in and out of the organization, including customers) are treated" (Burke, 2010, p. 222). As an example, in Melissa's case, many of her colleagues, her friends and support system, were transferred involuntarily to other schools. This administrative decision shattered the security and sense of support that could have been critical in the long-term healing of all school employees involved. In Mike's school, in contrast, staff unity was encouraged through social gatherings.

Family and Social Connectedness

A number of studies have shown that connectedness is a critical factor in how a witness to trauma heals and recovers. Lawrence and Fauerbach indicate that there is "evidence that a sense of belonging or connectedness is the most important variable in mediating stress" (Lawrence & Fauerbach, 2003, p. 65). Other studies have pointed out that "the amount of social support received did predict the extent of PTSD symptoms" (Agaibi & Wilson, 2005, p. 205).

In this study an important factor emerged in Melissa's story – her husband became a critical support system when her school administration did not respond with offers of psychological and job support systems. His reaching out to connect Melissa to psychological counseling proved to be invaluable to her healing process. As Agaibi and Wilson mention, family background is a critical element of coping with Post-Traumatic Stress Disorder. Other cases may have similar support systems, or they may be lacking. In addition, Melissa's school workmates, who had been a source of long-term support for years, could have been an important part of her healing, had they not all been transferred to other schools.

In Melissa's case, her family, post-trauma, was critical to what healing she was able to experience. She is generally an extrovert, and, most significantly, a biological factor, a struggle with post-partum depression, strongly contributed to the effects of PTSD.

Variability in Local and State Laws

Melissa's employment conditions operated under labor and educational laws in one state, and under the labor agreement between her district and the teachers employed in her district. Each state may have very different, laws and agreements regarding the investigation of a shooting, job re-assignments, rehabilitation and psychological disability pensions. Teacher unions across the country have variances in their contracts regarding such situations. Teacher retirement systems across the country may have different criteria regarding the use of psychological disability in approving an application for long-term payments.

Summary

While these factors explore a number of possible limitations, variables and implications for future studies of teachers witnessing school shootings, it is not meant to be all-inclusive. Each incident must be considered for its unique characteristics. The impact in the life of the teacher studied in this research may or may not be replicated in the lives of other teacher witnesses. As additional stories are gathered and catalogued, an over-arching studying comparing the factors discussed in this section could shed light on the interrelationship between the factors. This study was not designed to do this.

References

Agaibi, C., & Wilson, J. (2005, July). Trauma, PTSD, and resilience: A review of the literature. *Trauma Violence Abuse, 6*, 195–216. doi:10.1177/1524838005277438

Burke, W. W. (2010). *Organization change: Theory and practice* (3rd ed.). Thousand Oaks, CA: Sage.

Lawrence, J., & Fauerbach, J. (2003, January/February). Personality, coping, chronic stress, social support and PTSD symptoms among adult burn survivors: A Path Analysis. *Journal of Burn Care & Rehabilitation, 24*(1), 63–72.

· 1 2 ·

A QUESTION ABOUT WORKING
WITH PARTICIPANTS

"This brings up another question – how did you find your participants?" Janice asked.

"That took a bit of work. Of course, I had met Melissa, but I needed to expand my study group, for a variety of reasons."

"Why is that?"

"Well, for one thing, and this is important, if a participant wanted to drop out, they could, all the way up until the day I defended my research."

"Really? I had no idea."

"Yes. So, if one person dropped out and it was the only participant, I'd be back at square one."

"That's a great reason to expand!"

"Well, that and I started seeing something as I spoke to teachers – there could be value in comparing experiences. I debated on that for some time, because I was concerned that would make my study too big."

"I'll bet!"

"So, I decided to go with two participants. If one dropped out, I could still continue. Fortunately, they were all very much committed to participating."

"Why do you think that was?"

"When we're traumatized, being alone makes the trauma worse. When we reach out, connect with others who have experienced similar things, and receive affirmation. In addition, and I came to admire my participants – all of them hope this work could help someone else, in the future."

"I get it. So, back to what I asked – how did you find the teachers?"

An Answer

Recruitment and Access

One of the participants, Melissa, was a teacher that the investigator has known for a number of years. In a preliminary informal discussion, when the investigator started the Doctor of Education program at Northeastern University, he proposed the concept of telling Melissa's story through an interview process. Melissa was very enthusiastic about doing this – she expressed that by having her experience documented it would help in her healing process. She has always believed that this story could help future teachers who witness severe classroom violence.

As the formal process of creating this doctoral research project was begun, she was contacted along with a small number of other shooting witnesses by an introductory inquiry message. The approved IRB initial contact script was utilized to affirm her interest. The second participant, Mike, responded to the same short inquiry message and introductory script. All participant candidates were referred to the principal investigator. Once IRB approval was received, and within the guidelines that board expected, this interview process was begun.

· 1 3 ·

A QUESTION ABOUT THE INTERVIEWS
AND DATA

"I know that, in studies, you have to interview people, and gather data. How did you do that?" Janice asked.

An Answer

Data Collection

Data came from a number of primary sources, including interviews with the participants, medical documents regarding Melissa's disability, school letters and forms regarding the on-campus issues of both participants, court documents in the subsequent legal actions against the shooters, discussions with friends and relatives of the participants, as applicable and available, news items from the time of the incidents and campus visits, as practical and applicable. These sources were utilized to triangulate and corroborate the facts in the case and to understand themes and perspectives.

Interviews

The participants were questioned in a series of interviews. In the first phase of the interviews, a discussion of life up until the incident took place. The second phase focused on the shooting incidents witnessed. The final phase covered the period just after the incident, extending to approximately six months after the shooting.

The participants authorized their participation by use of an unsigned authorization form. This form stated that by starting the interview they consented to participation (see appendix). This form, recommended by the IRB board, allowed for maximum anonymity for the participants. In addition, state licensed psychological therapists were available before, during and after the interviews, for emotional and counseling support.

Their consent allowed the investigator to interview, to record the interviews, and to use the resulting transcripts in the process of developing the final report on this investigation. The participants also allowed the investigator to scan and use the documents they presented in this study. See the appendix for examples of these forms.

Documents

Numerous documents associated with Melissa's and Mike's cases were available during the investigation. These included reports from psychiatrists and mental health professionals, letters from school districts, legal documents surrounding the shootings, and subsequent legal actions, and newspaper reports. All of these were used to corroborate and add depth to these stories.

The Interviews

Interviews took place with Melissa and Mike, in places and times decided in consultation with them. The researcher deferred to their needs; what made them comfortable allowed for a more free exchange of information. State licensed mental health professionals were available before, during and after the interviews to provide psychological support if it was needed. The investigator arranged for a licensed professional as a back-up to the personal therapists arranged by the participants. No counseling support was requested in relation to the interviews.

The Emotional Climate of the Interview

In narrative research, Kohler-Riessman tells us, the specific wording of a question is "less important than the interviewer's emotional attentiveness and engagement and the degree of reciprocity in the conversation" (Kohler-Riessman, 2008, p. 24). The relationship between the participant and the interviewer is critical. As the Belmont Report urges, respect and openness have to serve as the foundations of the interviews. The researcher must stay involved in the discussion throughout.

The Questions in the Interview

First of all, in setting up the interview protocol, Butin urges the researcher to align interview questions with the research questions (Butin, 2010, p. 97). A list of these questions was with the researcher in the interviews, and was consulted as questions were posed. A sample of these questions is in the appendix of this report.

Secondly, it is important, in narrative research, to ask the right type of questions. As Butin describes, "... effective interviewing asks open-ended questions that elicit meaningful and deep responses" (Butin, 2010, p. 97). Butin urges the interviewer to make sure that the "last thing you want is to have people answer 'yes' or 'no' to your questions" (Butin, 2010, p. 97).

Initial questioning started with open-ended broad questions such as, "Tell me what happened on the day of the shooting," or "How did you feel about that?" The interviewer employed sub-questions, as needed depending on the responsiveness of the participant. Additional questions were structured in such a way that the participants were able to move in a diversity of directions. Indeed, their chosen directions were indicative of their perspectives. Their emotional responses indicated the importance and value of that perspective.

The other questions were structured to allow an exploration of one topic in depth, such as "Tell me more about your conversation with your principal that day," or they were used to explore previously untouched topics. If the participant did not mention, for example, how a number of substitutes were used while she was on maternity leave, a question such as, "How do you feel a revolving door of substitutes during your maternity leave affected your class?" was used. This question would be preferred to, "Did a string of substitutes during maternity leave affect your class?" The latter question would allow a simple "yes" or "no" answer, as Butin advises against. Very few of these questions were necessary.

Finally, Butin urges the researcher to "let them talk" (Butin, 2010, p. 97). He urges the questioner to use "subtle cues and prompts" (Butin, 2010, p. 97) to bring out the creative and thoughtful mind that can contribute ideas. The researcher needs to be emotionally and actively involved in the discussion and ready with those subtle prompts whenever the interview drifts or stalls.

In conclusion, the questions asked were aligned with the various research questions, they were not of the "yes" or "no" answerable variety, and the researcher allowed the participants to continue to speak. Throughout the process the researcher acknowledged that using these "rules" sparked new and creative perspectives on the situation. These allowed the participant to drive the direction of the data gathering to what he or she believes is important in the framework of this study.

References

Belmont Report. (1979). *The Belmont Report: Ethical principles and guidelines for the protection of human subjects of research.* Retrieved from hhs.gov/ohrp/humansubjects/guidance/belmont.html

Butin, D. (2010). *The education dissertation: A guide for practitioner scholars.* Thousand Oaks, CA: Corwin.

Kohler-Riessman, C. (2008). *Narrative methods for the human sciences* (2nd ed.). Thousand Oaks: Sage Publications.

· 1 4 ·

A QUESTION ABOUT CHECKING DATA

"If the participants could 'drive' the interviews, how can you make sure what they said is valid? How did you remember all that they said?" Janice asked.

"I used what we call transcription, and validation. The interviews were recorded."

"And then what?"

An Answer

Transcription and Validation

Once the interview data were electronically gathered, the responses to each question were transcribed into a Microsoft Word file. Phone calls and email correspondence served as validations of the transcribed material. These files were saved a second time; one file was used as the original transcript for each participant; the other was used for data coding. This component of the project was completed within one week.

Data Storage

Components of the Data

There were three major components of the data being acquired for this project: interview recordings and transcriptions, documents related to the experiences of Melissa and Mike, and notes taken by the investigator. During the process of developing the final research report (thesis), all three were kept isolated from everyone except the investigator and the investigator's committee.

All were stored in a separate folder in Microsoft Word format. As Creswell advises, "Always develop backup copies of computer files" (Creswell, 2012, p. 142); these files were backed up to online storage; this process was finished within a day of completing data gathering.

Data Storage During the Project

Electronic Recordings

The interviews were recorded through digital/electronic recording and through written notes. They were stored in MP3 format. During the process of creating the final research paper the digital recordings of the interviews and the transcribed records of the interviews were kept on two computers (a desktop and a laptop) accessed only by the investigator. In addition, one copy of these notes and recordings were kept in a safe deposit box with access held only by the investigator.

Documents

The documents related to the experiences of Melissa and Mike were scanned. The originals were immediately returned to the participants the same day. These scans were stored in a fashion similar to the electronic recordings of the interviews.

Data Storage After the Project is Completed

Once the final product (the research thesis) was completed and accepted, all of the data sources were stored in a safe deposit box for a period not to exceed three years. The data will be immediately erased from the two computers being used in the project, but maintained in the safe deposit box. After three years the data will be destroyed in all formats, paper and digital.

Data Confidentiality

No actual personal or place names were stored with the transcripts and recordings of the interviews. At the urging of the Northeastern University IRB committee, many non-essential facts were redacted to make it more difficult to pinpoint who are the actual participants. Scanned documents had personally identifying information redacted from the resultant scan. Once the project has been completed, all documents will be electronically destroyed or, if on paper, shredded.

References

Creswell, J. (2012). *Qualitative inquiry and research design: Choosing among the five approaches* (3rd ed.). Thousand Oaks, CA: Sage Publications.

· 1 5 ·

A QUESTION ABOUT ANALYZING DATA

"Every answer you give seems to generate one or two more questions!" Janice exclaimed.

"There' nothing wrong with that. I understood that myself as I did my study. The more I discovered, the more questions I had!"

"So, did the 'data,' or the interviews, help you prove your point?"

"Well, yes and no. You start out with an hypothesis, and then allow the data to sway your model. I started out with a 'guess,' but the more I worked on this the more I saw the answer was changing."

"What do you mean?"

"I have to admit that I came in feeling that how a teacher handles a school shooting is dependent on how the school deals with it."

"And it's not?"

"Well, again, yes and no. As I sifted and analyzed, I saw it was more complicated than that. In fact, a big chunk of my final chapter has to do with a 'formula' approach to answering how school shootings affect teachers. There are a lot of variables," I responded.

"Is that what's called 'inductive'?" Janice asked.

"Yes . . .," I began.

An Answer

Data Analysis

Suter states that "Qualitative data analysis often follows a general inductive approach (as opposed to a hypothetical-deductive one) in the sense that explicit theories are not imposed on the data in a test of a specific hypothesis. Rather, the data are allowed to speak for themselves by the emergence of conceptual categories and descriptive themes" (Suter, 2012, p. 346).

Data Acquisition and Transcription: Mechanics

Prior to the Interviews

After initial contact, using the script approved by the IRB board, a series of interviews took place, and they were recorded electronically. Prior to the commencement of interviewing, the participant met with the researcher to go over the details of how the study functioned, and to gain the participant's authorization to complete the study.

During the Interviews

While the interviews were underway, they were recorded digitally. At the same time the investigator made notes of expressions, body language or other considerations assisted in the transcription and analysis stages of the research.

After the Interviews

After the interviews were complete the investigator requested follow-up discussions. When these were finished, the investigator transcribed all interviews into an MS Word document, assigning appropriate line numbers for reference purposes. Non-essential personal identification information was redacted from the transcripts.

References

Suter, W. (2012). *Introduction to educational research: A critical thinking approach* (2nd ed.). Thousand Oaks, CA: Sage Publications.

· 1 6 ·

A QUESTION ABOUT CODING

"I get it. Again, another question comes to mind!" Janice exclaimed.

"And what is this one?" I asked.

"How the heck do you look through a transcript and try to find patterns, or clues?"

"That process is called 'coding,'" I responded.

An Answer

Data Coding

Data coding is described as the process in which "the researcher identifies one open category to focus on (called the 'core phenomenon'), and then goes back to the data and create categories around the core phenomenon" (Creswell, 2012, p. 64). It is important to note "There is no single right way to analyze qualitative data."

The methodology selected for this first cycle was *in vivo* coding, which is often used to "prioritize and honor the participant's voice" (Saldana, 2009, p. 74).

Axial Coding

Using constant comparison, an axial coding exercise was undertaken, blending the coding results from all interviews. Universal codes were assigned across the interview transcripts.

Saldana describes the purpose of axial coding as "to strategically reassemble data that were 'split' or 'fractured' during the Initial Coding process" (Saldana, 2009, p. 159). As additional interviews were brought into this process, codes were redefined and redeveloped to facilitate statements that did not fit the patterns of the first interview.

Strauss (1987) describes axial coding as consisting of "intense analysis done around one category [i.e., variable] at a time, in terms of paradigm items (conditions, consequences, and so forth)" (Strauss, 1987, p. 32). According to Glaser (1978), axial coding looks for "causes, contexts, contingencies, consequences, covariances, and conditions" (Glaser, 1978, p. 74). These searches are centered on a focal category.

Constant Comparison

The concept of constant comparison tells us that in principle, "data is organized by grouping like with like: data bits with data bits. After the bits are separated into piles, each bit is compared within each pile" (Dye, Schatz, Rosenberg, & Coleman, 2000, p. 1). In this exercise, components from the first interview's coding were compared with newly introduced interview data sets.

Overview of the Constant Comparison Process

After coding the subsequent interview data sets, the initial data set was recoded with changes in the code chart made after seeing the Second. This same process was repeated for all data sets, and the first two were modified as a result. Each additional re-coding, and constant comparison, produced fewer major modifications to the code list.

Continued analysis of new interviews produced more modifications, but few major changes to the main categories. Each new data set entailed a re-coding of earlier data sets to allow for new perspectives brought by new interviews.

Themes

As a result of coding, axial coding and constant comparison, themes arose, which are discussed in the "findings" section of this research paper. These data produced a "voice" for the participants, and a telling of their stories. As these themes arose, the influence of the elements of the constructs became apparent, allowing an assessment of the effects of Post-Traumatic Stress Disorder and Organizational Climate in the post-incident life of the teacher witnesses.

Trustworthiness

The trustworthiness and validity of this study was maximized through the use of several steps. These included member checking, prolonged engagement, triangulation, clarifying researcher bias, and rich, thick description.

Member Checking

Saldana describes "member checking" as the process by which the investigator consults "the participants themselves during analysis" (Saldana, 2009, p. 28). In this study the participants had a number of opportunities to review the data and the results of analysis. After the interviews were transcribed, Melissa and Mike had an opportunity to go over them and check for any factual errors. Once the coding was accomplished they had, once again, access to that information, and the opportunity to offer feedback.

Prolonged Engagement

Creswell stresses that prolonged engagement, the concept that the investigator and the participant have built a relationship over time, builds trust. This involves the investigator learning the background culture of the incident and participant, and the "checking for misinformation that stems from distortion introduced by the researcher or informants" (Creswell, 2012, p. 207).

The investigator has maintained a relationship with one participant, Melissa, for almost three years, and has been looking into the background of the incident, such as visiting the school where it happened, and watching the interactions of the participant with her family. Through the passage of time, and the interaction between the two, the investigator has come to understand the participant's culture, relationships, and personality, aspects that may influence the interviews.

The investigator has maintained a good relationship with Mike since concluding the interviews. It is anticipated that this will continue into the future.

Triangulation

Creswell describes triangulation as that process by which researchers "make use of multiple and different sources, methods, investigators, and theories to provide corroborating evidence". He continues by stating that "this process involves corroborating evidence from different sources to shed light on a theme or perspective" (Creswell, 2012, p. 208). In this study, numerous school, medical, and personal documents were made available to the investigator, as well as access to members of the participants' families. In addition, newspaper articles, district records, and court documents were consulted.

Clarifying Researcher Bias

Early in the report, the biases, experiences and background of the researcher were discussed, in addition to actions taken to minimize the influence of these biases in the analysis of the data presented. An outside auditor, recommended by Creswell (p. 209) was used to cross-check these biases.

Creswell recommends that the researcher "comments on past experiences, biases, prejudices, and orientations that have likely shaped the interpretation and approach to the study" (Creswell, 2012, p. 208). The investigator revealed that he has been a public school teacher in the same state as one of the participants and has witnessed school violence, albeit not as severe as that witnessed by the participants. He also revealed that he has had difficulties with members of school administration teams when dealing with school violence.

Rich, Thick Description

Creswell describes this aspect of validation as allowing the "readers to make decisions regarding transferability because the writer describes in detail the participants or setting under study" (Creswell, 2012, p. 209). Information can be transferred to other studies because of shared experiences. This was used extensively in this project; the participant's voice is "heard" throughout the final document.

References

Creswell, J. (2012). *Qualitative inquiry and research design: Choosing among the five approaches* (3rd ed.). Thousand Oaks, CA: Sage Publications.

Dye, J., Schatz, I., Rosenberg, B., & Coleman, S. (2000, January). Constant comparison method: A kaleidoscope of data. *The Qualitative Report, 4*(1). Retrieved from http://www.nova.edu/ssss/QR/QR3-4/dye.html

Glaser, B. G. (1978). *Theoretical sensitivity*. Mill Valley, CA: Sociology Press.

Saldana, J. (2009). *The coding manual for qualitative researchers*. Thousand Oaks, CA: Sage Publications.

Strauss, A. (1987). *Qualitative analysis for social scientists*. New York, NY: Cambridge University Press.

· 1 7 ·

A QUESTION ABOUT PROTECTING PARTICIPANTS

"It seems the voices of the participants, as you called them, is important in this kind of research. What did you say this type of qualitative research is called?" Janice asked.

"Narrative research, and yes, their voices, their messages, are critical."

"It seems so personal, since you had to leave out personal details that you thought did not affect the study."

"It was personal, yes." I responded.

"How did you protect them? I mean, their rights and privacy?"

"Well, first of all, as you know, I did not use real names."

"Right – I still find it hard to see her as 'Melissa!'" Janice chuckled.

"Well, that's a level of protection."

"I'm glad to hear that she was protected. What else did you do?" Janice asked.

"A lot, actually. And many of these protections go back over 70 years. In the middle of the twentieth century, researchers did all kinds of things with people, things that may have caused lifetime trauma, in the name of science. Laws were created, ones I strongly believe in, to protect participants."

"Tell me more . . ."

An Answer

Protection of Human Subjects

In this study the rights of the participants have been maintained and defended at all times. At various stages of the process the investigator checked with the participants to ensure that their well-being is strong and that if any questions or concerns arose he or she had the absolute right to bring these up and to cancel participation if desired. During formal contacts, such as the interviews with the participants, they had their own mental health professionals available, and the investigator had his own licensed therapist on call.

Ethical Consideration

The landmark Belmont Report identified three principles essential to the ethical conduct of research with humans. These are a respect for persons, beneficence, and justice.

Respect for Persons

The challenges in applying the Belmont principle of respect for persons are in making sure that potential participants comprehend the risks and potential benefits of participating in research, and avoiding influencing potential participants' decisions either through explicit or implied threats (coercion) or through excessive compensation (undue influence).

Beneficence

Two general rules have been articulated as complementary expressions of beneficent actions: do no harm, and maximize possible benefits and minimize possible harm. The challenge inherent in applying the Belmont principle of beneficence is how to determine when potential benefits outweigh considerations of risks and vice versa.

Justice

Justice requires that individuals and groups be treated fairly and equitably in terms of bearing the burdens and receiving the benefits of research. The principle of justice may arise in decisions about inclusion and exclusion criteria for participation in research and requires investigators to question whether groups are considered for inclusion simply because of their availability, their compromised position, or their vulnerability — rather than for reasons directly related to the problem being studied.

The challenge of applying the Belmont principle of justice is how to decide which criteria should be used to ensure that harm and benefit of research are equitably distributed to individuals and populations.

Informed Consent

The three fundamental aspects of informed consent are voluntariness, comprehension and disclosure. The participants voluntarily consented, via proper forms, to be the subjects of this research project. In addition, they comprehended this consent and the nature of the project. Finally, they had access to the data, of all kinds, and they understood how the data would be used. This was accomplished by the use of unsigned forms, an explanatory session on how the research was done, and what it was used for.

Confidentiality

The participant, and all parties involved in the research are identified by the use of pseudonyms. No real names, places, or unnecessary personal data are used in the analysis or report of the study. The use of dates, places, and names were carefully considered to ensure that little or no information is given out that would reveal the actual names, places, or dates involved with the incidents in question. Even the consent form is a recognized "unsigned" consent form – keeping the participants further shielded.

The participants had the opportunity to review information in this report and, indeed, the participants were allowed to review the report in its entirety to ensure that information was not inadvertently placed in the text that could identify him or her.

The IRB Process

The IRB approval process commenced after the initial three chapters of this paper were approved. All paperwork and documentation was prepared properly to meet all General Criteria for IRB Approval of Research (45 CFR 46.111). Official certification of this fact is included in the appendices of this report.

Risks

In this process, as much as possible, risks to human subjects were minimized. The availability of licensed psychological therapists before, during and after interviews mitigated these risks. Risks to the human subjects are reasonable in relation to anticipated benefits, if any, to human subjects and the importance of the knowledge that may reasonably be expected to result from the research. The selection of the human subjects was equitable and proper for the nature of the study.

Informed Consent: Other Parties

In addition to the participant, informed consent was sought from each prospective research participant or the prospective research participant's legally authorized representative in accordance with and to the extent required by the Health and Human Services (HHS) regulations (45 CFR 46.116). Informed consent is appropriately documented in accordance with and to the extent required by the HHS regulations (45 CFR 46.117) (see associated IRB appendix attached).

Data Monitoring

The research plan made adequate provision for monitoring the data collected to ensure the safety of the human subjects. When appropriate, there are adequate provisions to protect the privacy of human subjects and to maintain the confidentiality of data. HHS regulations require that studies involving human subjects should have a monitoring plan when appropriate (45 CFR 46.111). All data were made accessible to the Institutional Review Board and the research supervisor, as requested.

Since the NIH requires that all clinical trials supported by NIH have a Data and Safety Monitoring (DSM) plan, one was developed and provided, as required.

Conclusion

This study reviews the various components of the methodology proposed for a qualitative narrative study asking the central question, "How is a teacher's career affected by witnessing severe school violence?" The participants, teachers with the pseudonyms of Melissa and Mike, witnessed school shootings on their campus.

The study's methodology, research design, paradigm and tradition were discussed. In addition, there are sections describing participant recruitment and access. Finally, an overview of methods of data collection, storage and analysis, trustworthiness, and protection of human subjects is offered.

References

Belmont Report. (1979). *The Belmont Report: Ethical principles and guidelines for the protection of human subjects of research.* Retrieved from hhs.gov/ohrp/humansubjects/guidance/belmont. html

· 1 8 ·

IN MELISSA'S WORDS

"So, going back to your research question, and my biggest interest because she's my friend, what did Melissa tell you about what happened to her?" Janice asked.

"I think the best way to handle that question is to just let her use her words . . ." I responded.

Melissa McCarthy: Mother and Teacher

Becoming a Teacher

I've always loved being around kids, and I love books and writing, so a few years after my bachelor's degree I decided to go back to school to get a teaching credential. I was very excited about being a teacher. That was after my second daughter was born, in the late 1990s. Like any other teacher, you go to classes, and it seems like it takes forever to finish. I had to do my student teaching, but I was very lucky in that I was able to do that while actually getting paid; that was possible because of a shortage of teachers at the time.

I taught junior high school that student teaching year, 7th grade English and honors English. After that I thought I might like to teach high school;

I received a contract and taught 10th and 11th grade English. After I finished my student teaching, I'd thought, "After a year of junior high, maybe I would prefer older children." Junior high's a rough age to work with – the kids are going through so many changes in life and in their families.

Shortly after starting to work with the older kids I found out that, well, based on my demeanor, my age, and maybe my looks, I wasn't old enough to be a high school teacher. I felt like the older kids did not take me seriously. Obviously, at the junior high level, the kids think I'm old.

After that year, what I call my "high school" year, I started looking for another job and got really lucky. A local school district was hiring and that seemed, to me, like a great opportunity. It was closer to home – my commute would be almost nothing. I got a huge bump in pay because it's a low income area. They wanted a skilled teacher, and they figured that the more they pay, the better the teacher they'd get. I believe the district, at that time, felt like experienced teachers would provide the kids with a better education.

It was about this time that I finished up my master's degree, and it really bumped me up on the pay scale. I was able to quality for grants to help pay down some student loans and different things, so it was a win-win situation for me when I entered employment with my local district. That's when I started at Ash Tree Middle School, around the year 2000, I think.

Teaching at Ash Tree Middle School

They put me into English composition, and, well, basically I stayed there; I never deviated. I was never able to teach honors or GATE ("Gifted and Talented Education") class, or any of those kinds of classes; those seemed like they were special classes for special people who were part of the politically high echelon, and I was not in that group. I was a scrub and didn't care. I just wanted to get my tenure.

The year I started about seven English teachers came on board. They had just done a complete cleaning-out of the school, and all of us started at basically the same time. We were all on the same level in terms of tenure and assignments, but that was really unusual. It almost never happened that way.

So, at the beginning, I loved my school and my job. I loved where they put me – and nobody ever wanted to know anything. It was one of those positions where you were definitely on your own; you had to create your own safety net for help and networking with other teachers.

All my administration wanted to know was that everything was under control and that my kids weren't bugging them. I guess my students were mostly discipline problems, being lower-performing, non-GATE kids. Administration seemed to be happiest if I dealt with all of the problems in my classroom, and that's pretty much the way it worked out. As long as the office didn't get a phone call from or about you, they didn't want to know anything, and that's kind of the way they kept it.

If I had a problem, then yes, I would definitely go to them because there are just sometimes you had to. You would call home because, of course, the first rule in the rule book is, "Call the parents." Well, these weren't kids that you could call the parent because the parent either wasn't home, or the phone was disconnected, or there was no parent, or the parent didn't speak English, or the parent didn't care. You didn't have a parent to back you up with these kids.

Once in a great while you would, and those were truly the kids that didn't need to be in my class in the first place, for the most part. What I would usually do is, if there was a kid that showed promise or could actually read at his grade level, I would usually bump them to honors because I didn't teach at an 8th grade level. I taught about at a 3rd grade level on a regular basis.

Whatever was going on in the office, in my classroom I wanted to teach. I had one goal in mind – I wanted my students to succeed. I was driven by the thought, "Dang it, you are going to get to high school, and you are going to be able to write a four-paragraph essay." That was my primary goal, and, of course, to do decently on the various tests. I did everything in my power to make sure I accomplished these things.

Maternity Leave

So, it was a new school year at Ash Tree. At that point in my life I was the mother of a couple of daughters, and, funny enough, I found out I was pregnant. It was a surprise, and I did not expect to be a working mother by any means. I was one of those parents that was super lucky, and I was able to stay home with my kids in their early lives. I was able to stay home with both of my previous daughters, for at least a good year and a half to two years. When I found out I was pregnant I was panicked, to say the least. I knew I was going to have to work with this one, but I'm not a "put your kid in daycare" kind of mom, at least for those first two years.

This became a really big stressor on me, not to mention just teaching in and of itself. I went out on maternity leave in October, but before that

I spent a lot of time working on lesson plans, gathering materials, and setting up my room for a substitute, like every teacher would when she went on maternity leave.

I came back in January to find that none of the sub plans had been followed. They basically had had three different subs in there. My classroom had been raided. The kids had stolen books. The kids had stolen Sharpie pens. There was no part of my classroom that had not been disrupted.

It was disgusting. I walked into my classroom, and I started crying. I mean, you can chalk that up to just having a baby, whatever you want, but when I walked into that classroom I broke down. You see, I'm a very in-control, very organized teacher. I have a certain dialed-in way of working with my kids and my materials. I come back from maternity leave, and all of a sudden, adding in having a baby to the mix and then [the shape] my room was in, I was not ready for what I saw when I got back.

I couldn't find anything. None of the subs had left anything anywhere. I know that they tried to get a long-term sub in there, and not to discredit her, I think what had happened is she started pretty well; and a lot of the kids loved her. She was great, but she got sick.

After she got sick, the administration brought in substitute after substitute, you know, the day-to-day subs that screw everything up. These subs say, "Oh, I'm not going to follow this lesson." Even though everything was all set up, they still didn't follow it. So when I got back, it was a complete and utter mess. I realized I had to start all over.

All my teaching buddies (we had a great core group there) came in and picked me back up. They got me going, and set me up again. They helped me get back on my feet, but I was panicked at that point.

Rebuilding After Returning

So I started over in my lessons. They were supposed to have already had the unit on Anne Frank and tolerance. By the way, considering what happened, this, to me, is very ironic. Of course, they had gone through the tolerance unit very quickly and not significantly. I didn't have anything to gauge their levels or to assess them on, so I just took them back to the beginning of the unit. I figured it's a decent unit to start over on anyway.

That's where I started. A lot of them had had me for a month, a month and a half in September, so when I came back, now they'd been through all this and they pretty much had the attitude of, "We can do whatever we want."

I basically had to set the routine back up again, just like any teacher does, at the beginning of September. They say you shouldn't smile until December, and on this one I had to double do it because these kids had been running around crazy. At the same time, I had enough problems as it was dealing with things. I was breast-feeding and pumping and doing all kinds of crazy stuff, and trying to organize my classroom. Whew, I was a mess.

Many of my teacher buddies in the hallway would whisper something like, "We are so, so glad you are back because now we know there won't be kids standing in the hallway the whole time doing nothing but bugging us." It seemed that that's what the sub would do, "Just go stand in the hallway." Administration wouldn't help them.

It was sad. I had good kids in there. It was heart-breaking.

A New Student

We had been working on an essay on tolerance for almost three or four weeks, and it was at the point where they needed to have it done and finished. Strange; the essay focused on tolerance, and then we had this bullying. It's probably the one thing that never escapes me, but nobody else ever focused on that because it was on Anne Frank and Martin Luther King.

Also prior to this, three or four weeks prior, probably right about the time that we started this paper, that was the beginning of the quarter, and that's when Andrew was transferred into my classroom. All I got from administration when he came down to me was, "Oh, I'm giving you a gift. He's a gem." Basically, I got the idea that he's just a big jerk that isn't going to do anything; but I didn't get the understanding of why or what or how or any of the other details.

He came from GATE, and that was because he was a nonperformer. He was steadily going down, and of course, during the trial, once I had heard about some poem that he wrote about – about a little teddy bear or something and how it's going to disappear, that he had written in GATE. I thought, "How did anybody miss these things?"

Basically, it was a metaphor for this kid saying, "I don't like my life." Why wouldn't somebody have picked up that? To me, at that level, when these children write, if it shows even a small ounce of something like, well, that's a scream and you have to listen because they aren't going to walk up to you and say, "Hey, I'm feeling really crappy today. I think I might shoot someone." They don't do that. It can't be that blatant.

I've had that happen on more than one occasion with more than one student, and I've called in the counselors and the parents when I see it because I know. I know what it's like to be depressed. I know what it's like to be scared. You just don't mess around with these kids when that happens.

In the first day he came into my classroom without a backpack, didn't have paper or a pencil. He had nothing. I sent him to the office I said, "Andrew, you don't have anything to write with," and he replied, "No." I finished with, "Then go to the office and come back when you do."

On the second day he showed up again, with nothing. I was stuck. Remember, I'm setting the pace all over again from September with these students. I can't have somebody try and tell me, "Hey, I'm better than you." It isn't going to work like that with me. I told him, "Well, Andrew, you don't have anything to write with. You've got to understand this."

Again, I told him, "Go to the office. When you have something to write with, when you have something to do work with, fine, otherwise, look in this classroom. There are 29 other kids, Andrew, and I'm in charge of their education, too. I'm not going to let you sit in here with nothing to write or do when I'm giving a lesson because chances are you're going to be bugging them and goofing off." So I sent him back.

The office didn't want him sitting there again, so they gave him paper and a pencil and said that they would take care of it. Apparently they called his father, and his father had come in and picked him up because he had some dentist appointment or something. I know his father was beating him at home.

Finally he came back to class – and he's got his backpack, and some books, all he needs. He started working. Granted, I could tell he wasn't going to be the biggest performer in the world. He didn't want to be, and I was good with that. I was also understanding that, "Hey, this kid's really smart, and probably I'm rolling at a level way behind him." It didn't really matter in that respect.

I gave him a book. While I can't remember the name of the book, it was one of these soldier books where this kid is young and he's a soldier at war and going through whatever he's going through. So, after a struggle for a week or so he settled into a routine and started working.

The Shooting Incident: Like an Exploding Computer

I had taken roll in my classroom, and we were getting ready to slip into the computer lab to finish writing the essay. As we walked, and I usually follow behind everybody to make sure they all get there, Zachary was with me, and he was definitely subdued that day. He wasn't wearing his normal happy garb, just the uniform. I couldn't really tell if he looked beat up, but apparently other people thought he looked beat up. Maybe he had some marks on him. I don't know.

I spoke with him, and said, "Zachary, I need you to do this paper. You can't walk, you can't graduate, you can't go past 8th grade if you don't pass lit comp, and I need you to do this paper." He replied with, "Okay, I will, I will, I will, I will." Zach was very much like Andrew, but he was on the other side of it. He really couldn't do the work. He was a little lazier; it took him a while to do it.

I was worried about Zach. My girlfriend, Gloria, had told me, "Zach's pulling some really crazy stunts, and we're worried about his safety. A lot of the boys want to beat him up." There were rumors that Zach was a bully.

We got to the lab, and they all start, and they're basically done with these papers. They know what they're doing. They're writing. They're excited, and I'm hopeful. Those who weren't writing, they weren't writing because they didn't bring a book, or they hadn't brought the final draft of their paper which they should have had by now. I think Andrew had said, "No, I did it at home." I replied, "Okay, well, where is it? It's not here? Then you're not going to go on a computer today."

About four or five of them were sitting along the wall, and Andrew was one of them. Everybody else was seated at their tables. I just started walking around making sure people were working. It was nice – they were excited, doing what they were supposed to be doing. I had my back to that one side of the room, and of course, BAM, there was a pop. It literally sounded like a crash, like, well, I liken it to a computer exploding. I turned around to look in that direction.

I'm going to say I focused on Andrew because he was standing, but it's still fuzzy to me. These are just the bits and pieces that I remember, and that I go over; and, I think, are part of my memory because I go over them.

I turned around, looked at him, and yelled, "Andrew, what the hell are you doing?" I did this because he was standing up. Then all of a sudden I was able to process what had just happened, and at that moment he fired the gun again. That's probably when it all started going fuzzy in my brain.

If anybody ever interviewed the kids that were in there, I know some of them remember what was going on. I've never asked any of them because I know how traumatic it was for me to go back through what I went through back then, so I've never asked them; but a couple of the parents came up to me and said, "You saved my baby's life. Thank you!" All I remember thinking and yelling at that point was "Get in this door. Get in this door now. Everybody up and get out."

Andrew had dropped the gun and walked out, so I don't believe I had the imminent fear that we were all going to be killed at that point. I've got to believe it wasn't there. Who knows? God only knew at that point.

We ran into the other computer room and screamed our heads off. Someone called 911. Things moved fast. That's when all of a sudden your body just goes, well, it's like a wave, like a shock wave probably, when a bomb goes off and all of a sudden it hits you; and then you start to shake and you start to cry, but you're still an adult with all these little people and you can't do that. You can't lose it. You can't freak out.

I remember telling the nearby counselor, who was in the new room, "Zachary's in there. He shot Zach." I looked at the kids, and asked, "What did he, what was he doing?" Some of the kids who had seen it cried and said, "Mrs. McCarthy, he shot Zach!"

All I could think was, "Oh, no!" We had run in and locked the doors. The teacher whose classroom we ran into wouldn't let us unlock it, because it is protocol – once you lock, you don't unlock. The counselor in that room was determined. She said, "Oh, hell, no. I need to go in there because Zach's been shot. I need to get in there."

At that point a couple of other teachers and the school psychologist had come up on Zach, and they gave him first aid and everything. The counselor managed to get out of the locked room, but I stayed in with Mr. Farmer's class because he was just in there with all the kids.

I don't think I could have held it together if I actually would have seen Zach. I don't know what I would have done. I literally never actually saw his wounds because of my vantage point. The computer was in front of me, and so I don't know; but I do know that those kids, they, well, they actually had blood on them, the ones that were right there. I've got to admit it – I was scared.

The Aftermath

I'm still the most confused person in the world about the whole scenario that first week. What happened right after was the school district came to me and they were, well, good at the start. Some people might say, "Oh, well, they were supporting you this way." Okay, well, if this is the way you want to say it. I realized I couldn't keep working in my class. The administration said, "We're going to get you a substitute that's going to stay with you for the rest of the year, and she is basically you. If you have a bad day and you don't want to show up, she always understands. She knows what you're doing in class, and you're good to go."

The substitute was good. She was amazing. The problem was, I was a victim just like those students. The difficulty for me was figuring out how to relate to them as a teacher, which I shouldn't have done ever, but yet I was a victim. We were all peers in the process of dealing with our emotions, and I needed them, too. I didn't have anybody else. I had nobody else who was in the same area with me. My teacher friends, they had been at the school that day, but they hadn't been in the room. They hadn't processed anything. They hadn't felt it or seen it.

At the end of the month I decided to take days off, because I'd had my daughter and was overwhelmed with that. I looked at it as an opportunity. "Okay, so here's what I'll do. I'll work three days. I'll be in school on Monday, Wednesday and Friday, and I'll take Tuesdays and Thursdays off. My sub can handle that." The way that I had the days set up, remember that I was very organized so I knew what happened on each day, those were generally easier days like a library day or something like that, and I felt I could manage that.

Immediately when I did that, my first period was unhappy. "Wait, Mrs. McCarthy, what about us? No!" Am I responsible for them? No, I'm not. However, I felt it because nobody else was. I immediately panicked, and I didn't know what to do. The bottom line is, you look at the kids and you're thinking, "I can't leave. I want to leave. Everything's telling me to leave, but I can't."

I had to make the decision because I knew I was definitely failing my family in many, many ways. I wasn't sleeping, and it was a whole other situation when I got home. I went through the normal PTSD symptoms. The stress was compounded with struggles with post-partum depression.

I wouldn't ever have said, "Yeah, postpartum depression . . .," but also, over the last couple of years, there's been research now on Cesareans. That in and of itself creates a post-traumatic stress syndrome for the woman. All of a sudden I was amazed – that made so much sense to me because my daughter was an emergency Cesarean section.

I was going through all the hormones. I'll agree; they were rushing. Then you've got the post-traumatic stuff. Then I just felt like I was so responsible for so many little lives, and the parents were coming to me because they didn't know what to do, and the administration's coming to me saying, "Well, if you could have the parents fill these papers out and do this, and maybe they can go see the county," but there was no direct communications with the kids and the parents – nobody was really taking care of anything.

It was all mishmash. I'd get paperwork to somebody, and then nothing would happen; it would sit on their desk. If I'd make a phone call, and "Oh, we'll get back to you," but nothing got done. I'd get the, "We'll take care of it. Yes, we're on it. For sure. Whatever you need," lines.

That's just the way the whole thing went. Sometimes I sit and I look at it, and I think, "This has to be from a movie because this can't happen in real life." In real life, something like this happens, everybody takes care of it. There are procedures. There are protocols. Nothing was followed. Nothing was set up; nothing was followed.

They really did nothing. A little bit of counseling for about a week and a half. The kids kept requesting counseling and nobody would show up. Different organizations tried to volunteer and help, but here's where I'm going to say the legal situation bites people in the 'behinds.' That school would not let anything happen at that point, wouldn't approve or let anything happen that they thought put them in legal liability.

That was their bottom line. They were covering their asses for sure. It was not the welfare and safety of the children. It was ensuring that they didn't have to be liable in any way at any point for whatever, and that was evident big time. They gave me a 1–800 number and told me to call it. They brought in a week's worth of counseling triage, somewhat; but literally, again, what they did is they put out a handbook on how to address crisis situations, and that was it. I think we had two debriefings, but again, nothing happened in them; and that was it.

And I didn't see that when I was in it because I'm thinking, "You want whatever you can do to benefit these kids." Why wouldn't you? No. It took me time and that's when I learned, no, they didn't want it; they didn't care. I was the stupid one for even thinking that.

To me, the administration was supposed to be there for the students. I didn't see that they were fair and objective in taking care of the students and their well-being. Everything that happened in that classroom afterward was based on me, me seeking it out, me ensuring it came, me asking about it, or me inquiring about it. Again, they gave me a sub, but I think they did that as a matter of safety. Do you know what I mean? I think that was a political and safety issue. "We're covering our asses."

There were lots of excuses. I would ask an administrator, "Hey, Mark, maybe you can get a bus to take the kids to the memorial because there's a lot of press people that want to talk to them. I don't think the press should talk to them, at least my particular class." What was his response? "Oh, well, we can't do that. Getting a bus is too difficult, too much money."

What did I do? I walked. I walked with those kids through the streets, to the memorial and I walked them up to their own little row of seats. Half of them were scared shitless to sit. Granted, why wouldn't they be? I think only two parents showed up – only two parents.

Think about it. Your kids were involved in a shooting, and two parents show up with these kids, and go to the memorial. Do you see what I'm saying? I'm absolutely stunned at this whole situation.

I walk them through, I walk them back; and of course, the press is after them, but the press can't really tell who's who and what's what in the situation. I get in and out as quickly as possible. I managed to get little buttons for the class with Zachary's name on them and everything, and we donated them but nobody else thought of any of this stuff.

I'm thinking, "Why am I the only one?" It was remarkable to me.

The whole situation was completely overwhelming. That's what I was trying to convey to the people in charge, but then here's where you have to make a decision, and it was hard. Like I said, I had a substitute, and I was taking those two days off. I had to be there for the kids, but I needed help, too.

Then, at the end of the next month, it's my husband's birthday. I wanted a local company to come and bring cupcakes and have juice with the class, to celebrate my husband's birthday with me. I saw it as a positive. The school administration said, "No, that's just publicity for that company, and we don't want that. We don't want to draw that kind of publicity." I said, "What do you mean publicity? It's people who understand these kids went through something. Nobody else has done anything for them."

I had to take the kids to the park, because it couldn't be on campus, to meet the people from this company. The superintendent of the school district came and sat in his truck watching while we ate cupcakes.

It was so creepy. It was just creepiness to the nth degree. All I could think of is, "Why aren't you guys doing anything for these kids? Why? Why? And when I do it you threaten me?" Yeah, then they say, "You go ahead and authorize anything of this nature again, and it'll be your job." I was stunned and replied, "What are you talking about? These kids need help!"

I had called Columbine and asked them what to do. I was looking for any help I could get, any help whatsoever, because it was just me, alone, helping the kids. After a month they had some counseling service come through.

They were going to talk with the kids on a certain day, and it had taken a lot of work on my part to get the permission slips and everything.

I mean, oh, my God, I can't believe I finally did it. They had this counseling session happening. They put it in the bungalow directly across from where the shooting happened. I mean, it's literally 20 feet away.

There was an immediate problem. I had one little girl whose house is on the back street to the school – she has to walk in through this gate, past the computer lab door; it's in that back corridor, coming to school. Her mom came to me and said, "She won't come through. I have to drive her to the front of the school. She won't go through that area." So they want to have a counseling session now, and the bungalow was next to the shooting scene and I've got a little girl who won't even come to school from her house in that direction. I'm thinking, "Are you guys nuts?"

They put some of those kids right away back into the computer lab. I'm thinking, "Are you guys nuts?" Why isn't somebody on the phone to Apple or Costco and getting laptops in my room so we can work on computers in my room? I don't understand this. The kids shouldn't be in a lab at any point. At least give them the rest of their 8th grade year lab-free. No. Nothing.

They have this counseling session. The kids ask, "You're coming, right, Mrs. McCarthy?" and I respond, "Yes, I will be there. I'm coming. I'll go." Again, this is the first cohesive time that probably we as a group, other than the second day I think they brought in a couple of crisis counselors who, actually, I learned weren't crisis counselors; they were interns. We've been together and not processed anything or done anything together at this point.

I walked back there with the kids. I'm walking around the car and I get them in, and the school counselor comes to me and she said, "Melissa, you can't go in there." I respond with, "What are you talking about I can't go in there? Yeah, I can go in there."

The counselor responds with, "No, they'll process better without you." I shot back with "Are you kidding me? You really think they'll process better without me? I don't think so. They don't have any other adult in their life that actually processes with them. I'm the only one. I'm the one who's been doing their morning journaling and trying to talk to them about this. I'm the only one."

She simply responded with, "Well, you can't go." I said, "Really?" and that's when I turned around and said, "Well, you know what? Fuck you all." I walked into my classroom, got my shit, and walked out.

When I left, I think I was scared to face the fact that I'd let all their kids down. Then I was just scared in general. It was just this overwhelming fear of people and places. I felt like, "Oh, my God. They're all looking at me!"

I had a very negative view of the way people saw me. People basically, as far as I knew, thought I was the worst teacher in the world and I deserved everything I was getting because Zach had gotten killed. I was just a very negative presence in the world at that point.

It just got compounded to the point where I didn't want to leave my house. I would drive my little daughter, my middle daughter to work or to school, and then I'd pick her up. It took everything I had to do that, or to make it to the store and do the grocery shopping.

I could do it, but I hated it. I hated going out and doing anything. Of course, that took a toll on my marriage. My husband was working really long hours in a really high-stress lousy job, and I wasn't making it any easier on him. I kept having all sorts of fearful thoughts. I'd come to the realization that drugs would not help by any means, and I completely went off of those and just started working through things.

Then I had a series of counselors that had come through the school district's Workmen's Comp company. Obviously, Workmen's Comp wants you to see who they want you to see, and they were awful. I called Workmen's and I'm, "You need to get me somebody new. I refuse to work with this guy anymore."

That's when I went and filed Workmen's Compensation. I called because the union lawyer had taken me out and said, "Okay, you can file Workmen's Comp," and he goes through and he maps it all out. He advised me that I can take disability, and I have so long to do it because you're tenured, and it's your benefit. So I know at this point I can literally take the rest of the year off, and I'm good.

That's what I did. I filed the Workmen's Comp. I did this because this is what the lawyer told me to do. I filed Workmen's Comp, and then you file disability at the same time; but you can't actually. You can't do both at the same time, and I didn't know that – even though they told me to do it.

The Workmen's Comp process is probably what drove me nuttier than anything. That process was just evil, evil, evil. I had these women that weren't doctors, that weren't nurses that were like basically, "When are you going to get better and be over this?"

They said, "We don't want to pay; we aren't going to pay you for this." It got to the point where they were questioning whether or not I really had anything wrong with me.

I had to go to depositions with lawyers, and they brought up awful stuff. She's bringing up stuff I had told the counselor about my husband. It was a shock – that was my marriage! This didn't have anything to do with the school shooting, and she's asking, "Are you anorexic?" I respond with, "What? What are you guys talking about?" I literally didn't even know what they were coming up with at that point.

I got a lawyer, a Workmen's Comp lawyer, and they proposed a deal. "Okay, we'll offer you $25,000." What that basically was saying is, you quit your job that was going to be your career, and you were going to earn, let's just say I was going to earn over a million dollars in my lifetime as a teacher. "We're going to give you $25,000 for that, and that also should cover your medical expenses at the end of it." I looked at them and I said, "I don't think so. You're going to give me at least $250,000 – at least – and maybe I'll walk, but this is bullshit."

I never took this public. I never did anything too evil. I was trying to convince them that, "This is my life. I can't go back to teaching after this," because to go back to teaching, I mean, literally, I would have to relocate. That's what the principal told me, because he lost his job. They wouldn't say he lost his job, but he lost his job because of the shooting. He told me, "Melissa, you know, you have to relocate."

It was intense at that point, between the Workmen's Comp and the disability. I got a stipend or whatever, and I managed financially. My husband was working so he had insurance, and we were able to basically deal with it.

Once I finally signed the papers and officially quit and did it all, it hurt. To me I was saying, "No, I'm not going to be a teacher anymore. I'm on disability. It's permanent." It lasts as long as my disability lasts, but it pays me for me and it pays me for my minor children. I'm only allowed to earn up to a small amount a year outside of what they pay me. They always keep you on a funny little level there, but it's a steady income, and that's what allowed me to go looking or find another job or stay home with my new baby.

I'm not going to probably ever have a job that makes the money my education has me at or that I'm worth, but I've also learned I don't want that anymore. As long as I can still have benefits and be here for my children. That's what counts to me now, and that's how I've balanced my life.

I gave myself like two years of hell, and my family went through that with me. I think the emotional scars worry me the most. My youngest daughter is little, but she sees the effects a lot more than I think most kids her age do. She understands a lot more, and that's based on what she went through with me because we were together 24/7.

The impact on my family was huge. I mean, you have to think, "If my husband has to make money to support us as well, and the kids are still here, who's going to help pick up the pieces?"

This is why, when I see school shootings or I see these things happen, it's not just a simple little, "Hey, they'll go to a counselor," type thing. This is a lifetime – this is now who you are, and it is part of who you are. It is how you react to everything.

I'm one of the few who's had the benefit of making it a positive, but what if, I don't know, you have one of these guys in the war – I get it – his leg is off. Well, that's a physical reminder that he can't do something based on this awful situation he was in. I get it. I get that now.

Into the Future

Obviously, I have to make money. We are not wealthy and I want the opportunity to find a job that I'm going to be happy at and not stressed at.

Teaching, at least publicly, that thought in and of itself makes me so nervous that my stomach hurts. I don't know if that's a safety thing anymore. I don't know if that's just a public thing and how I can be perceived. I don't know if it's just that I'm so comfortable not being a teacher anymore and happy in that realm. I don't know what it is.

· 1 9 ·

IN MIKE'S WORDS

"Oh, Melissa . . . it is so hard to hear it from her." Janice said as she was crying – I could hear the sobs over the phone.

"I understand. It was the same feeling for me. She went through so much."

"What about the other participant, Mike? Are his words as hard to hear?"

"That's hard to answer. Yes - and no. Like we did with Melissa, I'll just
have you hear his words."

Mike Dougherty: Husband and Teacher

Becoming a Teacher

I graduated from college and then substitute taught for a while. After I finished my Bachelor's degree, which was in History and Social Sciences, there
weren't any jobs. I substituted for a while for a year. Principals would look at
me and say, "Well, I'd hire you if you were a Math teacher." So I went back
and got my Math certification. While I was working on my math certification
I went to work fulltime in middle school, including a stint as a teacher of the
gifted and talented.

After that I went back and got my Master's degree in Latin American studies. Next I taught in high school, and then taught on a satellite network for a couple of years. It was one of the first ones there was. When I was teaching on the satellite network, I finished up my teacher certification in Computer Science.

I moved to my current state and began working on another college degree, which I finished while I was still teaching at a small mountain school. That was when I went to work teaching at Pine Ridge Middle School. By the time the incident occurred, I had been there for nine years.

Teaching Style

The year before the incident, I was still teaching seventh grade. That was a group of students that, I guess you'd say I loved them more than any other group. I loved my students. I try to use love and logic techniques with them when I do discipline. I very, very rarely send anybody to the office. I usually just go out into the hallway and say, "What do you think?"

The kid goes, "I probably shouldn't be poking Suzie with the pencil."

"Yes probably. What do you think?"

The kid goes, "I'm not going to do it anymore."

"Probably not going to be able to measure a negative, you're going to have to do something to put some energy back into me, because I had to expend energy to come out here and deal with this."

The kid goes, "I'll come in, and I'll pick up trash in your room during lunch."

"Oh, okay," I go. "Have I been clear? Have I been fair? Have I been respectful? Because if I'm respectful to you, then you know how to treat me, if we're clear, then we know what we're supposed to do from here. I really want you to tell me if you think that I'm not fair."

This particular group of seventh graders was right after what the English teacher that was on my team called the "dream team." There were kids that just seemed to get it, seemed to get what you were trying to do. When you disciplined them it wasn't because you were being mean to them; it was because you felt like it would help them be successful.

The group that I had the year of the incident wasn't as good as the previous year that were then eight graders, but they were still really good kids. I would look at kids and go, "Hey, do you think maybe can do some math here, just for me because I'm cool here." The kids would go, "Yes, all right."

I might have sent one kid to the office in four years. That was usually because of something that went on in the hallway. It wasn't really my kid. I just saw this thing going on and go, "I'm going to have to write you up for this." It wasn't my classroom.

The Shooting Incident: A "bad guy sandwich"

It was just a typical school day; I was grading papers, teaching kids, seventh grade. I had three classes of regular seventh grade Math, one class of Pre-Algebra and one class of Algebra 1 in the seventh grade.

It was a Tuesday. I was, I guess, a little bit more dialed into going out for duty because if you're going to forget it on a Monday. It was in the afternoon, and I just, well, the bell rang and I hit the door. We end school at about 3:05; at about 3:06 I was out in the front.

I was actually proud of myself because I actually made it out to parking lot duty on time. We go out and supervise the kids, make sure they get across the street, make sure they don't run in front of the buses, different things like that. There are, I wrote one time that are 150 reasons why you don't want to get out to parking lot duty, they're called students.

They all want something. They all want something right now while you're trying to get out to duty. I actually went out, got out there very fast, went out through a side door and got out to the parking lot area that I handle on the crosswalk very quickly that day.

Out there was a kid that we called a "challenge kid." They are kids that have significant mental disabilities. He had moved on to high school. I said, "Hey, how you doing?" He was walking by. He was one of those kids that you talk to them and they just open a mental file. You never can really tell what they're going to say. He says, "Hey, Grandpa," because he used to always call me Grandpa when he was at school.

I talked to a kid who was sitting on the fence. He had a camouflage hat on. I said, "Did you go hunting this year?"

He said, "Yes, my dad got a mule deer."

I said, "I remember. You told me that in the fall." That was when I heard the shot. I was about 30 feet away.

I thought that some kid had set off a firecracker in a trash can. I'm walking over there thinking, "It's February. The kids should know they're not supposed to do this." I'm running through the list of usual suspects in my head.

At that moment I saw a man reloading a bolt-action rifle. I had to switch gears from condition white, I guess you would call it, to condition red immediately. I'm thinking, "It's a bolt-action rifle. He's reloading it." He shot again because I didn't have time to process it yet.

I'm thinking, "It's bolt-action, that means in between when he's reloading, effectively he doesn't have a gun." After he got the second shot off, and unfortunately, that's the one that hit Billy. I went for it.

I quickly passed one of my little seventh graders. She was frozen with her hands over her ears, dancing. As I go by her, she says, "What do we do? What do we do?" I said, "Run." I went for the guy as I was going past her.

From what I understand people in a crisis situation, some people time seems to slow to down for them. It seemed to slow down for me. It has always affected me this way. I felt like I had a lot of time. I'm sitting there going, "Okay, all right, bolt-action. Okay. I'm going to have to let him get off another shot so that that way I know." And that was when I went for it.

I had had one other situation when I was young that was a life or death situation. I had felt like I had a lot of time then too. It's my natural reaction for that.

When I was a kid, my father was chopping wood. He lost his grip on the axe and the axe was coming towards me. I'm standing there going, it's going to turn, it will turn one more, it will land right here. I can move my leg aside; because of the angle it's going to skip right underneath of me. I do that.

All of a sudden time is back in normal speed and my parents are on me going, "Are you okay?" They're feeling me to make sure that I am okay. I said, "I had a lot of time, I just dodged." They didn't know that.

A person who experiences slowed down time is not actually getting more input. That's my natural reaction when that stuff happens; all of a sudden I go, let's do, I got this. I'm thinking I got a lot of time, and everybody else is thinking I'm moving real fast.

One of the bus drivers who was one of the first guys to talk to the media said, "I've never seen anybody move that fast. I'm sitting there thinking, I got to wait for him to shoot again, actually, so that that way I can tackle him."

The bus driver must be one of those people that think time is moving quickly. I'm sitting there, and I'm one of those people that think time is moving slow.

Anyway, I ran up to him. There are people who understand how to fight and people who don't. He didn't know what to do when he didn't have a gun. When I grabbed him, you would think that he would use the fact that he's got a gun in his hand to at least jam, hit me with the rifle butt or something like that, but he just dropped it.

I grabbed him up by the lapels of his hoodie. He's pulling one way, and I'm pulling the other way. Fortunately, I outweighed him by quite a bit. I was quite a bit taller than he was. He said, "Just let me go."

I thought, "Wait a minute. There's an elementary school across the street. There's a bunch of houses. If I let him go, he could get away." That was when I thought, "I'm just going to wrap him up and go down to the ground."

My arms were wrapped around his arms, and my legs were wrapped around his legs. Not being very sophisticated about this stuff, I was on the bottom, which is the last place you want to be. I knew this, even when I was growing up playing sports, basketball was a much less contact sport than it is now. You just don't even know how to tackle a person.

He dropped the gun. Mary Burton, who was our assistant principal at the time, came out, took the gun and threw it inside. Jerry Morton, who was another Math teacher, he had actually been closer and had gotten inside the school, and then he came back out, and he got on top. We had a "bad guy sandwich" there.

From the time that our secretary called 911 until the guys were on the scene, was about 90 seconds. Everybody knew what to do when you lockdown – you're supposed to shelter because of a tornado or something, let people say shelter or whatever.

Actually the school had been trained in that like two weeks before. The thing that was strange was there was a substitute in the school. The substitute said later, everybody seemed to know what to do. We didn't really know what to do. We just all did something.

We always have our doors locked so that there's an electric lock. The school secretary was a very brave lady at his point. The guy is shooting at the school, and she is standing there not pressing the lockdown, watching him, making sure that all the kids can get inside and then presses the lockdown.

Of course when she presses the lockdown, that triggers all of the doors in all of the school, and they are all automatically go shut. We automatically have them locked all the time so that as they're shut, a person in the hallway is locked out.

So, back in the parking lot, I was on the bottom, and Jerry was on the top. Jerry was ticked off. Jerry was mad. Jerry has told me, he said, "I was doing my best to try and squeeze him and make him turn purple." He had his arm across the guy's chest, pulling. The guy was pulling all the time on Jerry's hand.

The guy was in fight-or-flight mode, and he was going to struggle no matter what. I'm fat and happy. I'm on the bottom, Jerry is taking all the, doing all of the squeezing. I'm just holding on to the guy. I'm just saying things like, "Hey, what's your name?"

I'm thinking if I can get him to start talking, maybe he won't struggle as much. I'm saying, "What's your name? Did you go to school here?" He's not very big. He only weighed like 132 pounds and not very tall.

One of the things that we have there is another school, a charter school. That's their pickup point for their bus. Every once in a while, we have one of those charter school kids that their parents are going to pick them up a little bit late or whatever. Sometimes there are kids there that are high school kids that we don't know.

I'm trying to ask the kid, the guy, turned out he was 32 years old. I didn't know that at the time. I'm just talking to him, trying to get him to relax a little bit.

Unknown to me, because my entire view of the whole incident was this guy's face from about three inches away. I mean, that's all I could see. Unknown to me, some people had come out. There was a heating and air conditioning guy there. He had come out and had gotten some zip ties and had zip tied the guy's legs together. A couple of bus drivers had come over to help, and a parent. He was pretty well secured.

The sheriff's guys came. There were two sheriff's guys. They were very specific with each other. They said, "Have you got him? Do you know where his hands are?"

One of them left to go inside. The other guy made sure that he had his hands and kneeled on his back. I'm still on the bottom. They're gradually peeling Jerry off, getting his hands, getting him hooked up, and then taking him away. I'm the last guy out of the bad guy sandwich. Because the sheriff's guys have way, way more experience with this, and they're thinking, "What if there's another shooter?"

When Mary threw the gun inside, the HVAC guy picked it up to make sure that it was unloaded. Some of the other teachers, all they see is a guy that they don't know with a rifle. They're screaming down the hallway telling everybody to lockdown. That was where some of the Internet reports came that there was maybe another shooter or maybe there were two.

The police guys are doing what they're supposed to do. They're making absolutely certain that there's not another guy. They're not assuming that he's the only guy like I did.

One girl had gotten wounded in her arm, and gotten inside the school, and just went screaming down the hallway, and all the way to the other end of the hallway, and had gotten locked down in the furthest room way away.

Two science teachers, they share an in-between utility room, they were sitting there going, "Pammy's bleeding out from her arm." They're trying to figure out what to do.

They're in lockdown. They know they're not supposed to make any noise, turn on any lights, anything like that. They get popsicles out of the freezer of the refrigerator that's between their room for science stuff, and put popsicles on Pammy's arm.

We didn't know that Pammy was wounded. We thought that maybe the bullet had just hit something on the door or something like that because there was a shattered window. We didn't know Pammy was wounded until they started evacuating people.

The only person we knew was wounded was Billy, and he was on his back in the snow. The bullet entered his right side, broke a rib, punctured a lung, and came out the front. It was lowish on his, well, kind of medium way up on his right side. Mary was there because after she saw that I didn't need any help, because she went to Billy. The thing that was very unusual is that an emergency room nurse was there – she had just picked up her kids.

She felt like that she needed to go back. That's how she describes it. She said, "I need to go back." She told her kids to lay down on the floor of her car, and then she was there helping Billy.

I just walked around crying because . . . well, every time I would walk over to see Billy, all I could see was his face. He was just bewildered and hurt and . . . in shock. All of that stuff. He was pretty much covered up by people trying to make sure that he wasn't going to bleed to death and all of that stuff.

Remember, he got hit in the back. When he was turned over, it was soft point hunting round from a .30 ought 6. I had seen that in deer. I knew that the trauma was probably about the size of a decent dessert plate.

All I can see is his face. I couldn't do anything to help him. I'm going back into the office. I called my wife. I called my Mom. Barry, I think it was Barry Hollis, I can't remember, said something like, "There are some kids at the gym that need to be supervised."

I said, "I can do that." I'm heading into the area and our sheriff's guys, they're good at this, unfortunately. There was a guy with an AR15, M16, whatever those weapons are, and a handgun. They're in a team, and they're behind a little insert. They say, "Wait a minute. You can't come in."

I said, "I'm sorry, you probably can't see my ID." I'm completely focused on I got to go help these kids that are in the gym. They're going, "I don't think you understand. This isn't your school anymore. This is our school until we know everybody is safe."

I walked away and started talking to the sergeant. They started asking me, "What happened?" They escorted me out through the gym to our exit point. They were evacuating all the kids to the elementary school right across the street, a couple hundred yards down the road, and across the street.

They're doing things like saying, "We want you to do a walk by. We want to walk by the guy in the . . . I'm looking around and I'm seeing guys with FBI on the back of their jackets . . ."

I'm thinking, "The FBI guys are making sure that of the, that nobody can say that this wasn't the right guy, and all of this stuff." I wanted to look at the guys and I wanted to say, the sheriff's guys, and I wanted to say, "Remember the guy you peeled off of me, that's him." I just walked by the squad car and said, "Okay, okay. That's him."

As I was walking out through the gym, I still don't know who this guy was. He was a sheriff's guy, sheriff's uniform and all of that stuff. I remember he had a really long scar on his arm. He looked at me, and he said, "You did good work today."

That actually helped me a lot, because I was thinking that I messed up, because I let Billy get shot. I couldn't think fast enough and the guy got off the second shot.

It was strange. Sometime before the incident I told my brother, when we talked about school shootings, that I was uncomfortable with the idea of just standing around being a target, and that I was going to do something if an incident like that had ever occurred.

I had talked with my students before, during lockdown drills, because afterwards they all want to play what if. I used to think, "They're just trying to get out of math." Really, it's a lot of scenario-based thinking that they're doing, even though they don't know that they're doing it. They would do things like, they would say, "What if somebody comes in the room?"

I would say, "I'm going to do something. You guys head for the other door."

They said, "What are you going to do?"

I said, "I don't know. Throw desks or something."

I was in the mindset of "I'm not going to just run. I'm going to do something."

The First Hours After the Shooting

After things settled down a bit, I called my wife. I told her that there was a shooting at our school that I was fine, but that one student got shot, and then my wife screamed.

I said I have to hang up. I called my mother and told her that you might hear about this, but that I'm fine. The thing that was weird was I got finished being interviewed at the sheriff's office, and then I called and said … I told the sheriff's guys, I said, "You don't need to use up a car taking me back or anything like that. You've got other things to do."

I called my wife at home and said, "Can you come and get me?" She loaded the kids in the car. There were already news trucks and everything outside of our house – and helicopters.

She said, "It was ludicrous." She had to stop for gas. There were three news trucks pulling in because a couple of them figured if we follow her that's probably where he is.

There were people wanting to interview afterwards and stuff like that. At some point you say, "Look, I'm just going to talk to these people just to get them to leave." I talked to a news lady right outside the Sheriff's office, and the sheriff and I talked about it. I went home. There were news people at the house already. I talked to a couple of them, and everything snowballed after that. I didn't get a whole lot of sleep that night.

The Day After: Faculty Reunification

We had a faculty and student reunification the next day at the elementary school down the street. I got to see that everybody was there and all of that stuff.

Mary, the vice principal, and I asked everybody, "How do you want to do this?" We talked to people as a faculty – all of us together. They said, "The news will want to talk to you guys." We said, "All right, how do you want to do this?" The group said, "We don't want to talk." I just want to get back to teaching school. Everyone else pretty much refused to talk to the media.

As a group we decided, "Two of us will talk to the media, Mary and Mike, and then maybe that will get them to leave everybody else alone because we'll feed them something." We interviewed with *People Magazine*. We had some really great and unfortunately experienced counselors in our district.

The counselors and the psychological trauma team, they were there at those early meetings – all of them.

One of the psychological counselors was saying, and Mary kept saying, "We have to go see Billy. I have to go see Billy." Because the vice principal had seen the wound, he had looked at her and said, "Am I going to die?"

She looked at him and said, "Not on my watch." We knew that he had gotten to Children's Hospital and that they had gotten him stabilized and everything like that. She had to see him.

Eventually we got there. We saw him later on in the day, which according to some of the people that saw him earlier, was way fortunate. He looked way worse in the morning than he was in the afternoon. Later on, after we saw Billy, we had a press conference arranged by the district people at the district office.

Of course, we couldn't get to our cars. All of the cars in front of the parking lot, none of the faculty has rides to school or has their car to get to school or anything like that because it took them two or three days before they went through all the cars and made sure which car was which and that stuff. They wanted to make sure there were no bombs or weapons left around.

The Friday After: School Reunification

We had a reunification day out in the front, and Mary our vice principal said, "We're meeting all of these kids out front. We're meeting them all out there with cookies. We're going to be out there because that's not– if we don't do that, then the shooter claims that space. That's not his space, that's our space."

There were special benches there – it was a special place. That was a space that we said was ours. We had posters, we met the kids; the kids came inside and signed stuff. They all went into my room because I'm still doing media crap. They are all signing my white board. They are doing stuff like that. That was a reunification day. Everyone was together.

It was a Friday. Tuesday the shooting happened, Wednesday we had faculty and stuff like that at the elementary school and kids could come if they wanted. We went back into our school on Friday.

I'm just sitting there going, "I want to teach and everything like that." Eventually, one of the counselors because they were very available; they just said, "Look, just go ahead and tell us when you need a break or whatever." The counselors just said, "Look, we're going for a walk."

Yes, they just said, "I don't care whether you say you need a break or not. You are going." Over the long term, they weren't there as much, but we could call them whenever we wanted.

Oh, and something unusual happened. We got phone calls. I was in the situation of just leave me alone and let me get to teach school. Ellen DeGeneres is sending me flowers. Oprah Winfrey's producer is calling. I'm thinking, "Just let me teach school." One of our staff members was saying, "Look, you got an opportunity where maybe you can do some good here."

Months and Years Later

Time has passed. They let me graduate to teaching at the eighth grade level – after 10 years. I'm still in the same classroom and all of that.

Since the shooting, if I needed to talk to counselor, I could call up a counselor, and he would be ready to talk to me today. Last June, we had what they called the briefing in the district. It's organized by a local foundation and our director of security.

We just get together and talk about what things happened and all of that stuff. Anybody who wants to attend and learn about school security can.

Let me give you an example of the support. I was at the briefing, and our security director was talking about the incident. I had to go to the bathroom, and I was going to speak next. I went out of the auditorium and went to the bathroom. The guy who is the Director of Psychological Services for the district discreetly followed me into the bathroom to make sure that I was okay. They're that available.

Since then I try to do things that have to do with school security. If anybody calls me and says, "Hey, look, there is a group of school security people, will you go and speak to them? Sure, I'm hard to get, all you got to do is ask me."

Into the Future

The future? I'm going to retire at the end of this year. I was originally thinking maybe if I teach until I can get 30 years in the state. I just feel like I'm burned out. I've been doing this for 36 years now. I've been teaching school for 36 years; 12 years in another state, but they still count.

I might still teach. I might tutor. I have retirement that's going to come in from public employees' retirement thing. I'm pretty much done teaching public school now.

I've thought about how much the incident has influenced this decision. I've thought, it was such an intense period that I'm wondering is this a, almost like a post-partum depression. I don't think so. I've just gotten to the point where I'm just burned out from teaching school.

Whenever I speak to a group of people I tell them I blame my mother. I start out by saying, "I blame my mother." I say, "Look, at times I'm going to get emotional here when I talk about this." What you find is, what I find is that when I get most emotional is when I think about Billy or Pammy or when I think about how brave people were. I think about teachers crawling around on the floor and not knowing whether there is a gunman roaming the hallways; other teachers treating the wounded.

I think about when Mary, our vice principal, came out and she just said, her husband looked at her and said, "What were you going to do?" She said, "I don't know, kick him between the legs, Mike needed help."

I think about Jerry being safe inside and then deciding to come back out to help. Of course, we will all turn all visions like a person who was a little bit more experienced with these things would understand that there could have been a second shooter, he could have had a knife, he could have had another gun, all these stuff that we never even thought of.

Advice for Other Teachers

What would I say to other teachers who experience this sort of thing? They are more than likely wanting to say, "I'm okay, just let me teach." Listen and talk to the counselors. Probably the most valuable thing that happened in terms of counseling was when that counselor just looked at me and just said, "We're going for a walk."

Principals and counselors said, "There is somebody here to cover your class. We're going for a walk." Talking about it helps, the fact that I've been lucky enough to have people say, "Will you come and speak?" I get to work through that. I get to work through those emotions. Of course, every time you talk about the incident, it becomes less traumatic. It's like letting the poison out of a boil.

During the incident, everybody is going to have a fight-or-flight reaction. If you decide to run, great, that's okay, help some kids along the way. Help them get to a safe place. If you decide to fight, be smart about it. Don't just soak up bullets.

One of the things that they did that we didn't get to because I was involved in interviews with the sheriff and stuff like that was the faculty met at one of the faculty people's house after, the day after. They all said, "This is what I was doing, this is what I was thinking." You need to get back together as a team – talk about it.

When the Sandy Hook thing happened, there were a number of people that know me that they call me and say, "Look, I was thinking about you when I heard about this." I'm not alone. You are not alone.

Advice for Schools

So, how do we stop this sort of stuff? If you train faculty people like security staff, the same way, tailor the curriculum to school based security, now you got a person who is fully trained like having a constable on campus – make it part of teacher license renewal. I know I have to do 90 clock hours every five years.

I have to do that anyway just to renew my certification, just make sure that that's a line in the certification renewal law. Instead of taking another course on how to teach Math that I've been doing for 30 years, I take a course in school security.

I'd take a course in self-defense or I do the local sheriff's program that I'm going to have to pay for the college course anyway. Just add a line in the certification laws, if I can get credit towards my certification for other training, why isn't there training to enhance school security?

Buses, that's an issue. You need to make sure that the bus people are trained too so that if they have to evacuate like that, they know where the evacuation place is because reunification with the parents and what kids have got, patching them up with their parents is a very important thing at the end.

Make sure that you know every kid – somebody in the school knows every kid. You know that their parents picked them up, all that stuff.

A Final Thought

We really need to be able to inform people about what we did because in my mind, it's pretty much of a textbook case of "what to do right." My school did it right.

· 2 0 ·

A QUESTION ABOUT FINDINGS: MELISSA

"I am so glad to hear that he got the support he needed. And I see why you decided to compare the two of them," Janice said.

"You do?" I asked.

"Yes, one person is still wrestling with a lot of pain, and she lost her profession, while another person was able to go back to work."

"True . . ."

"So, it makes me really want to ask, why were there two different outcomes?"

"Well, to answer that, we need to go back to my research questions, and apply them to the interviews," I responded.

An Answer

Melissa's Story

The Post-traumatic Stress Disorder Construct

Research Question 1: Melissa and Post-traumatic Stress Disorder

In research question 1, which of Hartman's 12 steps of PTSD affected Melissa in the weeks and months following the school shooting? These factors include the activating event, pain, confusion, guilt, shame, self-worth dissipation, anxiety, fear, anger, resentment, depression and acute anxiety. Melissa experienced all of the symptoms of Post-Traumatic Stress Disorder as time passed after the school shooting. Her attending psychologist diagnosed her as suffering from these issues, and evidence can be found in her interviews. From the perspective of her licensed therapist, and from academics, PTSD was definitely an effect and a factor in Melissa's resultant situation.

First, Melissa experienced an activating event – the shooting. Documents and news items verify that the event happened and that she was present. Her response right after the shooting is typical of the shock of a trauma. She said,

> That's when all of a sudden your body just goes, well, it's like a wave, like a shock wave probably, when a bomb goes off and all of a sudden it hits you; and then you start to shake and you start to cry . . .

Second, in conjunction with the activating event, she felt pain, physically and emotionally. As she just expressed, she felt something like "when a bomb goes off." The crying was an emotional expression of pain, while the physical reaction was manifested in the shaking.

Third, Melissa felt confusion. She expressed this as, "Then all of a sudden I was able to process what had just happened, and at that moment he fired the gun again. That's probably when it all started going nutty in my brain."

Fourth, Melissa felt guilt. She expressed this in her conflict over taking time for herself versus being there for her students. She said,

> . . . my first period was unhappy. "Wait, Mrs. McCarthy, what about us? No!" Am I responsible for them? No, I'm not. However, I felt it because nobody else was. I immediately panicked, and I didn't know what to do. The bottom line is, you look at the kids and you're thinking, "I can't leave. I want to leave. Everything's telling me to leave, but I can't."

She also felt guilt toward the parents of her students when she said, "When I left, I think I was scared to face the fact that I'd let all their kids down."

Fifth, Melissa felt shame. When she said, that the "difficulty for me was figuring out how to relate to them as a teacher, which I shouldn't have done ever, but yet I was a victim," she shook her head in the interview, and turned away. It was apparent that she felt shame, and felt that she let the children down. She felt she should have been stronger for them, but was unable to find the strength. She felt that she failed the kids.

Shame came from a sense of failing her family as well. She said, "I knew I was definitely failing my family in many, many ways. I wasn't sleeping, and it was a whole other situation when I got home." She shook her head in the same way as she did when she discussed her students. Melissa felt failure in every aspect of her life after the shooting.

In terms of the 6th and 11th steps, Melissa saw the erosion of her self-worth and a growing depression. She said,

> I had a very negative view of the way people saw me. People basically, as far as I knew, thought I was the worst teacher in the world and I deserved everything I was getting because Zach had gotten killed. Then you compound that with, "You know what? I think my people are better off without me because all I see is I'm just a very negative presence in the world at this point."

The seventh step is generalized anxiety, and the eighth is its cousin, fear. Melissa was overwhelmed. She was very clear when she said, "I was just scared in general. It was just this overwhelming fear of people and places. I felt like, 'Oh, my God. They're either all looking at me, or ... how do I know somebody's just not going to kill me?'" That general anxiety transitioned into the eighth aspect of PTSD, a real fear. She was terrified that someone might kill her.

The fear worsened over time – becoming the twelfth step, acute anxiety. According to her psychologist, she developed agoraphobia – a fear of going out in public. Melissa's world of safety shrank, ever smaller and smaller, when she expressed that,

> It just got compounded to the point where I didn't want to leave my house. I would drive my little daughter, my middle daughter, to work or to school, and then I'd pick her up. It took everything I had to do that.

The 10th and 11th steps, anger and resentment, arose in the interviews. Her voice pitch changed as she mentioned that the school administration officials ...

> ... were covering their asses for sure. It was not the welfare and safety of the children. It was ensuring that they didn't have to be liable in any way at any point for whatever, and that was evident big time.

Her anger was very apparent. On the day she walked off her job, after weeks of struggling with her school leadership, her last spoken words were those of severe anger, "'Well, you know what? Fuck you all.' I walked into my classroom, got my shit, and walked out." Later, she reflected on her experience with the district and found the moment her anger sprouted. In a tone that was almost a growl, Melissa said,

> And I didn't see that when I was in it because I'm thinking, "You want whatever you can do to benefit these kids." Why wouldn't you? No. It took me time and that's when I learned, no, they didn't want it, they didn't care. I was the stupid one for even thinking that.

Her ability to believe in those figures of authority was destroyed at that point. The resentment was apparent as one considers that she felt they had fooled her – "I was the stupid one for even thinking that."

Melissa and the Process of Adjustment to Trauma

As Lawrence and Fauerbach suggest, adjustment to trauma is a dynamic process influenced by "pre-trauma factors," "resilience-recovery variables," and "traumatic event characteristics" (Lawrence & Fauerbach, 2003). Melissa's most difficult issues were resilience-recovery variables; these focus on personality, social support and additional stressful life events. Her struggle with post-partum depression (an additional stressor) exposed her to deeper emotional trauma. This was in addition to a lack of support at her school after the shooting.

Melissa's own words pointed at prior issues: "I walked into my classroom, and I started crying. I mean, you can chalk that up to just having a baby, whatever you want, but when I walked into that classroom I broke down," and, "I had enough problems that I was dealing with. I was breast-feeding and pumping and doing all kinds of crazy stuff, and trying to organize my classroom. Whew, I was a mess." She came to realize this played a heavy role in her recovery . . .

> I wouldn't ever have said, "Yeah, postpartum depression . . .," but also, over the last couple of years, there's been research now on Cesarean sections and emergency Cesarean sections, and the fact that that in and of itself creates a post-traumatic stress syndrome for the woman. All of a sudden I was amazed, realizing, "Holy crap." That made so much sense to me because my daughter was an emergency Cesarean section.

Her social structure was cut in many areas. Beyond her disconnect with school administration, she found little connection with her co-workers. In her own words,

> I had nobody else who was in the same area with me. My teacher friends, they had been at the school that day, but they hadn't been in the room. They hadn't processed anything. They hadn't felt it or seen it.

Conclusion: Melissa and PTSD

In conclusion, the effects of the trauma event, the school shooting, produced strong symptoms of Post-Traumatic Stress Disorder for Melissa; this was verified by her licensed therapist. She experienced all of Hartman's 12 steps in the weeks and months after the shooting. This was the foundation of the disability that was to come. The PTSD was compounded by her post-partum depression and social isolation. This groundwork set up a situation in which a major emotional struggle would erupt – between Melissa and her employer, her students, her husband and children, and indeed, her own needs.

Melissa's experiences right after the school shooting reflect what Daniels, Bradley and Hays outline in their 2007 article. They describe the trauma of witnessing a school shooting as including "physical, behavioral, emotional, and cognitive responses" (Daniels, Bradley, & Hays, 2007, p. 653). Melissa described physical changes (shaking), behavioral changes (inability to go about her normal routine), emotional changes (a rise in fear, anxiety and anger) and cognitive responses (an inability to remember, to focus or go about her normal routines).

The Organizational Climate Construct

Research Question 2: Melissa and her Administrators

In research question 2, how Melissa's administrators dealt with her after the classroom trauma comes into focus. Did those actions affect her ability to function? Did those actions somehow contribute or alleviate post-trauma issues?

In the Burke-Litwin Model, leadership, or administrative actions, is defined as "persuasion, influence, serving followers, and acting as a role model" (Burke, 2010, p.220). What was the model prior to the shooting? The stage was set years in advance. Evidence indicates that there was a communications disconnect between Melissa and her administrators.

Burke, in discussing organizational climate, provides a corollary; he indicates that looking into the past is extremely valid in understanding the organization in the present. He writes that the history of an organization is "important for understanding culture, particularly knowing about the values and customs" (Burke, 2010, p.220). Extending, therefore, Burke's corollary, it can be asserted that the current culture of a school organization could serve as a clue as to how a school might handle a future shooting crisis – by recent administrative behavior.

As Melissa started her tenure with her school, she reported that "... the year I started about seven English teachers came on board. They had just done a complete cleaning-out of the school, and all of us started at basically the same time." Seven English teachers being replaced at one moderate sized middle school could be seen as unusual. Why so many at once?

That one piece of evidence in itself could be brushed aside, except there are other elements illustrating problems. Melissa described what she experienced after she started, in terms of administrative support. She said, "It was one of those positions where you were definitely on your own; you had to create your own safety net for help and networking with other teachers." That does not speak of support from the principal. She made her point by adding, "All my administration wanted to know was that everything was under control and that my kids weren't bugging them." The role model was one, it appears, of distance and a lack of involvement.

Further, an attitude of apathy seemed to exist on her campus. Melissa described what made her administrators most happy, who,

> ... seemed to be happiest if I dealt with all of the problems in my classroom, and that's pretty much the way it worked out. As long as the office didn't get a phone call from or about you, they didn't want to know anything, and that's kind of the way they kept it.

When she returned from maternity leave, getting closer to the shooting incident, this pattern continued. There was little control exerted by the principal or other administrators over their school's classrooms. She went out on maternity leave, "... but before that I spent a lot of time working on lesson plans, gathering materials, and setting up my room for a substitute, like every teacher would when she went on maternity leave."

Melissa left with everything in order in her room, but that's not what she found months later; she returned to find that,

> ... none of the sub plans had been followed. They basically had had three different subs in there. My classroom had been raided. The kids had stolen books. The kids had stolen Sharpie pens. There was no part of my classroom that had not been disrupted.

This chaotic situation crashed into her struggling emotions. She said, "I come back from maternity leave and, all of a sudden, adding in having a baby to the mix and then my room was in, I was not ready for what I saw when I got back." Here, also, before the shooting, was an indication that post-partum depression was interacting with her day-to-day life.

Moving to the trauma event itself, after she witnessed the shooting, she says that she was "the most confused person in the world about the whole scenario that first week." In this environment, she reported that the administration of her school told her that,

> We're going to get you a substitute that's going to stay with you for the rest of the year, and she is basically you. If you have a bad day and you don't want to show up, she always understands. She knows what you're doing in class, and you're good to go.

Unfortunately, this was not well thought out, in terms of her students. It was not easy for her to disconnect from her students if she had a bad day. She needed them emotionally, as they were the few who truly understood what she went through. She saw that she, too, was,

> ... a victim, just like those students. The difficulty for me was figuring out how to relate to them as a teacher, which I shouldn't have done ever, but yet I was a victim. We were all peers in the process of dealing with our emotions, and I needed them, too. I didn't have anybody else.

This was the starting point of an emotional wedge that was driven between Melissa and her students. She was forced to choose between her own health and the needs of her students. As she said, "I had to be there for the kids, but I needed help, too."

She described the panic in her classroom a week or two after the shooting, after announcing that she would start taking days off and allow her substitute to take over the class,

> "Wait, Mrs. McCarthy, what about us? No!" Am I responsible for them? No, I'm not. However, I felt it because nobody else was. I immediately panicked, and I didn't

know what to do.   The bottom line is, you look at the kids and you're thinking, "I can't leave. I want to leave. Everything's telling me to leave, but I can't."

Melissa felt that if she did not tend to the needs of her students, no one would. She did not see, at this point in the process, that administration had any substantial involvement in the recovery process. She describes how the school's front office even off-loaded work to her,

> I was going through all the hormones. I'll agree; they were rushing. Then you've got the post-traumatic stuff. Then I just felt like I was so responsible for so many little lives, and the parents were coming to me because they didn't know what to do, and the administration's coming to me saying, "Well, if you could have the parents fill these papers out and do this, and maybe they can go see the county," but there was no direct communications with the kids and the parents - nobody was really taking care of anything.

Throughout the weeks after the shooting, Melissa did her best to serve as an advocate for her students, but frustration grew as she saw nothing worked. Confusion, once again, reigned. All, for Melissa, was,

> . . . mishmash. I'd get paperwork to somebody, and then nothing would happen; it would sit on their desk. If I'd make a phone call, and 'Oh, we'll get back to you,' but nothing got done. I'd get the, "We'll take care of it. Yes, we're on it. For sure. Whatever you need," lines. That's just the way the whole thing went.

She became more desperate in her reaching out for help. She felt more and more isolated. Melissa called Columbine High School in Colorado and asked them what to do. She was, "looking for any help I could get, any help whatsoever, because it was just me, alone, helping the kids."

While Melissa was caught between her hormones, her post-traumatic stress symptoms, and her guilt toward her students, her administration increased their demands for paperwork and phone calls. Promises were made, but not much was carried out. She was doing more work, yet her additional tasks did not end in results that assisted her or her students. Confusion was joined with disorganization. She said,

> Sometimes I sit and I look at it, and I think, "This has to be from a movie because this can't happen in real life." In real life, something like this happens, everybody takes care of it. There are procedures. There are protocols. Nothing was followed. Nothing was set up, nothing was followed.

As the weeks dragged on, Melissa began to wear down; at one critical point, more than a month after the incident, it became apparent that the relationship between her and her administration had disintegrated. She wanted to have a cupcake-and-juice birthday party for her husband, and involve her students. Her principal denied the request.

Melissa saw cupcakes as a positive thing, but her school administration said, "No, that's just publicity for that company, and we don't want that. We don't want to draw that kind of publicity." Melissa replied with, "What do you mean publicity? Its people who understand these kids went through something. Nobody else has done anything for them."

She had to take the kids to the nearby park, because the principal said the party couldn't be on campus. As she celebrated with the kids, she noticed the superintendent of the school "came and sat in his truck watching while we ate cupcakes. It was so creepy. It was just creepiness to the nth degree. All I could think of is, 'Why aren't you guys doing anything for these kids? Why?'" When she returned to the school she was threatened with termination if she did such a thing again. Her superior said, "You go ahead and authorize anything of this nature again, and it'll be your job."

This appeared to be a "point of no return" in the relationship between the school and Melissa. With Melissa struggling with the anxiety and fear from Post-Traumatic Stress Disorder, having a distant administrator spy on a cupcake birthday party at the park added to her panic. Threatening her with her employment definitely added fuel to that fire. Melissa's expression as she described that moment reflected shock and panic.

Conclusion: The Effect of Administrative Actions After the Shooting

There appears to have been a history of administrative and teacher disconnection at this school, and that pattern seemed to play itself out again after the shooting incident. Administrators increased Melissa's burden (post-shooting) by requiring her to be responsible for additional paperwork and phone calls, all the while not following through on promises made. Melissa felt that there were no procedures, no systems, and no support structures in place to help her or her students. Finally, one administrative act of spying on a teacher providing cupcakes at a neighborhood park shattered what little trust and communications existed between this teacher and her superiors. As Blasé and Blasé explain, "the reward of a trusting environment is immeasurable, yet the price of lack of trust is dear" (Blasé & Blasé, 2001, p. 23). The price in Melissa's case appears to have been "dear."

The verdict at this point is that administrative actions, or often inactions, strongly contributed to the stress and effects of PTSD. Melissa's story validates the assertion of Daniels that ". . . teachers and other school personnel may not receive the support they need following mass trauma" (Daniels, 2007, p. 657). Melissa did not receive the support she needed, and, in fact, dealt with conditions that exacerbated her struggle.

Research Question 3: Melissa and School District Practices

In research question 3, the effects of policies, practices and procedures used by the school districts are addressed. Did these affect Melissa's ability to function? Did the process itself somehow feed into or alleviate Melissa's problems?

In the Burke-Litwin Model, practices refer to "a particular set of specific behaviors" (Burke, 2010, p. 221). These behaviors may include positive feedback, "pats on the backs" and challenges to grow a subordinate's abilities.

As to positive feedback, there is very little evidence of that in the interviews. There was one prominent practice by district administration that stands out as being very detrimental to Melissa's ability to function. The practice of "hands-off" administration, as previously described, contributed heavily to Melissa's struggles. The policy and practice for this particular school district appears to be one of delegation with no follow-through.

In one example, prior to the incident but after she returned to her classroom, a few of her teacher friends whispered that they were glad she was back because ". . . now we know there won't be kids standing in the hallway the whole time doing nothing but bugging us." Melissa's substitute would just send troublesome kids out into the hallway. As she said, "Administration wouldn't help them."

When Melissa asked for some counseling assistance, the district, once again, displayed a disconnection. They gave her a 1–800 number and brought in a week's worth of counseling triage, but what they truly did was, as Melissa said, "put out a handbook on how to address crisis situations, and that was it. I think we had two debriefings, but again, nothing happened in them; and that was it." The process seemed quite mechanical.

The district had a very cumbersome procedure for arranging trauma support to assist the students – or, actually, to refer the students to external support. After her continued prodding about therapy for her students, the leadership approached Melissa and asked, "Well, if you could have the parents fill these papers out and do this, and maybe they can go see the county."

She followed through on the paperwork, but, "I'd get paperwork to somebody, and then nothing would happen; it would sit on their desk. If I'd make a phone call, and 'Oh, we'll get back to you,' but nothing got done. I'd get the, 'We'll take care of it. Yes, we're on it. For sure. Whatever you need,' lines."

To Melissa, the administration was supposed to be there for the students. Over time a different view arose, however. She said,

> I didn't see that they were fair and objective in taking care of the students and their well-being. Everything that happened in that classroom afterward was based on me, me seeking it out, me ensuring it came, me asking about it, or me inquiring about it.

Over time, she believed that her school administration protected itself, at all cost, no matter how it hurt the children or her. Political posturing, to her, was the main motivation of the district and school administration. She continued,

> Again, they gave me a sub, but I think they did that as a matter of safety. Do you know what I mean? I think that was a political and safety issue. "We're covering our ass."

As the relationship degraded, she felt like responses from the office sounded more and more like excuses, and more of a worry about money rather than kids. She explained that, "I would ask an administrator, 'Hey, Mark, maybe you can get a bus to take the kids to the memorial because there's a lot of press people that want to talk to them. I don't think the press should talk to them, at least my particular class.' What was his response? 'Oh, well, we can't do that. Getting a bus is too difficult, too much money.'"

More and more, Melissa felt isolated. After explaining about her struggle to arrange a school bus to attend the memorial for their slain classmate, she sat and asked herself, "Why am I the only one?" At this moment, Melissa began to echo the wisdom of the Dalai Lama. He saw that when people neglect the well-being of others, ". . . and ignore the universal dimension of our actions, it is inevitable that we will come to see our interests as separate from theirs" (Lama, 1999, p. 163). She felt the district was not working toward the same goals that she was focused on; they were separate. To her, the district was playing a political survival game. She was worried about her survival and the well-being of her students.

Conclusion: The Effect of Policies and Practices After the Shooting

Early on Melissa came to feel that her desire to help her students did not fit into the school district's primary focus, which appears to be political damage control. The district was very worried about allowing a cupcake catering company to get near the students involved in the shooting – more worried about the publicity a cupcake company would receive than the comfort they'd serve to the children.

Follow-through problems are a recurring theme in Melissa's discussion. There were many requests made of the school and district, and little was accomplished, yet much was asked of Melissa, in terms of paperwork and calls. The appearance is that a lot of paperwork was completed, but there was not much to show for that paper trail; there were expressed concerns for the costs involved in helping students, but little discussion about the benefits possible.

The verdict, in terms of school policies and practices, is that the district was highly concerned about publicity, costs, creating a document trail and political survival. The effect on Melissa was symbolized by her haunting question, "Why am I the only one?" She felt more isolated, pressured and alone because of school district policies and practices.

Research Question 4: Melissa and Fairness

In research question 4, the concern is regarding Melissa believing she was dealt with fairly by administration. Did Melissa ever feel there was a hidden agenda, or an agenda that was not to her benefit, going on behind the scenes?

The Burke-Litwin Model describes leadership as being about "vision, change, using one's intuition, influence, persuasive and presentation skills, and rewarding people with personal praise and providing opportunities to learn new skills" (Burke, 2010, p.220). Fairness is an important component of this factor (Burke, 2010, p.222). What was Melissa's leadership like?

One of the most insightful comments made by Melissa regarding her dealings with her administration after the shooting, and in regards to fairness and a hidden agenda was,

> I'm thinking, "You want whatever you can do to benefit these kids." Why wouldn't you? No. It took me time and that's when I learned, no, they didn't want it, they didn't care. I was the stupid one for even thinking that.

This statement is revealing in three ways. First, she shows that she started by believing that her administration wanted the same thing for the students affected by the shooting that she did. Second, over time, through her experiences with her administration, she came to believe that there was a hidden agenda – meaning purposes are hidden from all except a few in control. She came to question their motives and trustworthiness. Finally, Melissa felt humiliated to discover that a hidden agenda existed. She felt fooled. None of the positive Burke-Litwin leadership attributes can be described using words from Melissa's interviews.

She noticed that the district provided little assistance as she realized that "Everything that happened in that classroom afterward was based on me, me seeking it out, me ensuring it came, me asking about it, or me inquiring about it." This contributed heavily to her feelings of being overwhelmed. While she expressed feelings that she did a lot, she also said that, from the school and district, "There were lots of excuses." Melissa started her journey trusting that she could believe in the administration, but this trust quickly fell through.

One of the most telling experiences, and one that she readily admits injured her immensely, was her battle with the school district's worker's compensation representative after she realized she could no longer continue in the classroom. Melissa said that the "Workmen's Comp process is probably what drove me nuttier than anything." In her state, an insurance company is retained by school districts to represent the school in cases where an employee has been injured; they act as agents for the schools.

The gloves came off between the school district and her during that process. Melissa felt her work with that company was ". . . evil, evil, evil. I had these women that weren't doctors, that weren't nurses that were like basically, 'When are you going to get better and be over this?'" They doubted her struggle, her illness. Early on they said, "We don't want to pay; we aren't going to pay you for this."

She went to depositions with lawyers, who brought up emotionally difficult issues that often had little to do with the school shooting. She went to one deposition in which the interviewer is "bringing up stuff I had told the counselor about my husband. It was a shock - that was my marriage! This didn't have anything to do with the school shooting . . ." Melissa said she "literally didn't even know what they were coming up with at this point."

Finally, the district's company proposed a deal. They offered her a total of $25,000; what they asked in return was that Melissa would give up her career. The math startled her. She considered that she was,

> . . . going to earn over a million dollars in my lifetime as a teacher. "We're going to give you $25,000 for that, and that also should cover your medical expenses at the

end of it." I looked at them and I said, "I don't think so. You're going to give me at least $250,000 - at least - and maybe I'll walk, but this is bullshit."

It was open warfare after that point. It was no longer about compassion, or healing, or working on solutions. The district was basically bargaining for her exit.

Conclusion: The Effect of a Question of Fairness and Hidden Agendas

Melissa started the process to heal and rebuild after the shooting; she believed that the school district wanted the same results she did. After receiving excuse after excuse, and realizing that her work was all that was being done for the students or herself, she began to doubt the real intentions of the school district. She recognized excuses. When she provided cupcakes for her students, and was spied on and threatened for it, the trust crumbled. When she was confronted by the coarseness and money-based horse-trading of the worker's compensation process, she saw herself as needing to fight for what she perceived was right for her, as her employer was not concerned about her needs.

If ethics are as Albert Schweitzer describes, as a "sense of duty toward others," (Hansen, 2007, p. 158) then Melissa did not feel as if she were being ethically treated. She did not experience any "sense of duty" toward her by her district or the district's representative.

The verdict on fairness in this case is negative. Struggling with Post-Traumatic Stress Disorder, buffeted by a disconnected administration, coping with a distant and unresponsive set of district policies and practices, Melissa was hit with a battle for the Burke-Litwin Model's factor of fairness. Early on it became apparent to her that fairness was not a part of the relationship between the school and her. This increased the probability that she would not be able to easily recover from the trauma of witnessing a school shooting.

Research Question 5: Melissa and Motivation

In research question 5, the focus is on Melissa's interaction with administrators and motivation. As she struggled after the classroom shootings, did she struggle with motivation because of anything her superiors did or said?

The critical element in the Burke-Litwin Model concerning positive motivation is, "congruence between the goals and values of the organization and the individual's needs and values" (Burke, Organization Change, p.223).

Having this congruence contributes significantly to workplace motivation. One might ask, "Does staff feel motivated to take the action necessary to achieve the organization's strategy?"

As discussed in research question 4, early on Melissa realized there was a disconnection between her agenda and that of the organization, her school. The school seemed more focused on political ramifications, financial impact and distancing itself from the shooting, whereas Melissa had to deal, on a day-to-day basis, with the emotional trauma experienced by her students and herself.

Newman et al. (2004) found that school administrators feel a need to get their schools "back to normal" as soon as possible after a school trauma. As Roberts (2007) describes, the weeks following a school shooting is a "period of psychological disequilibria," which very much reflects the emotions Melissa felt during that time. Her need to deal with the emotions of the shooting clashed with the desire of the administration to distance itself from that trauma and return to such mundane considerations as the cost of arranging for a bus to transport students to the memorial for the student slain in Melissa's classroom. Her principal's response after that request spoke of priorities when he said, "We can't do that. Getting a bus is too difficult, too much money."

Conclusion: The Effect of Values and Motivation

So, in terms of the Burke-Litwin Model, were values aligned or in conflict? For Melissa, her concern was for the well-being of her students. For her principal, the concern was about the bureaucratic effort and cost of arranging for a school bus to transport those students to an emotional moment such as a memorial. This is a conflict, not an alignment.

Melissa's motivation, her passion, would be blunted as she asked for resources to act upon her values. In many instances, as she tried to get help for her charges, she was blunted with denial. A cupcake party and a bus request are examples of such a blunting of motivation. The verdict in the question of motivation is negative – this factor would not have assisted in Melissa's recovery or healing.

Research Question 6: Melissa and School Unity

In research question 6, the concern is about Melissa believing that her administration looked after her needs after the school shooting. Was there a unified school culture after the shooting, one in which all sides took care of each other?

The Burke-Litwin Model delves into the roots of this concept, a sense of support, by looking at an idea called culture, which is defined as "the way we do things around here" (Burke, 2010, p.220). The model describes two important components of "culture" – explicit rules and implicit rules. Explicit rules address such issues as hours of work and a dress code. Implicit rules are followed, but rarely talked about. One aspect of this is how openly subordinates communicate with a supervisor – does the culture allow for disagreement, or do employees simply say what the boss wants to hear?

Again, the seeds of this condition could be seen in the years prior to the shooting incident. There was no culture of unity, openness and support before the incident. As Melissa returned from maternity leave, there was some evidence that she had co-worker support. Her room was a mess, and had been ransacked by substitutes allowing kids to run loose. Her colleagues, "... (We had a great core group there) came in and picked me back up. They got me going, and set me up again." But when she speaks of her superiors prior to the incident, there are indications of absence and a desire to not want to be bothered. If they "didn't get a phone call from or about you, they didn't want to know anything, and that's kind of the way they kept it."

Melissa, the subordinate, felt that her superiors "didn't want to know anything;" that signaled a closure in communications. This indicates there were really a minimum of two cultures operating in her school. Her colleagues were approachable, and she could count on them when things got tough, but her administrators could not be counted on. The implicit rule in her school was, by her own words, don't bother the administration and your life will be smooth. Conversely, if you bother the administration you will find problems. This was the climate at the school at the time of the shooting – the administration did not want to be involved in the issues or problems of the day-to-day lives of the teachers.

Considering the underlying paradigm in this research, social constructivism, the goal of this form of research, again as described by Creswell, is "to rely as much as possible on the participants' view of the situation" (Creswell, 2012, p. 20). Sometimes what is not said speaks as loudly, or louder, about that view than what is said. While there is much to quote from Melissa's interviews, it is very difficult to find anywhere in the transcript any significant expression that she saw worthwhile support from her administration throughout this ordeal.

There is one noticeable exception, an expression of concern for this wounded teacher – the school district called in a substitute to work alongside her for the rest of the year. That was a commitment of money and resources to Melissa's needs; one could argue that her superiors were looking after her needs. But the view of the teacher who is being assisted is odd; she didn't see this assistance as a positive. Melissa said,

> Some people might say, "Oh, well, they were supporting you this way." Okay, well, if this is the way you want to say it. I realized I couldn't keep working in my class. The administration said, "We're going to get you a substitute that's going to stay with you for the rest of the year, and she is basically you."

What is noticeable about her statement was the early sentence of, "Okay, if this is the way you want to say it." There is an undertone of sarcasm. There's a sense that not all that appears as a positive is, indeed, a positive. Once again, a portrait of mistrust, distant leadership, double messages, hidden messages, and disconnection from day-to-day life was Melissa's view.

Conclusion: The Effect of Culture and Melissa's Needs

What's the verdict in this factor? It's mixed. On the positive side, there was some unity in her school – among her colleagues prior to the shooting. On the negative side, the question of Melissa feeling a sense of support from her superiors was answered simply and succinctly with,

> They were covering their asses for sure. It was not the welfare and safety of the children. It was ensuring that they didn't have to be liable in any way at any point for whatever, and that was evident big time.

So, she saw that the administration was focused on their liability. In other situations, such as with arranging bus transportation, they had little resources, time or interest in looking after Melissa's interests. From a social constructivist point of view, the administration failed, but one must acknowledge that there was one expression of interest in her needs with the provision of a substitute to "be her" for the rest of the year.

Research Question 7: Melissa and a Sense of Safety

In question 7, the issue of Melissa feeling safe while in her school after the shooting trauma is addressed. Did the school district take actions to make her feel safe?

The Burke-Litwin Model describes "the need for security" (Burke, 2010, p. 222) as being critical for motivation and productive work. Considering

Melissa's struggle with Post-Traumatic Stress Disorder, this sense of security is paramount. As Kazdin wrote, people with PTSD "may relive the event via intrusive memories, flashbacks and nightmares; avoid anything that reminds them of the trauma; and have anxious feelings they didn't have before that are so intense their lives are disrupted" (Kazdin, 2000, p.251). The trauma happened at school – flashbacks and anxiety would be presented on or near the campus. Two incidents recounted by Melissa indicate that an atmosphere of disregard for a feeling of safety, and an attitude of mistrust, pervaded the campus.

First, Melissa was astounded when administrators "put some of those kids right away back into the computer lab. I'm thinking, 'Are you guys nuts?'" She knew the demands of Post-Traumatic Stress Disorder, and she recognized what this placement of the children who witnessed the murder back into the very site of the murder could do. Kazdin's words rang true – the children, and Melissa, needed to avoid anything that reminded them of the trauma, but they were forced to confront the reminders in that computer lab. This was, to her, a blatant disregard for the emotional need to feel safe.

Second, as described, Melissa took her class to the nearby park for cupcakes because the administration did not want to allow a publicity opportunity for the cupcake bakery. A surreal spy movie scene presented itself as Melissa noticed that "the superintendent of the school came and sat in his truck watching while we ate cupcakes. It was so creepy. It was just creepiness to the nth degree." It is difficult to find a sense of safety as one is being secretly watched.

Conclusion: The Effect of Safety on Campus

This disregard by the organization for the need to be safe collided with the symptoms of Post-Traumatic Stress Disorder; fear exploded. By the end of her time in her school, "I was just scared in general. It was just this overwhelming fear of people and places. I felt like, oh, my God. They're either all looking at me, or ... how do I know somebody's just not going to kill me?"

The verdict in this factor is, simply, negative. Attitudes and actions by her administration produced less and less of a feeling of safety and security on her school campus.

Research Question 8: Melissa and the Fairness of the Process

In research question 8, Melissa had to deal with a bureaucratic process to establish her injury and to move her toward resuming her pre-incident life.

Did she believe that her school district's system treated her fairly after the trauma?

Lawrence and Fauerbach indicate that "a sense of belonging or connectedness is the most important variable in mediating stress" (Lawrence & Fauerbach, 2003, p. 65). As described, a gulf existed between administration and the teachers, one that started years before the incident in question. This disconnection continued after the incident, and led to conflict in two major processes that occurred in the recovery period – arranging counseling for the students who witnessed the murder and in Melissa's processing with the school district's worker's compensation agent.

Recalling a principle of PTSD, Seligman described that the more out of control a person feels in a stressful event the more traumatic it will prove to be in the long term (Seligman, 1972). In these conflicts it is apparent that Melissa had little or no control, or even input, on how these situations would be resolved.

In the first conflict, during the process to obtain counseling services for the students exposed to the murder, Melissa and her class were called to an on-campus center that was established to initiate that process. As they were preparing to leave the classroom for the meeting, her students asked her if she would be there for them. The kids ask, "You're coming, right, Mrs. McCarthy?" She responded with, "Yes, I will be there. I'm coming. I'll go."

She walked her charges to the center and, as she entered, the school counselor called out to her, "Melissa, you can't go in there." Melissa was startled and responded with, "What are you talking about I can't go in there? Yeah, I can go in there."

A tense exchange ensued, in front of the students. The counselor answered back by saying, "No, they'll process better without you." Melissa immediately lashed out with,

> Are you kidding me? You really think they'll process better without me? I don't think so. They don't have any other adult in their life that actually processes with them. I'm the only one. I'm the one who's been doing their morning journaling and trying to talk to them about this. I'm the only one.

The counselor, without explanation or consideration of Melissa's point, said, "Well, you can't go." Melissa made her final statement as a teacher at that point, overflowing with frustration and a sense of not having been kept informed. She faced the counselor and said, "Well, you know what? Fuck you all." She then walked into her classroom, got her "shit," and walked off the campus. Melissa's use of two obscenities indicated her extreme level of frustration.

The fact that Melissa was not informed of how the counseling process would occur prior to the event itself added to the gulf between administration and her. Also, she probably should have been involved in the design and set-up of the event. Her input was not asked for. She was not aware of the conditions of the counseling. In this instance, Melissa felt outside of, and unaccepted by, the administrative process. She felt more and more out of control.

In the second process, she is faced with dealing with the district's agent, the worker's compensation company. She experienced more disconnection, more "out of control" feelings, and more perceived unfairness. They questioned whether she even had any emotional issue at all, in spite of professional psychological assessments. Melissa describes that process as "just evil, evil, evil." The officials in that organization continued to ask, "When are you going to get better and be over this?" The process became a confrontation; they weren't going to pay, at first, then Melissa was required to make legal depositions. The administration does not present to her a welcoming and fair process – the questioners even brought up "stuff I had told the counselor about my husband. It was a shock - that was my marriage! This didn't have anything to do with the school shooting."

Recalling Seligman's concern, she feels out of control in her words, "What are you guys talking about? I literally didn't even know what they were coming up with at this point."

Melissa felt that the process was so unfair that she needed to retain a lawyer. At that point, the district's representative proposed that, "we'll offer you $25,000." She was insulted. She countered with the argument that they were asking her to quit her job,

> ... that was going to be your career and you were going to earn, let's just say I was going to earn over a million dollars in my lifetime as a teacher. "We're going to give you $25,000 for that, and that also should cover your medical expenses at the end of it." I looked at them and I said, "I don't think so. You're going to give me at least $250,000 - at least - and maybe I'll walk, but this is bullshit."

Again, she was so upset she resorted to the use of an obscenity.

Conclusion: The Effect of the Process on Melissa's Future

Van der Kolk describes the challenges that victims of trauma face if proper therapy and support are not provided at the earliest appropriate opportunities.

These victims can "degrade into rigid thinking, paranoia, defensiveness, over-reactivity and health problems" (Van der Kolk, 1993, p. 231). In Melissa's struggles with the counselor, when she took her class to the room at the school to be used for therapy, she expressed defensive words and behavior. That was a moment of confrontation, not a moment of support. This same behavior was deepened with her tense discussions with the district's agent for worker's compensation. That was a situation of battle, of argument, not one of compassion.

There is no evidence that Lawrence and Fauerbach's principle that a sense of belonging or connectedness existed in Melissa's post-trauma period. While a sense of connectedness is important to the PTSD healing process, it did not happen for her.

The verdict in this question is not good. The processes Melissa experienced after the trauma left her more defensive, and with more rigid thinking.

Research Question 9: Melissa and Task Performance

In question 9, Melissa's emotional, physical and intellectual skills are investigated in relation to her ability to perform the tasks at hand after the shooting. Were there difficult issues that prevented her from being successful in her classroom?

In the construct of Post-Traumatic Stress Disorder, the element of fear is a serious component of that struggle. Elliott, Hamburg, & Williams (1998) reported that fear and heightened levels of stress lead to burnout and less effective work. It could be argued that, as previously described, Melissa's therapist-diagnosed struggle with PTSD after the shooting and her additional problem of Post-Partum Depression significantly impaired her competence.

Turning to the Burke-Litwin Model, the "knowledge, skills and abilities (competence or talent)" (Burke, 2010, p. 222) of the individual are critical elements of being able to perform the tasks assigned. Competence is an important consideration. Melissa's ability to perform tasks that she had been able to accomplish prior to the shooting incident was seriously diminished by fear and feeling out of control. Up to the day of the shooting, Melissa had enough problems she was dealing with. "I was breast-feeding and pumping and doing all kinds of crazy stuff, and trying to organize my classroom. Whew, I was a mess."

In addition, throughout her discourse a theme emerged about her ability to count on her superiors – expressed simply as, "administration wouldn't help." This was explicitly mentioned about her relationship with her principal prior to the shooting. On the day of the shooting, before the trauma, Melissa was overwhelmed and isolated. In a number of statements in her interviews, she expressed that her students "don't have any other adult in their life that actually processes with them. I'm the only one. I'm the one who's been doing their morning journaling and trying to talk to them about this. I'm the only one." Notice the repetition of the phrase "the only one."

The shooting brought trauma, which brought the 12 steps of PTSD, which included a heavy burden of fear and anxiety. From the moment of the shooting, Melissa felt overwhelmed and out of control. After she had herded her charges to another room, immediately after the shooting, the gravity of what had just happened hit her full-force. In her own words,

> That's when all of a sudden your body just goes, well, it's like a wave, like a shock wave probably, when a bomb goes off and all of a sudden it hits you; and then you start to shake and you start to cry, but you're still an adult with all these little people and you can't do that. You can't lose it. You can't freak out.

Melissa's ability to function was compromised at this very point. An old academic illustration, passed around by mental health professionals, likens the human ability to cope with a cup of water. As more and more water is poured in, there's less and less space to cope with additional water. At the moment of the shooting, from her words above, she fought hard to keep her cup from running over. One can see that this was the point from words she spoke moments later, "I don't think I could have held it together if I actually would have seen Zach. I don't know what I would have done." She had been pushed to the edge of her emotional cup.

Consider, again, the concept that fear and heightened levels of stress lead to burnout and less effective work. An error on the part of school leadership was made, weeks after the shooting, which contributed significantly to this: Melissa and her class were ordered back into the very same computer lab where she and the children witnessed the murder. Her response was incredulity. She said, "They put some of those kids right away back into the computer lab. I'm thinking, 'Are you guys nuts?'" She knew that the stress and fear would be heightened if they returned to that room; it is incomprehensible that leadership would not have seen this as an issue.

Conclusion: The Effect of Stress on Melissa's Competence

The verdict in this question rests heavily on an assessment of Melissa's condition in light of Elliott, Hamburg, and William's concept that fear and heightened levels of stress lead to burnout and less effective work. Melissa had felt fear, as expressed in her interviews and by diagnosis of her psychologist, and a strongly heightened level of stress. Therefore, she was heading, immediately after the shooting, toward burnout. The diminishment of her competence, due to fear and burnout, contributed to the decline toward her disability.

Research Question 10: Melissa and Organizational Processes

In research question 10 a summary of the actions of the school district is built to describe how Melissa arrived at the outcome of her struggle, disability. What organizational processes contributed to the final disposition of Melissa's situation?

Like tree species, the roots of the disposition of Melissa's case can be found hidden deep underground, in this case, in the past. Melissa's struggles began well before the shooting; she was struggling with her school principal's policies and practices for years. There was no nurturing, supportive environment on her campus. Her administrators "didn't want to know" what was going on, or about problems. Administrative apathy was felt by many. Melissa knew before she left on maternity leave that she was alone; her substitute did not get much support from the office. She returned dealing with Post-Partum Depression and with all the demands that come with babies. On the first day back she was overwhelmed by the state of her classroom – it had been ransacked. She turned to her friends in her building for rescue, not to her administration.

Like an ash tree, when the plant is young it is supple and able to bend; it is more able to sway with the blowing of the wind. This is a simile for Melissa's situation in the weeks after the shooting. This new way of life, after the shooting, could have gone in many different directions. If she had been nurtured and protected, like that young ash tree, she could have returned to growing straight, strong and true. Unfortunately, her surroundings presented her with hostility, anxiety, fear, loneliness and desperation. She felt out of control. There were insufficient communications, as seen in the class visit to the counseling arrangements. Her superiors threatened her with her job and they spied on her as she provided cupcakes for her students. These examples can be seen as an indicator of fear and anxiety on the part of her administrators.

Just as a tree grows in a place of storms, she hardened into a defensive posture. As Van der Kolk pointed out, this harsh environment forced permanent changes. The "rigid thinking, paranoia, defensiveness, over-reactivity and health problems" (Van der Kolk, 1993, p. 231) began. Melissa showed some of these symptoms at each step of the process.

When a tree breaks after a fierce storm, scavengers sweep in to dissect the remains, to clean the debris from the forest. After Melissa "broke," leaving her position with an obscene verbal expression, she immediately had to fend off attacks by the school's worker's compensation agent. When they realized she would not get better, they turned to hardball dollar negotiations – offering a paltry sum for her to leave. That money was supposed to cover her medical needs, her earnings requirements and part of her retirement income (considering lost contributions from that point forth). She fought back. She gained more money, but not enough for the lifetime of a woman not yet in middle age.

Conclusion: The Effect of the Process on Melissa's Case

If there had been a nurturing school climate in her life or if proper psychological assistance had been offered early on, or if there had been better communications after the shooting, or if the district had presented a relationship of trust and compassion, there could have been a different outcome to this case. The verdict is that school administration could have, at any point along the line, recognized the course of the process and offered to step out of a "cover their ass" mentality. The process, continuing as it did with no willful alteration in course, contributed to Melissa's eventual disability.

Conclusion: What Caused Melissa's Disability?

It is clear that one solitary factor did not transport Melissa into disability – many forces created the disposition of this case. She struggled with personal and professional issues. Just before the shooting Melissa carried a burden of Post-Partum Depression, her own psychological past (as anyone carries), the demands and responsibilities of a new baby, and the weight of a non-nurturing school environment. These were described by her psychologist. She worked in a school that dealt with struggling families. As she said, there were few adults active in the lives of the children in her class.

From the moment of the shooting on, Melissa was forced to deal with an extraordinary trauma event. As the first construct (Post-Traumatic Stress Disorder) outlines, she exhibited the symptoms of PTSD, including pain, confusion, guilt, shame, self-worth dissipation, anxiety, fear, anger, resentment, depression and acute anxiety. Her struggle with these symptoms degraded her ability to attend to her professional responsibilities.

From the moment of the shooting on, the second construct impacted Melissa's ability to recover and continue in her role as a classroom teacher; the Burke-Litwin Model's concept of organizational climate came into play. Management practices, policies, actions and policies shaped her perceptions of her working environment, affecting her motivation. She didn't feel safe. She didn't feel as if she could trust her superiors. She didn't believe that her agenda was the same as that of her school leadership. A lack of trust and communications was seen in many vignettes. Decisions were made, such as making the students return to the very computer lab in which the murder occurred, that confused, frightened and angered Melissa.

From the moment she left her school, Melissa had to fight a defensive battle with her school's worker's compensation agent. She particularly noted that process as, "evil, evil, evil." As Melissa was in the throes of dealing with her own psychological pain she was forced into a battle for her own financial survival.

Melissa was forced into leaving her chosen profession because of the interaction of all of these factors from the two constructs of this study. The interaction of Post-Traumatic Stress Disorder and Organizational Climate in her situation caused Melissa's disability. Even the fact of her going out on disability was painful. As she said, "Once I finally signed the papers and officially quit and did it all, it hurt. To me I was saying, 'No, I'm not going to be a teacher anymore. I'm on disability. It's permanent.'"

References

Blasé, J., & Blasé, J. (2001). *Empowering teachers: What successful principals do* (2nd ed.). Thousand Oaks, California: Corwin Press.

Burke, W. W. (2010). *Organization change: Theory and practice* (3rd ed.). Thousand Oaks, CA: Sage.

Creswell, J. (2012). *Qualitative inquiry and research design: Choosing among the five approaches* (3rd ed.). Thousand Oaks, CA: Sage Publications.

Daniels, J., Bradley, M., & Hays, M. (2007, December). The impact of school violence on school personnel: Implications for psychologists. *Professional Psychology: Research and Practice, 38*(6), 652–659.

Elliot, D., Hamburg, B., & Williams, K. (1998). *Violence in American schools: A new perspective.* Cambridge: Cambridge University Press.

Hansen, D. T. (Ed.) (2007). *Ethical visions of education: Philosophies in practice.* New York City: Teachers College Press.

Hartman, R. J. (2011). *The twelve steps to the formation of PTSD*. Retrieved from http://aaph.org/rjhartman/articles/twelve_steps_to_PTSD

Kazdin, A. (Ed.) (2000). *Encyclopedia of psychology*. New York: Oxford University Press (USA).

Lama, D. (1999). *Ethics for the new millennium*. New York City: Riverhead Books.

Lawrence, J., & Fauerbach, J. (2003, January/February). Personality, coping, chronic stress, social support and PTSD symptoms among adult burn survivors: A path analysis. *Journal of Burn Care & Rehabilitation, 24*(1), 63–72.

Newman, K., Fox, C., Roth, W., & Mehta, J. (2004). *Rampage: The social roots of school shootings*. New York, NY: Basic Books.

Roberts, A. R. (2007). *Crisis intervention handbook: Assessment, treatment and research* (2nd ed.). New York: Oxford University Press.

Seligman, M. (1972). *Helplessness: On depression, development and death*. San Francisco: Freeman and Company.

Van der Kolk, B. (1993). Biological considerations about emotions, trauma, memory and the brain. In S. Ablon, D. Brown, & J. Mack (Eds.), *Human feelings: Explorations in affect development and meaning*. New York: Routledge.

· 2 1 ·

A QUESTION ABOUT FINDINGS: MIKE

"Oh, my. It seems like a 'perfect storm' (sorry to use that cliché) hit Melissa," Janice said.

"That's a good way of thinking about it, and that describes trauma, in many ways," I responded.

"How is that?"

"One perspective on trauma is that one feels like something was out of his or her control. All of these factors hitting Melissa at that time would have felt out of control to her."

"Did you have similar findings about the other teacher, Mike?" Janice asked.

"Similar, and some were different. Let's look at his story . . ."

An Answer

Mike's Story

The Post-traumatic Stress Disorder Construct

Research Question 1: Mike and Post-traumatic Stress Disorder

Addressing research question 1 in light of Mike Dougherty's experiences, which of Hartman's 12 steps of PTSD affected him in the months following the school shooting? These factors include the activating event, pain, confusion, guilt, shame, self-worth dissipation, anxiety, fear, anger, resentment, depression and acute anxiety.

With PTSD, the journey begins with an activating event, in this case a shooting at Mike's school. The law enforcement reports and news items document the incident, and it happened as Mike described it. In his own words:

> That was when I heard the shots. I was about 30 feet away. I thought that some kid had set off a firecracker in a trash can. I'm walking over there thinking, 'It's February. The kids should know they're not supposed to do this.' I'm running through the list of usual suspects in my head.
>
> At that moment I saw a man reloading a bolt-action rifle. I had to switch gears from condition white, I guess you would call it, to condition red immediately. I'm thinking, 'It's a bolt-action rifle. He's reloading it.' He shot again because I didn't have time to process it yet.

From an academic point of view, not one of a therapist, for Mike the journey began the moment he "switched gears" from condition white to condition red. At that point, what he calls "condition red" is a condition of alarm as he realizes that a traumatic event is happening. He continues by describing another emotion of being confronted with a life-threatening situation,

> During the incident, everybody is going to have a fight-or-flight reaction. If you decide to run, great that's okay, help some kids along the way. Help them get to a safe place. If you decide to fight, be smart about it. Don't just soak up bullets.

Mike decided to not run, and he definitely did not become one who would "soak up bullets." He moved toward the gunman, confronting the source of trauma head on. The resulting scene was, indeed, a moment of heroics. In his words,

I ran up to him. There are people who understand how to fight and people who don't. He didn't know what to do when he didn't have a gun. When I grabbed him, you would think that he would use the fact that he's got a gun in his hand to at least jam, hit me with the rifle butt or something like that, but he just dropped it.

Mike did not know how the gunman would react. This was not a rash act, as before he ran toward the man he timed his actions carefully. In his mind,

I'm thinking, "It's bolt-action, that means in between when he's reloading, effectively he doesn't have a gun." After he got the second shot off - and unfortunately, that's the one that hit Billy. I went for it.

As Mike came into contact with the gunman,

I grabbed him up by the lapels of his hoodie. He's pulling one way and I'm pulling the other way. Fortunately, I outweighed him by quite a bit. I was quite a bit taller than he was. I thought, "I'm just going to wrap him up and go down to the ground."
My arms were wrapped around his arms, and my legs were wrapped around his legs.

Mike was not alone. As he took the assailant down to the ground, others rushed over to assist him.

He dropped the gun. Mary Burton, who was our assistant principal at the time, came out, took the gun and threw it inside. Jerry Morton, who was another Math teacher, he had actually been closer and had gotten inside the school, and then he came back out and he got on top. We had a "bad guy sandwich" there.

The descriptions Mike provided match the definition of an activating event in Post-Traumatic Stress Disorder. He was definitely confronted with trauma.

Second and third in the list of steps of PTSD, one experiences pain and confusion. One moment of confusion came as he watched the shooter. Mike could not process what he was seeing. He said, "He shot again because I didn't have time to process it yet." The assailant was able to fire another round, Mike believed, because he did not understand what he was seeing.

He experienced pain and helplessness just after the shooting. Mike expressed these feelings in more than words. He had difficulty speaking, needing to pause from time to time and take a breath as he described how,

I just walked around crying because . . . well, every time I would walk over to see Billy, all I could see was his face. He was just bewildered and hurt and . . . in shock. All of that stuff. He was pretty much covered up by people trying to make sure that he wasn't going to bleed to death and all of that stuff.

The pain continued with a sense of helplessness. Mike had hunted and knew the impact of bullets on animals. He was confronted with that image, only with a wounded boy before him. In the interview, Mike's voice changed. He grew quieter as he said,

> Remember, he got hit in the back. When he was turned over, it was soft point hunting round from a .30 ought 6. I had seen that in deer. I knew that the trauma was probably about the size of a decent dessert plate.
> All I can see is his face. I couldn't do anything to help him.

Mike felt helpless and in emotional pain. While it was but a momentary flash of confusion as he tried to comprehend what was happening before him, it was confusion.

Guilt is the fourth step of PTSD, and Mike was afflicted with this. After the scene had been secured by law enforcement, and he was walking out of the building through the gym, Mike was confronted by

> I still don't know who this guy was. He was a sheriff's guy, sheriff's uniform and all of that stuff. I remember he had a really long scar on his arm. He looked at me and he said, "You did good work today."
> That actually helped me a lot, because I was thinking that I messed up, because I let Billy get shot. I couldn't think fast enough and the guy got off the second shot.

During the interviews Mike became most emotional when he discussed the elements of the incident involving the two children hurt in the shooting. He cannot forget that there were two children affected. In his words,

> Look, at times I'm going to get emotional here when I talk about this. What you find is, what I find is that when I get most emotional is when I think about Billy or Pammy or when I think about how brave people were.

From Mike's tone of voice during the interview, one could tell that Mike needed the words of the law enforcement officer, and he hangs on to those words. Still, however, he may still carry a sense of guilt – perhaps he wonders why he couldn't have stopped the gunman earlier. Maybe Billy and Pammy would not have been injured at all if he had been faster. His tone of voice says this may haunt him for some time to come.

Elements of the fifth step of Post-Traumatic Stress Disorder, shame, cannot be readily found in Mike's interview. It's possible that he avoided a longer-term, debilitating sense of shame because of one sentence from a law enforcement officer. When that officer said, "You did good work today," it happened early in the healing process, within the first hour.

Jordan (2003) indicates that emotional support coming quickly after a traumatic event is critical to long-term healing. This simple pronouncement from law enforcement could be good medicine, well dosed, at a very opportune time. Mike was still processing what he went through, and the implanting of this idea, that he had done "good work," was valuable in the long term.

Indeed, this pronouncement of a job well done may have produced the results in the sixth step of PTSD, as there is no indication anywhere of a dissipation of self-worth. Mike continues to teach, as of the writing of this paper, but not much longer. When he spoke of his plans for the future, he said he was planning on retiring. He explains,

> I was originally thinking maybe if I teach until I can get 30 years in the state. I just feel like I'm burned out. I've been doing this for 36 years now. I've been teaching school for 36 years; twelve years in another state, but they still count.

After he expressed his plans for the near future, he was asked if the shooting had any influence on this choice. His response was telling,

> I've thought about how much the incident has influenced this decision. I've thought, it was such an intense period that I'm wondering is this a, almost like a postpartum depression. I don't think so. I've just gotten to the point where I'm just burned out from teaching school.

Many teachers experience this feeling after more than thirty years in the classroom. There is no sign of long-term dissipation of self-worth or depression, just a sense of it's time to do something new. In fact, Mike discussed ideas for new directions. He explored new directions by saying, "I might tutor. I have retirement that's going to come in from public employees' retirement thing." He's looking forward to the freedom to choose a new direction.

Mike has also been reaching out to others, to any audience who will hear him. He advises that,

> Talking about it helps; the fact that I've been lucky enough to have people say, "Will you come and speak?" I get to work through that. I get to work through those emotions. Of course every time you talk about the incident, it becomes less traumatic. It's like letting the poison out of a boil.

The impression Mike leaves is one of an extrovert, someone who thrives upon interacting with other people. He has decided to act on this, and speaks frequently. Years after the shooting incident, he still reaches out to others. After the recent shooting in Newtown, Connecticut,

> When the Sandy Hook thing happened, there were a number of people that know me that they call me and say, 'Look, I was thinking about you when I heard about this.' I'm not alone. You are not alone.

A social support system, mentioned by a number of PTSD experts, bolstered and supported Mike on his road to recovery. He is not alone.

In terms of PTSD steps 7 and 8, anxiety and fear, Mike said he struggled with both of those elements. He admitted that after the shooting he "didn't get a whole lot of sleep that night." Adrenalin from the incident, anxiety over whether or not the two students would be okay, and concern for his wife ran through his mind. As he was still processing the incident, only minutes after it had finished, he said, "I called my wife. I told her that there was a shooting at our school, that I was fine, but that one student got shot and then my wife screamed. I said I have to hang up."

He also admits to dealing with the "flight-or-fight reaction," which is symptomatic of fear. He said, "If you decide to run, great that's okay, help some kids along the way. Help them get to a safe place. If you decide to fight, be smart about it. Don't just soak up bullets." While he dealt with fear, there is nothing in his interviews that indicates this fear became overwhelming. Again, Mike continued teaching in the same school long after the incident was over.

Another act by law enforcement may prove to have been critical in Mike's long-term recovery. After the shooting, as he walked through the school hallway and was stopped by an officer, Mike presented his school identification and told the officer that it was all right for Mike to pass, as it was his school. The officer responded with, "This is our school until we know everybody is safe." This sense that proper authorities were in control throughout the period after the shooting pervades many of Mike's statements. He knew the right people were in charge at that moment. He was able to put fear out of his mind.

In terms of PTSD steps 9 and 10, anger and resentment, there's little evidence of these after the shooting. Indeed, the opposite could be asserted. Mike was so level-headed during the incident that while trapping the assailant in a bear hug, waiting for support, he had the presence of mind to engage him in conversation. He said,

> The guy was in fight-or-flight mode and he was going to struggle no matter what. I'm fat and happy. I'm on the bottom, Jerry is taking all the, doing all of the squeezing. I'm just holding on to the guy. I'm just saying things like, "Hey, what's your name?"

> I'm thinking if I can get him to start talking, maybe he won't struggle as much. I'm saying, "What's your name? Did you go to school here?"

It is possible that Mike's easy-going attitude in those crucial minutes after the shooting helped keep the gunman calmer than what would have been possible if he had erupted in anger. Mike's stated intent was if he got him to start talking, "maybe he won't struggle as much."

Finally, in terms of PTSD steps 11 and 12, there is no indication of symptoms of depression or anxiety in any of the interviews provided. Mike has stayed active, and perhaps this explains why. He said,

> Since then I try to do things that have to do with school security. If anybody calls me and says, "Hey, look, there is a group of school security people, will you go and speak to them?" Sure, I'm hard to get, all you got to do is ask me.

There's no depression here – to the contrary, he seems to have found a new sense of purpose. He has even spent a lot of time outlining what could help future schools that have to cope with shootings:

> So, how do we stop this sort of stuff? If you train faculty people like security staff, the same way, tailor the curriculum to school based security, now you got a person who is fully trained like having a constable on campus - make it part of teacher license renewal. I know I have to do 90 clock hours every five years.
>
> I have to do that anyway just to renew my certification, just make sure that that's a line in the certification renewal law. Instead of taking another course on how to teach Math that I've been doing for 30 years, I take a course in school security.

Mike has a long list of ideas to fight back against the scourge of school shootings, and he's anxious to get the word out. He has thought of every angle, from dealing with students on busses to making sure that "you know every kid – somebody in the school knows every kid." This is not the sign of a man struggling with long-term depression.

Conclusion: Mike and PTSD

In an academic analysis of Mike's incident in light of Hartman's 12 steps of Post-Traumatic Stress Disorder, a review of factors (the activating event, pain, confusion, guilt, shame, self-worth dissipation, anxiety, fear, anger, resentment, depression and acute anxiety) shows that Mike was affected by many of these, but not all. He was confronted with a trauma and the resultant steps of pain, confusion, guilt, anxiety, and fear, but Mike struggled with a more moderate form of PTSD. He did not confront significant levels of the more difficult and longer-lasting steps, including shame, dissipation of self-worth, anger, resentment, depression or severe anxiety.

The Organizational Climate Construct

Research Question 2: Mike and his Administrators

In research question 2, the way Mike's administrators dealt with him after the school trauma comes into focus. Did those actions affect his ability to function? Did those actions somehow contribute or alleviate post-trauma issues?

Returning to the Burke-Litwin Model, leadership, through administrative actions, is "persuasion, influence, serving followers, and acting as a role model" (Burke, 2010, p.220). One indicator of leadership prior to the incident is that Mike's school held regular emergency drills and allowed open discussion of the possibility of such an emergency. His school administration had made emergency preparedness a priority, but Mike showed leadership with his own students by supporting this school-wide effort and allowing his charges to explore what might happen.

He said, "I had talked with my students before, during lockdown drills, because afterwards they all want to play 'what if.'" His students asked, "What if somebody comes in the room?" His response showed openness, "I'm going to do something. You guys head for the other door." The give-and-take continued with the kids asking, "What are you going to do?" He answered with, "I don't know. Throw desks or something."

There was a sense that the school was prepared for an emergency. Mike said that "Everybody knew what to do when you lockdown - you're supposed to shelter because of a tornado or something, let people say shelter or whatever."

Mike indicated there were no unusual conflicts with administration prior to the incident. A review of interview transcripts failed to uncover any real complaints about his principals. In fact, when asked about any issues on the day of the shooting, prior to the incident, Mike responded with, "It was just a typical school day; I was grading papers, teaching kids, seventh grade." He describes a "typical" school day as one that focuses on his students, their work and his teaching – he does not mention any administrative clashes.

On the day of the incident, one witnessed real teamwork, a meshing of the efforts of a teacher with an administrator. After Mike grabbed the gunman, and after the assailant dropped the gun, "Mary Burton, who was our

assistant principal at the time, came out, took the gun and threw it inside."
She didn't have to ask Mike what to do; she knew Mike well enough to see
he had the situation in hand and she knew how to contribute to the safety
of her school – by removing the weapon. After the weapon was removed, the
assistant principal returned to check on Mike, and "she saw that I didn't need
any help, because she went to Billy." This administrator spent a lot of time
checking on peoples' well-being. She was actively involved.

Mike feels very strongly about how his assistant principal came to his
assistance. He said,

> I think about when Mary, our vice principal, came out and she just said, her husband
> looked at her and said, "What were you going to do?" She said, "I don't know, kick
> him between the legs. Mike needed help."

Here was a strong statement from an administrator – "Mike needed help."
She was concerned about her teacher. Mary approached, and then saw that he
had it under control. She then went to check on the wounded boy.

Just after the shooting, when the staff gathered to figure out the next
steps, such as dealing with the press and re-opening the school, the assistant
principal, Mary, showed a strong sense of leadership when she asked, in conjunction with Mike, "How do you want to do this?" Then the two of them,
in unity, addressed how the staff wanted to deal with the press. "We" refers to
Mike and the assistant principal.

> We talked to people as a faculty – all of us together. They said, "The news will want to
> talk to you guys." ' We said, "All right, how do you want to do this?" The group said,
> "We don't want to talk." As a group we decided, "Two of us will talk to the media,
> Mary and Mike, and then maybe that will get them to leave everybody else alone
> because we'll feed them something."

This conversation points to a very democratic and collaborative staff –
and that only comes from leadership that nurtures collaboration. Mike used
the phrase "all of us together." He didn't say "administration and teachers" or
"us and them." As the seeds of current relationships are built in the past, this
indicates that there was a close working relationship before the incident.

This conversation also points to the Burke-Litwin concept of leadership
"serving" the followers. The assistant principal asked the staff, "How do you
want to do this?" She was sensitive to staff needs. She did not say, "This is how
we're going to do this." One other sentence bolsters this assertion of unity –
"as a group we decided."

This discussion was held at a faculty reunion, held at the elementary school down the street – arranged for by the administration. They held the meeting in a place that felt safe, to plan the steps for a return to normalcy. As Newman found, school administrators often feel a need to get their schools back in session as soon as possible (Daniels, 2007, p. 654). Nowhere in the interviews or associated documents is there a sign that the leadership wished to rush such a movement. In fact, in this meeting there are indicators that leadership was heavily concerned with what worked best for the entire staff.

Mike expressed that he "got to see that everybody was there." He wanted to know that everyone was doing well. There was empathy and compassion for his fellow staff members.

After the meeting, Mike wanted to see Billy in the hospital; he felt a need to make sure the boy was alive and well. A district-level person, the site administrator and Mike, a teacher, were on the same wavelength, emotionally. Mike said,

> One of the psychological counselors was saying, and Mary kept saying, "We have to go see Billy. I have to go see Billy." Because the vice principal had seen the wound, he had looked at her and said, "Am I going to die?"
>
> She looked at him and said, "Not on my watch." We knew that he had gotten to Children's Hospital and that they had gotten him stabilized and everything like that. She had to see him.

This speaks strongly to a connection between the administrator, the teacher and the students. Mary needed to know about Billy, as Mike did. There was a strong sense of compassion evident that day. The assistant principal showed incredible leadership by stating that Billy would not die "on my watch." This is a person who looks after her subordinates.

In the months that followed the shooting, Mike felt a lot of support from school and district administration. On a regular basis, there were visitors in his classroom. Every now and then, a principal or a counselor would approach him and say, "There is somebody here to cover your class. We're going for a walk." The "walk" consisted of a stroll around the campus, with the counselor or principal asking Mike how he was doing, and then just listening.

Mike's school district knew they could not hide the shooting from the press or the people of the community. Mike describes a press conference, arranged by the school district and held at the district offices. This, again, indicates a leadership structure not trying to "sweep the incident under the rug," but willing to address it head on.

As the months stretched out after the shooting, the support remained. Mike describes how the district remained responsive to his needs. "Yes, they just said, 'I don't care whether you say you need a break or not. You are going.' Over the long term, they weren't there as much but we could call them whenever we wanted."

This assertion that the teacher would take breaks, whether or not the teacher believed he needed them, sent a strong signal to Mike – his well-being was monitored. He was not alone.

One of the most extreme examples of support came long after the incident – almost a year later. Mike was,

> ... at the briefing and our security director was talking about the incident. I had to go to the bathroom and I was going to speak next. I went out of the auditorium and went to the bathroom. The guy who is the Director of Psychological Services for the district discreetly followed me into the bathroom to make sure that I was okay. They're that available.

Conclusion: The Effect of Administrative Actions After the Shooting

The verdict in Mike's case regarding administrative leadership and support is clear – the model of behavior was a positive one and contributed to the recovery of the school and Mike. In the years prior to the shooting, a collegial, supportive atmosphere was built, one that paid off on the day of crisis. The school held emergency drills – people knew what to do if there was a crisis. During the shooting, administration and teachers worked together to subdue the assailant and control the scene until law enforcement arrived. In the long-term, over months, Mike knew administrators and counselors were there for him, and that he could get help whenever he needed it. Administrative support before and after the shooting made a world of difference.

Daniels recommended that "... in their efforts to provide assistance to the student body, psychologists not overlook opportunities to provide aid to teachers and other school staff who have been traumatized" (Daniels, 2007, p. 657). Mike's school district took heed of this wisdom and put it into practice.

Finally, Mike's own words echo that the verdict should be a positive one in this area when he said, "We really need to be able to inform people about what we did because in my mind, it's pretty much of a textbook case of 'what to do right.' My school did it right." Mike's choice of the pronoun "we" says a lot about how things worked during the incident and after.

Research Question 3: Mike and School District Practices

In research question 3, the effects of policies, practices and procedures used by the school districts are addressed. Did these affect Mike's ability to function? Did the process itself somehow feed into or alleviate Mike's problems?

Practices, according to the Burke-Litwin Model, refer to "a particular set of specific behaviors" (Burke, 2010, p. 221). These behaviors may include positive feedback, "pats on the backs" and challenges to grow a subordinate's abilities.

When Mike's superiors came into his classroom after the shooting to check on him, saying, "We're going for a walk," what they were doing was challenging him. They wanted to look into his emotional struggles, and determine if he was growing after the shooting.

When the school district was trying to determine when to reopen the school, they checked on the opinion of the staff. They offered flexibility to everyone involved. As Mike said, "Tuesday the shooting happened, Wednesday we had faculty and stuff like that at the elementary school and kids could come if they wanted. We went back into our school on Friday." The district allowed time to pass before trying to re-start the school schedule and program.

Mary, the assistant principal, showed compassion and flexibility as they re-opened the school. She did not rely on rigid pre-established and out-of-touch policies when she said,

> We're meeting all of these kids out front. We're meeting them all out there with cookies. We're going to be out there because that's not, if we don't do that, then the shooter claims that space. That's not his space, that's our space.

She indicated that formal policies were not dictating how to deal with a situation outside of normal human experiences when she asked her faculty at a reunification meeting, "How do you want to do this?" The recovery process was not dictated by board policies, but by the needs of the human beings involved at the time.

This sense of positive feedback and challenges to grow a subordinate's abilities can be seen, first and foremost, in Mike's attitude toward students who presented problems to him in the classroom. When disciplining a student, Mike asks the person, ". . . if I'm respectful to you, then you know how to treat me, if we're clear, then we know what we're supposed to do from here."

This was the example offered at the school, how things were done all over campus.

Preparedness was a policy and a practice at school, and that preparedness paid off on the day of crisis. As Mike said, "Everybody knew what to do when you lockdown - you're supposed to shelter because of a tornado or something, let people say shelter or whatever. Actually the school had been trained in that like two weeks before." They drilled for what had happened that day. Mike had discussed "what-ifs" with his students.

The physical plant at the school was ready for such an emergency as well. Mike tells us that, "We always have our doors locked so that there's an electric lock." Administration had put school security as a high priority on campus.

As the shooting went on, the school secretary showed courage and presence of mind. She knew what to do. She understood how to use the school security system, installed by the school district, for the advantage of the students and staff. Mike said that,

> The school secretary was a very brave lady at this point. The guy is shooting at the school and she is standing there not pressing the lockdown, watching him, making sure that all the kids can get inside and then presses the lockdown. Of course when she presses the lockdown, that triggers all of the doors in all of the school and they are all automatically go shut. We automatically have them locked all the time so that as they're shut, a person in the hallway is locked out.

Conclusion: The Effect of Policies and Practices After the Shooting

Pine Ridge Middle School, where Mike taught, had two practices and policies that contributed to the positive outcome the day of the shooting, and to the healing of Mike and his colleagues. One started well before the incident and one evolved after the incident.

First, the school was well prepared for any kind of emergency. They had lockdown drills and security systems installed across the campus. The secretary was well-trained on how to use the system. The staff knew what to do when they heard an alarm. Teachers, such as Mike, talked to their kids about a possible attack on the school well before any incident occurred.

Second, his administration showed flexibility and compassion in dealing with the staff in restarting school activities after the incident. In addition, they showed flexibility and compassion by providing substitutes to take over his class so a counselor or an administrator could take Mike outside and check on his well-being.

Research Question 4: Mike and Fairness

In research question 4, the concern is about Mike believing he was dealt with fairly by administration. Did Mike feel there was a hidden agenda, or an agenda that was not to his benefit, going on behind the scenes?

There is one story involving Mike that is telling about the atmosphere at the school. When disciplining a student, Mike asks that person,

> Have I been clear? Have I been fair? Have I been respectful? Because if I'm respectful to you, then you know how to treat me, if we're clear, then we know what we're supposed to do from here. I really want you to tell me if you think that I'm not fair.

Mike indicated in one conversation that this attitude, this theme, permeated the entire campus. From the top down fairness and respect were expected to be displayed by everyone. Mike worked hard to ensure that his students knew this was a priority for him. At the root of all of this was caring – caring to do what is right.

His assistant principal, Mary, showed the same caring and involvement when she jumped in and grabbed the gun from the shooter – exposing herself. She was concerned about someone else on her campus being shot. Mike did not forgot what Mary said to her husband when he asked what she would have done if the shooter had come after her, "I don't know, kick him between the legs. Mike needed help." The words "Mike needed help" were emphasized in the interview. Mike has taken those words to heart – he knew he was not alone.

Conclusion: The Effect of a Question of Fairness and Hidden Agendas

Fairness was an integral part of Pine Ridge Middle School's climate, and this had a huge effect on Mike's recovery from the shooting incident. Mike knew his assistant principal cared about him. She rushed to the struggle after the shooting and pulled the gun away. She publicly stated that one of the reasons she did that was because "Mike needed help."

As the leadership and the staff planned for a re-opening of the school after the shooting, the principals asked for input from the staff – and acted on that input. They did not have a hidden agenda, it was one that was shared with the staff and incorporated input from the staff.

Another telling moment, previously described, was when the assistant principal wished to have a reunion out in front of the school, involving the students. She said that, "We're going to be out there because that's not, if we don't do that, then the shooter claims that space. That's not his space, that's our space." Her use of the pronoun "our" speaks strongly about her sense that the whole group is a team, not divided. It was not spoken as "the students' space" or "the school's space," it was "our space."

Again, Albert Schweitzer described ethics as a "sense of duty toward others," (Hansen, 2007, p. 158). The administration of Pine Ridge Middle School had a sense of duty toward others, and it permeated Mike's attitude toward his students as well.

Research Question 5: Mike and Motivation

In research question 5, the focus is on Mike's interaction with administrators and motivation. As he struggled after the school shootings, did he struggle with motivation because of anything his superiors did or said?

As mentioned, the Burke-Litwin Model critical element in terms of positive motivation is, "congruence between the goals and values of the organization and the individual's needs and values" (Burke, 2010, p.223). Do the members of an organization feel motivated to take the actions necessary to achieve the organization's goals?

In the interviews when he was asked if he felt supported throughout the ordeal after the incident, Mike focused on one extreme example of that support. It happened almost a year after the incident. Mike said,

> Let me give you an example of the support. I was at the briefing and our security director was talking about the incident. I had to go to the bathroom and I was going to speak next. I went out of the auditorium and went to the bathroom. The guy who is the Director of Psychological Services for the district discreetly followed me into the bathroom to make sure that I was okay. They're that available.

From the beginning Mike knew people were there for him. He expressed that "We had some really great and unfortunately experienced counselors in our district. The counselors and the psychological trauma team, they were there at those early meetings – all of them." He went on to say that, "Probably the most valuable thing that happened in terms of counseling was when that counselor just looked at me and just said, 'We're going for a walk.'"

Mike was able to see that his assistant principal, Mary, cared for everyone, not just for him, when she discussed Billy, the student who was seriously injured in the shooting. His voice sounded very determined as he described what his superior said, "We have to go see Billy. I have to go see Billy." When Billy asked Mary if he was going to die, she responded with, "Not on my watch." These are words of determination, and of honest emotions. She was not afraid to express how she truly felt in front of a subordinate.

Mike knew that there were no hidden agendas, not only from words but from actions. When the staff was confronted with how to deal with the press after the shooting, the leadership of the school asked, "How do you want to do this?" Their actions after gathering the answers validated that they truly wanted to do as the staff wished – the two people elected to speak to the press were the ones who did. There were no substitutes or changes not discussed with the staff.

Conclusion: The Effect of Values and Motivation

Mike believed in his organization. He knew there was congruence between his needs and the needs of the school district. The effect of this congruence was, indeed, a deeper commitment to his organization and a better path to healing.

Research Question 6: Mike and School Unity

In research question 6, the concern is about Mike believing that his administration looked after his needs after the school shooting. Was there a unified school culture after the shooting, one in which all sides took care of each other?

When considering the Burke-Litwin Model, an idea called culture arises, as mentioned earlier. This is defined as "the way we do things around here" (Burke, 2010, p.220). There are two important components of "culture" – explicit and implicit rules. Explicit rules tend to be "up front" and visible, such as hours of work and a dress code. Implicit rules are followed, but rarely talked about. So, did the culture of Mike's school allow for open expression, or did employees just say what the boss wanted to hear?

There was openness and unity at Pine Ridge Middle School. Once again, when the staff was confronted with how to deal with the press after the shooting, the assistant principal of the school asked, "How do you want to do this?" The administrator listened – the two people elected to speak to the press were, indeed, the ones who spoke. The entire staff of the school was allowed to vote, their wishes were heard and administration carried out the directive.

In addition, when the school held a reunification meeting, the administration set it up solely for the benefit of the people at the school – they knew that people needed to find out what happened to everyone else. Mike described it as a "faculty and student reunification the next day at the elementary school down the street. I got to see that everybody was there and all of that stuff." Mike seemed relieved, even years later, when he said he got to see that everybody was there. It sounded like he was relieved to see that "nobody had been killed." The school did this reunification, and unity was strengthened.

Conclusion: The Effect of Culture and Mike's Needs

"The way things are done around here," as the Burke-Litwin model describes it, can be described as "openness, unity, and caring" at Mike's Pine Ridge Middle School. The verdict on this point is clear: there was a culture of nurturing and openness at the school that strongly contributed to Mike's healing and, indeed, the healing of all involved in the shooting incident.

Research Question 7: Mike and a Sense of Safety

In question 7, the issue of Mike feeling safe while in his school after the shooting trauma is addressed. Did the school district take actions to make him feel safe?

As the Burke-Litwin Model mentions, safety is critical for productive work. Considering Mike's introduction to Post-Traumatic Stress Disorder after the shooting, security is critical. As Kazdin wrote, people with PTSD "may relive the event via intrusive memories, flashbacks and nightmares; avoid anything that reminds them of the trauma; and have anxious feelings they didn't have before that are so intense their lives are disrupted" (Kazdin, 2000, p.251). The trauma happened at school – flashbacks and anxiety could be presented on or near the campus.

As mentioned, school principals and counselors came by frequently as the weeks went by and said, "We're going for a walk." The walk was a de-facto counseling session.

Morale was a concern for the administration. In the school reunification days there were balloons and posters. The school staff, in Mike's words,

> ... met the kids, the kids came inside and signed stuff. They all went into my room because I'm still doing media crap. They are all signing my white board. They are doing stuff like that. That was a reunification day. Everyone was together.

This sent out a message that people are welcome; it is a time to celebrate coming back together, and unity in the school. It was not a time of fear, anxiety and disconnection. On the big day when everyone returned to campus, the school assistant principal pronounced that,

> We're meeting all of these kids out front. We're meeting them all out there with cookies. We're going to be out there because that's not, if we don't do that, then the shooter claims that space. That's not his space, that's our space.

The message was clear with the inclusion of cookies for the kids – a humanizing touch, a treat, and a sweet token that says, "Welcome back." Essentially, the balloons, posters, signing of whiteboards, and cookies, were a way of saying, "we want you back, you are safe here, and we are excited to see you."

In addition, the school's security system was still fully functional. Staff and students alike knew that it had worked before, as the heroic secretary waited for students to rush into the building before pushing the lockdown button, the button that left the shooter outside.

Conclusion: The Effect of School Safety

Mike felt emotionally and physically safe at school because of three factors. These included a nurturing and supportive social system, a functional lockdown security system in place, and counseling support that extended over a long period of time. He had seen all of these components work; he knew they could protect him, because they had once already. The verdict? Mike felt safe in returning to his school; these factors played a big role in this fact. An important piece of evidence was that he was still teaching there at the time of the interviews for this paper.

Research Question 8: Mike and the Fairness of the Process

In research question 8, Mike had to deal with a bureaucracy for him to resume his pre-incident life. Did he believe that his school district's system treated him fairly after the trauma?

As Lawrence and Fauerbach indicated, there is "evidence that a sense of belonging or connectedness is the most important variable in mediating stress" (Lawrence & Fauerbach, 2003, p. 65). After the shooting, Mike was involved in a process to restore the school, as well as his sense of equilibrium.

As described in a number of scenes discussed in all of the research questions, Mike felt a part of a compassionate, caring organization. He felt that he belonged to the school, and that the school valued his connection to the organization. He was elected, along with the assistant principal, to be the spokesperson to the press for the school – they saw his value.

He saw the value in being a part of a close, nurturing organization. The day after the shooting, the faculty met at a member's house. They discussed what had happened. They listened to each others' stories. In Mike's words, "This is what I was doing; this is what I was thinking." He found a truth about cohesiveness and unity that day – "You need to get back together as a team – talk about it."

Conclusion: The Effect of the Process on Mike's Future

Throughout the process after the shooting, Mike felt cared for by his school. As reported, they sent counselors and administrators to his room repeatedly. Nowhere in the transcript did he mention one meeting in which he felt threatened or interrogated, except by law enforcement personnel after the shooting. The verdict is that the process preserved a future for Mike.

Research Question 9: Mike and Task Performance

In question 9, Mike's emotional, physical and intellectual skills are investigated in relation to his ability to perform the tasks at hand after the shooting. Were there difficult issues that prevented him from being successful in his classroom?

As mentioned, Elliott, Hamburg, & Williams (1998) reported that fear and heightened levels of stress lead to burnout and less effective work. In Mike's case, the long-term provision of counseling and administrative support convinced him that he was cared for – reducing his stress.

He knew that he did not have to push himself past a point where the stress was getting the better of him. Many excerpts from his interviews describe how he knew support was always there. He said, "I'm just sitting there going, 'I want to teach and everything like that.' Eventually, one of the counselors because they were very available; they just said, 'Look, just go ahead and tell us when you need a break or whatever.'"

This didn't happen once only. Mike knew that, "Since the shooting, if I needed to talk to counselor, I could call up a counselor and he would be ready to talk to me today." The door for help, for relief, was always open for Mike.

Mike was inspired by the actions of others as well – he knew he could count on others to come to his aid. One of his co-workers ran out of the building to help Mike grapple with the shooter. In the interviews, his voice trembled as he mentioned, "Jerry being safe inside and then deciding to come back out to help." He knew he was not alone.

In the years since, he has received many messages of support. Recently, as Mike describes, "When the Sandy Hook thing happened, there were a number of people that know me that they call me and say, 'Look, I was thinking about you when I heard about this.' I'm not alone." This is a recurring theme in his message, applicable across all of the research sub-questions – he is not alone.

Conclusion: The Effect of Stress on Mike's Competence

With all of the support Mike had after the shooting, from counselors, administrators, fellow educators, his colleagues at Pine Ridge Middle School, and from friends everywhere, he did not feel alone. Lawrence and Fauerbach describe a social support system as being one of the most critical factors that determines the outcome of a struggle with Post Traumatic Stress Disorder (Lawrence & Fauerbach, 2003, p. 63). This social support can reduce the stress, or a lack of support can increase it. The verdict is that the stress, because of the developed support system, did not affect Mike's competence. Again, a strong piece of evidence is that he remained teaching at the same school for years after the shooting incident.

Research Question 10: Mike and Organizational Processes

In research question 10 a summary of the actions of the school district is built to describe how Mike arrived at the outcome of his struggle, a return to his classroom. What organizational processes contributed to the final disposition of Mike's situation?

Revisiting Van der Kolk's assertion, harsh environments over time force permanent changes. These changes include degradation into "rigid thinking, paranoia, defensiveness, over-reactivity and health problems" (Van der Kolk, 1993, p. 231). In Mike's situation, the entire process seemed like one set up to protect and nurture him, not to investigate, isolate or burden him. Mike did not have to face a "harsh environment" in his organizational processes.

Returning to an analogy of a tree, Mike was able to weather the storm because other trees in his forest, less affected by the cold winds of the situation, rallied around him. Those in authority gave him "carte blanche" in terms of support – they told him to "just go ahead and tell us when you need a break or whatever."

Mike received counseling, over a long period of time. Mike experienced reunification. He was able to visit the shooting victim in the hospital. He was able to watch as his superior expressed concern for him and for his student.

He was encouraged. Those around him urged him to talk about his experience, and to not shut down. He got some unusual phone calls. At times he wanted people to,

> ... just leave me alone and let me get to teach school. Ellen DeGeneres is sending me flowers. Oprah Winfrey's producer is calling. I'm thinking, "Just let me teach school." One of our staff members was saying, "Look, you got an opportunity where maybe you can do some good here."

The leadership around him believed in his abilities, and they knew he could reach out to others so afflicted. He took up their suggestion and started speaking at a number of venues.

The process has led him to develop ideas that might help other schools prevent or recover from school shootings. Mike has gone beyond dealing with the process – he is developing new ideas to create a new process for school security. Mike is reaching out to create something good from something terrible.

He outlines ideas such as teacher certification in school security and self-defense classes. Teachers would receive in-service training, similar to classroom management courses, on how to secure a school, or how to defend themselves from violent students or intruders.

He also calls for the ensuring of a relationship between every kid and at least one adult – making sure every child feels safe and making sure staff members check on student well-being before and after a crisis event. He even has ideas for securing a school bus during a crisis.

Conclusion: The Effect of the Process on Mike's Case

This is a man whose roots have deepened, who has decided to give back to his community, and who has decided to create a new organizational process that would make a difference in a future school shooting. One could argue that this is a worthwhile return for the investment of some counseling, nurturing, time off, reunification meetings, balloons, posters and cookies. The verdict? When a man endures the trauma of a school shooting and then decides to develop new processes to help others recover, one could say that this organizational process was a success. Again, the final verdict, worth repeating, comes from words of Mike's own choosing, "My school did it right."

Conclusion: What Enabled Mike's Return to his Classroom?

Construct 1: Post-traumatic Stress Disorder

Mike had to deal with PTSD, but critical to his recovery was the fact that throughout his post-shooting experiences there was access to mental health professionals. From moments after the shooting, administrators, counselors and law enforcement professionals checked on his condition and encouraged him. He was not left alone – and never felt alone.

Counselors pulled him out of the classroom regularly. A year after the incident, one met him in a private place during a public meeting to check on him informally just before he was to give a talk on the incident.

In addition, Mike had a social support network that functioned. He was allowed quick and open access to his wife and mother – providing a connection to his personal support network. Mike knew his fellow teachers and his administrators were there for him, and he was there for them. In many examples, people listened to Mike and his needs, and acted, as in the discussion of how to deal with the media after the shooting. He felt valued.

There are no indications that Mike had major pre-existing traumatic conditions that would have impacted his dealing with PTSD. Mike was allowed to deal with the trauma. Indeed, it was expected that he would be dealing with PTSD. This acceptance of PTSD and a regular dealing with the steps and symptoms of this condition proved to be valuable to Mike's recovery.

Construct 2: Organizational Climate

Simply put, Mike saw his organization as "being there" for him – before the incident, during it, and well after. He believed in his organization.

Before the incident, Mike's school held drills. They prepared for any problem that could arise. Mike felt that he had a good relationship with his supervisors. He cared about his students, and believed his leadership cared about him. The school had teachers supervising in the parking lot – there were adults watching the kids as they left campus. That fact in itself may have saved a lot of lives.

This support and teamwork started well before the incident. The school had lockdown drills. They openly discussed "what if" scenarios. They were already working well as a team, and someone had worked hard to develop that.

During the incident, the drills and relationship building paid off. He knew he was in the parking lot to watch the kids, and he knew the school supported him in his assignment. He believed in what he was doing – his values were congruent with those of the organization. All of the staff members were in the recovery together.

Conclusion

Mike is recovering because his Post-Traumatic Stress Disorder was dealt with quickly, and help was provided over a long period of time. In addition, he was a part of a supportive organization. He believed in the school, his administrators were involved and he was socially and behaviorally prepared for a crisis.

References

Burke, W. W. (2010). *Organization change: Theory and practice* (3rd ed.). Thousand Oaks, CA: Sage.

Daniels, J., Bradley, M., & Hays, M. (2007, December). The impact of school violence on school personnel: Implications for psychologists. *Professional Psychology: Research and Practice, 38*(6), 652–659.

Elliot, D., Hamburg, B., & Williams, K. (1998). *Violence in American schools: A new perspective.* Cambridge: Cambridge University Press.

Hansen, D. T. (Ed.) (2007). *Ethical visions of education: Philosophies in practice.* New York City: Teachers College Press.

Hartman, R. J. (2011). *The twelve steps to the formation of PTSD.* Retrieved from http://aaph.org/rjhartman/articles/twelve_steps_to_PTSD

Jordan, K. (2003). A trauma and recovery model for victims and their families after a catastrophic school shooting: Focusing on behavioral, cognitive, and psychological effects and needs. *Brief Treatment and Crisis Intervention, 3*(4), 397–411. https://doi.org/10.1093/brief-treatment/mhg031.

Kazdin, A. (Ed.) (2000). *Encyclopedia of psychology.* New York: Oxford University Press (USA).

Lawrence, J., & Fauerbach, J. (2003, January/February). Personality, coping, chronic stress, social support and PTSD symptoms among adult burn survivors: A path analysis. *Journal of Burn Care & Rehabilitation, 24*(1), 63–72.

Newman, K., Fox, C., Roth, W., & Mehta, J. (2004). *Rampage: The social roots of school shootings.* New York, NY: Basic Books.

Van der Kolk, B. (1993). Biological considerations about emotions, trauma, memory and the brain. In S. Ablon, D. Brown, & J. Mack (Eds.), *Human feelings: Explorations in affect development and meaning.* New York: Routledge.

CONTRASTING THE TWO TEACHERS

"This is overwhelming. So many similarities and differences. Can you summarize them?" Janice asked.

"Of course. Let's summarize using my research questions as a framework . . ." I started.

An Answer

Two Teachers: Contrasts

To understand the effects of witnessing a school shooting, the differences between the two cases should be explored. These were not "duplicate" teachers working in the same environment.

The Teachers and Their Schools

Mike and Melissa were both teachers, but they were in different places in life when the incidents occurred. One was a new mother; the other already had children in the midst of growing up. Mike was considering retirement while

Melissa considered herself to be in the earlier stages of her career. One had a contributing psychological issue, while the other did not.

Mike worked in a school with a very different socioeconomic description from Melissa. They dealt with different class sizes, as prescribed by their districts and state funding. Melissa's school was an older facility while Mike's offered more amenities, such as an electronic lockdown system.

Research Question 1: Post-traumatic Stress Disorder

In Melissa's case, she started the day, before the incident, struggling with new parenthood and the challenge of therapist pre-diagnosed Post-Partum Depression. As pointed out, pre-existing issues can increase the impact of witnessing trauma. In Mike's situation, he had no issues of this magnitude. This difference affected the outcome significantly.

Research Question 2: Administrators

In Melissa's case, she felt as if her administrators were disconnected and uninterested in the "goings-on" in her classroom. They did not communicate about many issues, including an arrangement for counseling service. They did not hear her concern about the students returning to the computer lab in which the murder happened. Melissa's principal presented her with paperwork to be completed, and was unwilling to procure a bus to transport students to a memorial service for the slain student.

In Mike's situation, he felt his administrators were engaged and a part of the school climate. They asked for input from staff and acted on the input. Mike's vice principal checked in on how he was doing; counselors went into Mike's room, frequently, to check on his well-being.

The differences in administrations were marked. These differences played a significant role in Mike's successful return to teaching, and in Melissa's disability.

Research Question 3: School District Practices

In Melissa's case, the district swamped Melissa with paperwork, and imposed rules and orders on her to the point where they threatened her job. Mike had no such issues. In fact, the district supported him in his desire to speak at meetings and reach out to tell his story.

Research Question 4: Fairness

Throughout his interviews, Mike portrayed his vice principal and other administrators in his school district as fair and as people who listened. He expressed no opinion that shed a negative light on any decisions made by his superiors. This relationship was built over the years prior to the incident. On the other hand, Melissa never, even before the shooting, saw her superiors as fair. That relationship was built over the preceding years as well. Indeed, she questioned what the real agenda was in the heads of her principal and super-intendent. For Melissa, trust was hard to come by, even early on.

The issue of trust and fairness can be seen as a foundation to the outcomes of these two cases. Mike trusted his superiors while Melissa doubted the intentions of her administrators.

Research Question 5: Motivation

Motivation can be seen as shared values and interests. In Mike's case, he agreed with the recovery steps taken after the shooting, and his opinion was valued by leadership. Since he saw their goals as being his own, his motivation was high. On the other hand, Melissa questioned the agenda of her superiors. She did not believe the two were congruent; her motivation suffered.

The difference in motivation played a significant role in recovery in both of these cases. Mike aligned with the intentions of his superiors, and worked with them to find help for all involved. Melissa, on the other hand, felt there were different agendas in every corner of her school, none of which matched her needs.

Research Question 6: School Unity

In Melissa's situation, there was division across the school. The counselors called in to work with her students did not agree with Melissa on her role in the sessions. Melissa had been pushed so far at that point that she used an obscenity as she quit. But that was not the only moment of division. She felt her administrators were disconnected from her needs. She felt spied upon as she fed cupcakes to her students. She was threatened with her job.

On the other hand, Mike's vice principal brought the sweet baked goods. His administrators offered a reunification day, and set up a meeting for every-one to debrief and talk the incident out. She wanted to reclaim the area in front of the school, as it belonged to the school, not the shooter. This was a unified school, and it made a world of difference for Mike.

Research Question 7: A Sense of Safety

With a lockdown system, and a school reunification, Mike had the advantage in this research issue. In addition, he did not have the shooting happen in his own computer lab – it was in the parking lot. With the constant stream of counselors and principals checking on him, he knew someone was looking out for him. On the other hand, Melissa's administrators pushed her class back into using the same computer lab in which the murder had happened. That showed no regard for emotional safety whatsoever. This factor was difficult for Melissa and played a large role in the disposition of her case. One could say the same for Mike's incident.

Research Question 8: Fairness of the Process

For Melissa, relations with her employer quickly turned sour. Her dealing with her employer's compensation agent turned ugly and confrontational, but this relationship of subterfuge and manipulation was exemplified by the superintendent spying on her from a truck while she fed cupcakes to her students. At every turn, from early on, the process, she felt, was not working in her favor.

Mike had a different experience. Nowhere in his interviews could unfair issues be found. He felt supported by his leadership. This helped him to remain in teaching.

Research Question 9: Task Performance

Melissa was overwhelmed by paperwork, mistrust, miscommunications and a sense that her school did not support what she wanted to do for her students or herself. These things, combined with the symptoms of PTSD, such as sleep difficulties, anxieties and fear, degraded her ability to perform the tasks she had easily accomplished before. Mike, on the other hand, felt as if his superiors were watching over him, and always there to help him. Because of this, his ability to perform tasks at hand was not significantly degraded.

Research Question 10: Organizational Processes

The concept of organizational processes can be put more simply as the gentleness or harshness of the environment. The changes when one is exposed to a harsh environment include degradation into Van der Kolk's ideas of rigid thinking, paranoia, defensiveness, over-reactivity and health problems. Melissa, overall, had to deal with harshness; she became defensive. She developed health problems. Mike, on the other hand, was given gentleness, and the difference between these two experiences had immense impact on the outcome of these cases.

Conclusion

To wrap up the comparison, Mike was not dealing with the psychological struggle that Melissa had, Post-Partum Depression. He was also not working with a disconnected administration that seemed to throw obstacles to healing and growth before him, as Melissa did. These differences meant the continued employment in the profession to one – and emotional disability for the other.

References

Van der Kolk, B. (1993). Biological considerations about emotions, trauma, memory and the brain. In S. Ablon, D. Brown, & J. Mack (Eds.), *Human feelings: Explorations in affect development and meaning.* New York: Routledge.

· 2 3 ·

THE BIG QUESTION

"I am seeing where this is going. So, let's go back to your big question, the one your other professor told you that you needed – what are the effects of witnessing a school shooting on a teacher's career?" Janice asked.

"Okay, like in a movie, let's get to the climax – answering the big question." I responded.

"Yes!"

"Unfortunately, while I did a qualitative analysis on this question, I discovered that using terms familiar to qualitative people makes more sense in describing how we can understand the effects."

"I don't follow you . . ." Janice sounded confused.

"Simply put, we can use the analogy of a math formula to understand what happened. There are too many variables that one short sentence wouldn't really describe things."

"Uh-oh. We have to use math?"

"Well, not really, but keep the idea behind variables in a math formula in the front of your mind."

An Answer

Answering the Question: The Effects of Witnessing a School Shooting on a Teacher's Career

This research started with one clear question – what are the effects of witnessing a school shooting on a teacher's career? In order to summarize this report and answer this question succinctly, a sort of construct, or framework, is necessary. The best frame could be one of how a young person learns mathematics.

A Framework: The Concept of Variables in a Math Formula

Through the years, as students learn mathematics, they begin with simple absolutes, such as the idea that 1 of something plus 2 other items of something equals 3 items, thus $1 + 2 = 3$. Unfortunately, there are few such absolutes in this research. Later, advancing to the next level, these same students learn about single variable formulas. Again, this is not as useful to an understanding of the effects. Finally, when a student enters the world of mathematics with multiple variables then they have found a language that can explain teachers and school shootings.

In the mathematic land of multiple variables, the outcome is dependent on how a number of symbols interact, not on any one symbol. These variables could be weighted differently as well –case by case. The same can be said about the effects of school shootings on the careers and lives of teachers.

The Variables of Teachers and School Shootings

As discussed in the general study, two major constructs, or "families of variables" in the analysis here, exist in a study of the effects of a teacher witnessing school shootings. These families of variables can be called "Post-Traumatic Stress Disorder" (PTSD) and "Organizational Climate".

Putting It Together: An Example

As a math teacher would demonstrate a sample formula on the board in front of his or her class, a similar activity might be of value here. Let's step through a multiple variable equation.

Within the PTSD family, variables such as "pre-trauma factors," "resilience-recovery variables," and "traumatic event characteristics" could be measured and assigned a value as they are diagnosed by a licensed psychologist. If a teacher witnessing a school shooting was struggling with a "pre-trauma factor," such as Melissa with Post-Partum Depression, he or she might have a lower index number in that category, for example. Mike had a higher number as he had fewer pre-trauma factors. The other PTSD variables could be assessed similarly.

Within the Organizational Climate family, variables such as leadership characteristics, a supportive school, and pre-existing conditions at the school being considered would come into play, among others. Melissa would have a lower index for leadership characteristics since she often cited the disconnection between her and her principal. Mike would have a higher index in that same area. Mike's school would have a higher index in preparedness; Melissa's would have been lower. Also, Mike's vice principal and the district's counselors would earn a high score here. Melissa's administrators would earn her variable a low index number.

So, if one were to assemble the variables, Mike's numbers would all be much higher than Melissa's. If a higher number, or result of solving the multiple variable equation, indicates lower effects on a teacher's career, then Mike would be expected to weather a school shooting better, and this was the case in these two studies.

The Answer

Many students, after working through a math problem, like to have a clear and straight solution. The answer to the this question of, "What are the effects of witnessing a school shooting on a teacher's career?" is, simplified, dependent on how all of the variables involved in Post-Traumatic Stress Disorder and the variables inherent in Organizational Climate interact.

The more that issues surrounding Post-Traumatic Stress Disorder present themselves as difficult or overwhelming, and the more the issues within Organizational Climate present themselves as problematic, the higher the probability will be that the effects on the teacher will be stronger and more difficult to overcome. Conversely, less difficult issues and their "scores" could increase the probability that the effects on the teacher could be weathered and overcome.

Conclusion: Simply Stated

Simply put, the effects on a teacher would vary. A teacher with few psychological issues beforehand, and with empathetic school leadership and a support system, would be likely to recover rather quickly. On the other hand, a teacher with pre-existing psychological issues and disconnected school leadership and support systems might struggle for years.

One teacher in this study was able to stay in his career while the other was forced to leave with a psychological disability. To answer the question, the effects, such as a teacher staying in his or her career, or leaving with a disability, would depend on how the psychological and organizational variables of this equation add up for that particular teacher.

· 2 4 ·

WHAT CAN SCHOOLS AND COMMUNITIES DO?

"That is overwhelming! The effects would vary by each teacher!" Janice exclaimed.

"That's true. While we have some commonalities, there are a number of variables, too." I replied.

"Going a bit off the subject – I'm kind of reeling from all of this – what the heck can we do to help these people?"

"There are a number of things we can do – before, during and after a shooting event."

"Before?"

"Yes. Being prepared would help a lot."

An Answer

Implications for Practice

Before a School Shooting

Research and the experiences of these two teachers indicate preparation for a crisis is the best start to healing from a school shooting. There are two implications for practice – for the individual and for the school.

On the individual level, as described, Lawrence and Fauerbach inform us that successfully dealing with PTSD is heavily influenced by "pre-trauma factors" (Lawrence & Fauerbach, 2003, p. 63). Psychological and experiential issues from before the trauma can and will come into play after a shooting incident.

Implication: Make Pre-incident Counseling Available

In one of our case studies, the impact of pre-existing psychological issues was important to Melissa; she was struggling with Post-Partum Depression. An important implication for practice is that schools offering and encouraging ongoing and available counseling for all staff members could identify and, perhaps reduce, the impact of pre-existing mental health issues.

Implication: Build a Supportive School Climate

Encouraging social connection between staff members could pay dividends after a school shooting. Melissa's return from maternity leave was a disaster; her classroom had been ransacked. Her teacher friends came through for her by providing supplies and encouragement. While she felt that she could not rely on her administration, she felt she had someone to turn to.

As described, social support is critical in the post-trauma recovery period. Actively encouraging the development of a supportive social system in a school, with activities such as tailgate parties before school athletic events, dinners at staff member houses, and outings in off-hours, could help after a shooting as teachers see the people around them as people they can reach out to and confide in, not strangers performing tasks in similar classrooms.

Implication: Build an Involved and Serving School Administration

Mike felt connected to his assistant principal, Mary. He described, in a number of statements, how he knew she was concerned about him. Her pronouncement that no one will die on her watch was a statement of, "Your safety and well-being are paramount to me." When asked what she would have done if Mike had not had the shooter subdued, she replied with, "I don't know, kick him in between the legs. Mike needs help." Again, she focused on Mike.

Melissa portrayed her administrators as cold and not involved in her day-to-day life. In Melissa's case, this could have contributed to a gulf between the two sides, and a lack of communications which led to such misunderstandings as the counseling session in which she used an obscenity to renounce the school and leave her job. To her, at that moment, she felt disconnected from the process and the people working the process on the school's side.

An administration that is seen as being there to serve the school community, not one that is disconnected from it, could prove to be a critical factor in post-traumatic healing. Mike's leaders provided that element; Melissa's did not.

Implication: Hold Regular Emergency Drills

In the other case study, Mike recalled a moment in his childhood in which he had to respond to a sudden emergency. He believed that his early experience helped him to respond to the crisis of a school shooting. As he described,

> When I was a kid, my father was chopping wood. He lost his grip on the axe and the axe was coming towards me. I'm standing there going, it's going to turn, it will turn one more, it will land right here. I can move my leg aside, because of the angle it's going to skip right underneath of me. I do that.

What can be learned from this? Perhaps training sessions for dealing with school shootings would be advantageous for educators responding to such an emergency. Mike also mentioned, a few times, that lockdown drills helped to ensure that everyone knew what to do in such a situation as a school shooting (or an earthquake or a tornado). His school's secretary was trained and was able to lock the school's security system down after she believed all students and staff had come inside for safety. This could prevent a lot of injuries and, perhaps, deaths.

Implication: Beef up School Security Systems

While most security systems would not have assisted Melissa in her situation, perhaps a functioning metal detector as students entered her campus would have detected the gun that Andrew carried in his backpack. In Mike's situation, a school-wide door lock system could have proven to have been lifesaving, if he had not tackled the shooter. If the shooter could not have entered the campus, or if the system had slowed him down, lives could have been saved.

Implication: Develop Student/Staff Relationships

In both of our cases, the relationships between teachers and students came into play after the shootings. Emotional connections between all individuals at a school should be developed and encouraged. Administration needs to realize that these relationships are critical to everyone on campus. The mechanisms of how the teachers and the students work together emotionally need to be taken into consideration after the incident when staff and facility changes are being considered. Prior to any shooting, encourage teachers to build emotional connections with kids.

In Melissa's situation, her students expressed how important she was to them. They saw her as the main adult support system after the incident. She was the one who allowed them to talk about it, and to process it. She was also the one who felt guilt when she was so wracked with pain that she had to leave her class. Her administration tried to block the use of cupcakes and juice as a relationship bonding tool – but the kids saw that someone cared about them. This type of disconnect has to be removed.

In Mike's case, he grew emotional as he recalled how his students wrote thank you notes on his classroom's whiteboard. The staff of his school brought cookies to the kids on what they called their "reunification day." Not only did Mike's administration not block the use of sweets on a special day, they pushed for it and actually paid for it.

Implication: Have Adults Around Before and After School

Mike's school had adult supervision after school; this may have saved a lot of lives. Because there were a number of adults present they were able to stop the shooter. Have adults supervising students in various campus activities, before, during and after school.

Implication: Be Aware of Post-traumatic Stress Disorder

It would be advantageous for those in leadership, and perhaps all on campus, to be aware of the steps and symptoms of Post-Traumatic Stress Disorder. As the incident unfolds, and just after, this awareness may allow leadership to shelter the witnesses from further injury. Melissa noted that she did not know how she would have reacted if she had actually seen Zach's wounds. She wondered if it would have sent her over an emotional edge. Fortunately, it didn't happen. Perhaps, in Mike's case, someone keeping him from seeing Billy just after the shooting could have shielded him from further pain.

During a School Shooting

On the day of a crisis, it's difficult to prescribe a set of staff and administrative behaviors as the variety of factors surrounding a shooting are immense.

However, drawing on our case studies, one can find a couple of valuable threads.

Implication: Provide Personal Time For Witnesses

Administration should be sensitive that the staff member who witnessed the shooting is emotionally overwhelmed. They don't need more paperwork or responsibilities; they should be protected emotionally. They'll be dealing with law enforcement. In Mike's case, he was given time to call his wife and his mother, to reassure them that he was okay. Mike's voice in the interview at that moment indicated that this was important to him. Give them a chance to communicate with their loved one.

Implication: Prepare "witness shadows"

Create a team of "witness shadows" to ensure that the well-being of the teacher witness after a school shooting. These people could just "be there" for the teacher witness – be available at all times for almost any purpose the witness needs. Someone pre-identified as a member of the witness's social support system could serve in this capacity.

After a School Shooting

There are three types of implications for the time after a school shooting that could prove valuable. These implications include psychological, administrative and long-term issues.

Implication: Provide Quick Access to Professional Counselors

In the psychological realm, quick and frequent access to qualified and licensed counseling was important to Mike. A lack of that access was damaging to Melissa.

Implication: Consult with Crisis Management Specialists

As outlined in the literature review section, there are crisis management teams that are familiar with handling occupational episodes of violence, albeit there are none at this time set up for school violence. As soon as possible, contact and discuss the school shooting just experienced with psychologists and crisis managers – and listen to them.

Implication: Budget Expenses for Crisis Recovery

There will be expenses after a shooting, such as arranging for bus services to transport students to a public memorial for a slain classmate, as in Melissa's case. As soon as possible after the shooting, school financial management people should identify funding sources and possible expenditures. Be flexible – expenditures may not be able to be predicted.

Implication: Be Sensitive to the Demands of Post-traumatic Stress Disorder

After the traumatic event, be aware of the symptoms and issues presented by PTSD. Reminders of trauma are all over campus after the event; consider this when scheduling facility use after the trauma. Consult an expert in PTSD as soon as possible to identify incident-specific issues on campus that could present problems for witnesses. In Melissa's case, setting up counseling sessions near the site of the shooting may have contributed to her problems. Pushing classes to return to the same computer lab where the shooting occurred played right into allowing flashbacks and painful memories to return.

Implication: Don't See the Problems Disappearing After a Week

As mentioned, Newman, et al. (2004) found that school administrators feel a need to get their schools "back to normal" as soon as possible after a school trauma. However, as Roberts (2007) described, the months after a school shooting are a "period of psychological disequilibria." Administration should consult, on a regular basis, a counselor or psychologist familiar with Post-Traumatic Stress Disorder to determine when and what should get "back to normal" over the long term. As each traumatic event has a number of variables involved, there is no "prescribed" length of time in which healing will occur.

Conclusion: Over-Arching Implications

If there were two implications that could be drawn from all of these described here, they would be, first, consult an expert in Post-Traumatic Stress Disorder before a shooting, just after a shooting, and long after a shooting. In conjunction with this, see staff members on campus as human beings with emotional needs. The second over-arching implication is that being prepared for a school shooting can contain the damages much better than not being prepared. Plan for what might happen, use the lessons during the event, and for months after.

The researcher, while biased from the perspective of a classroom teacher, urges all parties invested in a school to work together as a team. No one group can be "blamed" for the incident, or the function or dysfunction of school relationships; all need to step up and work together.

References

Lawrence, J., & Fauerbach, J. (2003, January/February). Personality, coping, chronic stress, social support and PTSD symptoms among adult burn survivors: A path analysis. *Journal of Burn Care & Rehabilitation, 24*(1), 63–72.

Newman, K., Fox, C., Roth, W., & Mehta, J. (2004). *Rampage: The social roots of school shootings.* New York, NY: Basic Books.

Roberts, A. R. (2007). *Crisis intervention handbook: Assessment, treatment and research* (2nd ed.). New York: Oxford University Press.

· 2 5 ·

OPPORTUNITIES FOR OTHER RESEARCH

"We have so much work to do, it sounds like," Janice said.

"You're right," I responded.

"But what about you? Have you figured out everything about school shootings and how they affect teachers?"

"Oh, my, no. Sadly, the more I dug into this, the more I realized there was a lot to understand."

"Like what?" Janice asked.

An Answer

Opportunities for Further Research

Five opportunities for additional research, and one institute, arose from the completion of this study. These include the development of an Educator Trauma Recovery Index Model (Ed-TRIM), the design of an Educator Career Intervention System (ECIS), a repetition of the methodology of this study with other participants who have dealt with school shootings, a repetition of this study after more than a decade, looking for long-term implications, and an over-arching project comparing the various participants of all of the studies. The institute, tentatively labeled "iVAST" – The Institute for the Study of Violence and School Teachers, is a concept surrounding the development of a research team based at a university that would focus on the study of violence and teachers.

A Proposed Educator Trauma Recovery Index Model

The Concept

Utilizing factors outlined in Lawrence and Fauerbach's study of coping, stress and support among trauma survivors, and elements from the Burke-Litwin model of organizational culture, it is conceivable that an Educator Trauma Recovery Index Model (Ed-TRIM) could be developed to compare, measure and, possibly, predict the effect of different trauma incidents on teachers. In this model, an assessment by a licensed therapist along with a researcher could be made, scoring the teacher, the organization and the incident on a numeric scale, arriving at a composite index number representing a relative value indicating possible recovery from, or avoidance of, long lasting psychological struggles.

Three general areas of assessment could be made – psychological factors, organizational factors, and elements from the incident in question. The psychological factors could present a Personal Recovery Index (PRI) while the organizational elements would provide an Organizational Recovery Index (ORI). The incident would be rated to create an Incident Intensity Index (III). Together, weighted appropriately, one could arrive at a Trauma Recovery Index (TRI) for a particular teacher.

The Psychological Factors

The psychological factors could be assessed using Lawrence and Fauerbach's factors that heavily influence the adjustment to trauma: "low socioeconomic status, family instability, early trauma history, resilience-recovery variables, personality, coping strategies, social support and additional stressful life events" (Lawrence & Fauerbach, 2003, p. 63). Together, these would represent the PRI.

The Organizational Factors

In the Burke-Litwin Model, important organizational climate factors affecting employee performance are listed as management practices, structure, policies and procedures, work unit climate, motivation, individual needs and values, task requirements and individual skills, and individual and organizational performance. In this model these would be the elements contributing to the ORI.

The Incident Factors

Pulling, again, from Lawrence and Fauerbach's factors regarding incidents, the elements of this component of the Ed-TRIM would be: intensity and duration of exposure, perceived threat, exposure to atrocities or abusive behavior, and injury (Lawrence & Fauerbach, 2003, p. 63). These elements would create the III.

Bringing It Together: The TRI

In developing a Trauma Recovery Index, the researcher would rate a teacher, an organization and an incident on a scale of 1–5 in each sub-category. Through repeated analysis over time, with a number of different teachers, organizations and incidents, weighting could be applied to each factor to more closely represent the relative impact of trauma on a teacher. Eventually, as this model evolves, develops and is honed, it could be used to predict possible responses in schools, with different teachers. A teacher with a lower index number would have a greater vulnerability to severe long-term trauma than one with a higher index number.

Using a score chart, the researcher would score each element and tally to create this TRI. Five would be considered "HIGH" or positive, while 0 would be considered "LOW" or negative. As seen in sample chart "A", below, Teacher Able has a composite TRI of 71 out of 100 possible points.

Looking at a different teacher, as seen in the chart below, Teacher Baker's TRI score comes in much lower, at 54 out of 100 points on the Trauma Recovery Index. This could suggest that Teacher Baker is more susceptible to long-term post-traumatic stress issues.

Arriving at the Assessments

The researcher, in gathering assessments of the various components of the three main areas of the index, could utilize the services of a psychologist in rating the Personal Recovery Index and in the Incident Intensity Index. An organizational structure researcher could be consulted to rate an institution on the Organizational Recovery Index elements.

Figure 2: Teacher Able's Trauma Recovery Index scoring.

TEACHER ABLE

Element	Personal Index	Organizational Index	Incident Index	Total
Socioeconomics	3			
Family stability	4			
Trauma history	3			
Coping strategies	4			
Social support	4			
Additional stress	2			
Management practices		4		
Structure		4		
Policies and procedures		4		
Work unit climate		4		
Motivation		5		
Individual needs and values		4		
Task requirements and individual skills		5		
Individual and organizational performance		4		
Event intensity			3	
Event length			2	
Perceived threat			4	
Atrocities			2	
Abusive behavior			3	
Injury			3	
TOTAL PRI	20			
TOTAL ORI		34		
TOTAL III			17	
TOTAL TRI				71

Further research and testing could contribute to the weighting of each element of the three components of the model. A caveat must be offered; this is a proposal for analysis, and is considered hypothetical at this point in time. This model is not offered as a trusted tool for understanding trauma; this discussion is meant as a starting point for a dialogue on the idea only.

Figure 3: Teacher Baker's Trauma Recovery Index scoring.

TEACHER BAKER

Element	Personal Index	Organizational Index	Incident Index	Total
Socioeconomics	2			
Family stability	2			
Trauma history	2			
Coping strategies	3			
Social support	3			
Additional stress	3			
Management practices		3		
Structure		3		
Policies and procedures		3		
Work unit climate		2		
Motivation		2		
Individual needs and values		2		
Task requirements and individual skills		4		
Individual and organizational performance		4		
Event intensity			4	
Event length			3	
Perceived threat			4	
Atrocities			1	
Abusive behavior			2	
Injury			2	
TOTAL PRI	15			
TOTAL ORI		23		
TOTAL III			16	
TOTAL TRI				54

Conclusion

It is conceivable that an Educator Trauma Recovery Index Model (Ed-TRIM) could be developed to compare, measure and, possibly, predict the effect of different trauma incidents on teachers. In this model, an assessment could be made, scoring the teacher, the organization and the incident on a numeric scale, arriving at a composite index number representing a relative value showing vulnerability to deeper, long lasting psychological struggles. This conceptual model is offered as a starting point for discussion, not as a definitive model ready to be tested.

An Educator Career Intervention System (ECIS)

While researching Melissa's story it became apparent that a number of job modifications, if they had been considered and implemented, could have strongly assisted her recovery from the trauma of witnessing a classroom murder. Noting that each episode of school violence has great variability, an Educator Career Intervention System could be designed to allow for flexible use of job modifications such as a change in room, grade level, building, and class size. In addition, the use of classroom aides to give the teacher opportunities to break from her class when it is needed might be helpful. Shifting to half-time status for a short duration might be a viable option for some educators. This ECIS would present a menu-style listing to be discussed and agreed upon by the school and the teacher in question, with input from a psychological consultant. An example of such a menu-style system of career interventions follows – perhaps this particular assessment would have helped Melissa in her recovery.

A Repetition of the Methodology of this Study

With every scenario being unique, a repetition of the methodology of this study with other teachers who have experienced school shootings would provide valuable information for an over-arching comparison of similarities and

Figure 4: Job modifications worksheet.

Modification	Useful	Not useful
Room change	X	
Grade level change	X	
Building or site change		X
Class size reduction	X	
Teacher aide use	X	
Job hour modification		X

differences in the recovery and handling of the trauma between the teachers and their respective school system.

An Over-arching Comparison of Teacher Experiences

Once additional narratives have been gathered, a comparison of similarities and differences could be undertaken. Differences in teacher personality, organizational behavior and incident intensity could be explored. Questions in this project could include, "How did the way the teacher in this study cope with the shooting compared to the other cases?", "How did the school system deal with the teacher after the shooting compared to the other cases?", and, "How did the intensity of the incident compare to the shootings in the other cases?"

iVAST: The Institute for the Study of Violence and School Teachers

The proposed institute, tentatively labeled "iVAST" – The Institute for the Study of Violence and School Teachers, is a concept surrounding the development of a research team based at a university that would focus on the study of violence and teachers. This would expand to include the development of resources to support these teachers and their school systems. Finally, a central nexus would develop, one connecting educator victims of violence with crisis experts, experienced counselors, literature and local support structures. The ECIS could serve as the foundation of the development of this institute, guiding the team toward connecting school violence victims and appropriate support systems.

Beyond Opportunities: Mike's Ideas

Mike Dougherty has some good ideas. While they are outside of the scope of this research direction, assistance for teachers affected by school shootings, his ideas are worth consideration in the long run, in dealing with school shooting prevention.

He outlines ideas such as teacher certification in school security and self-defense classes. Perhaps state legislatures should consider this. Why not have people working at school aware of security and safety? Why not integrate these needs into teacher certification processes?

He also calls for the ensuring of a relationship between every kid and at least one adult – making sure every child feels safe and making sure staff members check on student well-being before and after a crisis event. It could be speculated that closer relationships could allow schools to spot potential shooters before they "erupt." Perhaps teens who are school shooters would be less likely to turn to gunplay because they have built positive relationships with the people they may shoot.

He even has ideas for securing a school bus during a crisis. Why not look beyond the campus and realize that others are affected by school shootings?

Conclusion

Five new opportunities for research presented themselves over the course of this study – and an opportunity for a research institute. These would include the creation of an Educator Trauma Recovery Index Model (Ed-TRIM), an Educator Career Intervention System (ECIS), a repetition of the methodology of this study with other participants who have dealt with school shootings, and an over-arching study comparing the various participants of the proposed new studies. In addition, an institute focusing on violence and school teachers could be established.

References

Burke, W. W. (2010). *Organization change: Theory and practice* (3rd ed.). Thousand Oaks, CA: Sage.

Butin, D. (2010). *The education dissertation: A guide for practitioner scholars.* Thousand Oaks, CA: Corwin.

Lawrence, J., & Fauerbach, J. (2003, January/February). Personality, coping, chronic stress, social support and PTSD symptoms among adult burn survivors: A path analysis. *Journal of Burn Care & Rehabilitation, 24*(1), 63–72.

· 2 6 ·

REFLECTING

"It seems you've thought this out really well, Ed." Janice said.

"Not perfectly, but I believe our work has value, and could help someone going into the future."

"Why did you say, 'our work?'" Janice asked.

"I feel like Melissa, Mike, and a number of other people, contributed a lot. They hung in there with me and were always willing to answer questions."

"I can imagine this was not easy for them, re-hashing what happened."

"No, I am sure it wasn't, but I will tell you that they had great courage and strength. I admire them a lot." I responded.

"Look at the time! I can't believe we've been talking about this for hours! I didn't think I'd keep you like this!" Janice exclaimed.

"No harm, Janice. I appreciate anyone who is willing to hear the stories of these two people. I'm grateful you were willing to be a 'good ear'."

"One last question, and then I really have to go."

"Sure, what is it?"

"How do you see all of this, kind of like, you know, briefly? In one sentence, or two? Or a paragraph?"

An Answer

Conclusion

The effects of witnessing a school shooting on a teacher's career vary by the type of psychological and organizational experiences offered to a teacher before, during and after a school shooting. Some teachers will be able to weather the storm, with proper help, and return; others, with less support and bigger psychological issues, will not be as fortunate.

If education needs an example of what to do after a school shooting, study Mike's case. In his words, "We really need to be able to inform people about what we did because in my mind, it's pretty much of a textbook case of 'what to do right.' My school did it right."

· 2 7 ·

THE LAST TIME I SAW MELISSA

"Thanks, Ed. That helps me understand the effects a lot," Janice said.

"You're welcome. If I've helped you, I'm thrilled."

"When was the last time you saw Melissa?"

An Answer

My Story: A Final Reflection

As we closed our final interview, I felt a bit of emotion as I watched Melissa and her daughter walk in the parking lot outside. Her little girl was skipping along and showing an assortment of toys to her mother. I felt a smile coming on; that was nice, but the world and all of time seemed to slow down in the next moment. The flowers, blowing in the gentle wind, paused as I noticed a growing grin on Melissa's face. Her daughter slowly, at least it seemed that way to me, held up a brightly colored doll, and Melissa reached for it, feigning to play with it. That smile, that moment of simple joy, gave me more peace than I can say. It was a moment of hope, a moment that indicated that this wonderful lady was healing.

As they disappeared around the corner, I noticed that my papers were neatly arranged on the table in front of me. Unknowingly, I had watched Melissa before me; I wanted to watch for some sort of sign that Melissa had a new life, one of hope. Watching those two happily walking together was, for me, like opening a Christmas gift.

In the years since the shooting, Melissa has been able to return to part-time work, although not in a public school. That may never happen again, but she has found a rewarding new position. The shorter hours give her the chance to find happiness in being a mother; she's able to dedicate time to her children.

Melissa and her husband often travel on short vacations, and find happiness in a variety of outdoor activities. It's not about money to her; it's about finding simple joys. Most importantly, she has found ways to smile and laugh now.

As I gathered my possessions, I realized I have walked away from this project with more than I could have imagined. I have new friends. I have shared in the lives of two people who I am now very proud to know. I have learned that it is a remarkable thing to do qualitative research, to delve into a human story, albeit a painful one. I could not help but be touched by the power of these human experiences. I will admit I shed a tear that day.

While it was good to finish the project, I didn't want the relationships to end. I suppose that is my new task – to keep these people, Mike and Melissa, in my life as people I care about. After all, that is one of the desired outcomes of this work – to find the empathy and compassion to reach out to teachers who have witnessed severe school violence, and to not leave them to the cold winds of a harsh world.

I gently slid the papers into my briefcase, and one item caught my eye. Lying on the table was a small piece of paper. I opened it – and, in flowing writing were the following words . . .

> Dear Ed,
>
>   Thanks for always thinking of me. I am just so excited to even have a small part in such an important part of your education! I can't reiterate enough how important your work is for so many - not just students, but teachers. I am blessed that you are a good man with a vision to seek the truth, regardless, and make sure others learn from it. You are one of the wisest people in my life. The honor in this is all mine and I am just happy to even be a small part of what you are doing!
>
>   I am here to help you however I can. I am hopeful. I do know that you have chosen a situation that needs attention brought to it in so many ways and for so many reasons! I am so honored to be able to help you make a positive somehow, hopefully,

out of such a negative - really! It is always easy to support you however I can, you have a heart that shows clearly where your intentions are coming from and going to! It seems that a true educator shows himself regardless of the circumstance!

    Melissa

Needless to say, driving home that afternoon was delayed by an hour. It's tough for me to drive with overflowing emotions.

The message in between the lines of this research paper, one of compassion, is for you, Melissa and Mike. Thank you for sharing your stories and your friendship.

· 2 8 ·

THE CALL ENDS

"Thanks for taking the time to talk about all of this, Ed," Janice said in a quiet voice.

"Thanks for listening. She's had a hard time with this," I responded.

"Do you know what's strange?" Janice asked.

"Well, I could probably list a few dozen things from what she went through, but what do you mean?"

"It's something you didn't mention in your study, and there's probably no way to really get this in there ..."

"Get what in there?" I asked.

"For as long as I live, I will never be able to forget the look on her face that day. I saw her about an hour after the shooting. I'm not sure how you could quantify that moment."

"I think you're right. There's no way I could have seen that piece of evidence. I know what she looked like from our meetings, but I can believe the expressions she had during our time together lacked the, well, I guess I could call it 'rawness'."

"Raw is the word. She looked disoriented ..."

"Shock, I'm sure ..."

"But there was more. Scared was mixed in."

"Oh, yes."

"But a different kind of scared, more of a deep-down lost look."

"Trauma like what Melissa experienced can dig right into your foundation, make you unsure about your safety, or much else. That's why trauma is so hard to treat – and I'm not the one who does that. I just study it."

"I think that's it. She looked more than hurt, and scared. It was deeper."

"Notice that after the shooting, she retreated into her house for a long time."

"Yes . . ."

"In a way, you can think of it as her retreating to an early stage of life – searching, looking, to find how she could be safe again. Like when we were kids, looking for mommy when we were in a strange place," I answered.

"I can believe that. I've seen that look in my little ones, when they're scared," Janice responded.

"It's not quite the same, but I think that can help us get a grasp on how she felt."

"I'm not sure we can really, fully, understand what she felt back then."

"No, but we can find it in our hearts to be compassionate, to listen, and to find ways to help, as much as we can," I said as I took a deep breath.

"Oh, hey, listen, I've really taken up a lot of your time. I'm sorry . . ." Janice sounded like she was in a hurry.

"Oh, no! I'm sorry. My sigh came out of wishing I could do more, not because I'm talking with you."

"I know, but I just saw the time. I have to get dinner going!"

"Oh, wow – you're right!" I looked up at my clock.

"I can't tell you how much this meant to me, to see what happened in a new light."

"And it meant a lot to me, that you'd want to hear about it."

"Again, thanks. I have to go. Good-b . . ." Janice started.

"Wait . . . wait. Melissa. Can you get a hold of her?"

"Oh, that's right. After hearing this, now I want to. I'll see what I can do, but we've been out of touch for so long."

"That would mean a lot to me. For me, it was more than just a research project. I came to feel for these teachers, all of them. I need to know how she's doing."

"Give me a week or two. I'll make some calls, and send out some messages online."

"Thanks, Janice."

"Now, really, I have to get to the kitchen! Bye!"

"Bye!" I smiled as I disconnected the call.

EPILOG

It was hard to turn away from the baseball game I was watching, but my phone kept ringing. I didn't recognize the number, so I decided that, in the top of the ninth inning, with the score tied, I'd let it go to voicemail.

My team won, and I had forgotten about the call. While in the kitchen making a sandwich, my wife asked me who had called. She pointed ay my phone. As I took a bite, I shook my head.

"What call?" I asked after swallowing.

"I know the phone rang." She responded.

I turned and looked at my cell phone, and, sure enough, the message light was shining. I walked over to the counter and picked up the phone.

"Looks like you're right. I think it was some telemarketer or something. I'll check," I said as I put down my sandwich, then typed in the code for retrieving messages. There was one, and I listened to it. A familiar voice came through the speaker.

"Hi, Ed, it's Melissa. Janice tracked me down and let me know you wanted to re-connect. I appreciate that you still remember me ..." I took a deep breath.

"Whoa!" I exclaimed. My wife turned toward me.

"Who was it? Is everything okay?" She asked.

"Yeah, hold on … trying to get a phone number from the message …"
I paused the message as I signaled for a pen, and she handed me one. I re-
started the message, and then scribbled the number on an envelope.

"Hi, Ed, it's Melissa. Janice tracked me down and let me know you wanted
to re-connect. I appreciate that you still remember me! So, you want to know
how I'm doing. It's been hard, and a lot has changed, but I'm getting by.
I wouldn't wish what has happened to me since the shooting on anyone,"
there was a pause and I heard a long sigh, "but, anyway, if you want to talk,
my phone is …"

I wrote her number down, then added "Melissa" to the note. Hanging up
slowly, I turned toward my wife.

"It was Melissa, Carrie," I responded to her earlier question.

"Do you mean Melissa from your research?" Shae asked, as we didn't know
anyone with that name in our social circles. I nodded.

"Yes, that Melissa."

"Wow. How long has it been?"

"We first talked a decade ago, and that school shooting was about twelve
years ago."

"How's she doing?"

"Not sure from her message. But I can guess she'd not doing well. Her
words say that she's getting by and a lot has changed, but the sigh I heard told
me she's had a rough time." I sighed.

"I can only imagine. I'm not sure how anyone could cope with what she
went through," Carrie responded.

"Even after doing my study, I feel that way. Coping is rough, no matter
what you've been through in your life."

"So, are you going to call her back?" Carrie asked.

"Oh, yes. Let me get to my computer and pull up some notes. I want to
re-focus and be able to ask some direct, but sensitive, questions."

"Yes, be sensitive … as I know you will."

"I'll probably mostly just listen. Oh, and be supportive …"

I walked into my office, sat down and pulled up my school shooting
research file. After looking it over, I pulled out Melissa's number and dialed
the phone. I tapped a pen on my desk as the phone rang. It seemed to ring for
a long time. Just as I was about to hang up, I heard a familiar voice.

"Hello?"

"Hello … Melissa?" I responded.

"Yes. Is that you? Ed? Or do you still prefer 'Edward?'" The tone of her voice went up.

"Yes! You remember me! And Edward or Ed is fine." I smiled.

"How could I forget? You listened to my whole story! And that was a brutal time of my life . . ."

"I know. And I haven't forgotten, either."

"I can tell. It was strange to get a call from my old friend Janice. We talked for over an hour. Then she gave me your number and email address."

"I'm glad you were able to re-connect with Janice. She seems like a good friend. She was really interested in my research, and about the effects of witnessing a school shooting."

"She mentioned that. Janice said after you two last spoke she went online and downloaded your dissertation. She now sounds like an expert!" I could hear the smile across the phone line. It was in the tone of her voice.

"I hope you two are back together again. For her to listen to everything about the study, she must really care about you," I answered.

"She does. It was her phone call that made me see that our friendship is still there. We're planning on having lunch together, when I get back there."

"Didn't she live like only a block or two away from you? Does that mean you moved?" I asked.

"Yeah. That changed, too."

" 'Too?' It sounds like you've been through a few changes."

"I'll say. How much time do you have?" She asked.

"Don't worry about that. Fill me in. I have time for you."

"Where do I begin?" Melissa asked.

"Well, you moved. Tell me about that."

"Yeah, I'm now about forty miles away. That happened kind of suddenly."

"Something happened with your house?"

"Well, no. My marriage." There was a pause. Melissa's voice grew quieter.

"Oh, no. Are you two apart?"

"Yeah. Divorced."

"Oh, Melissa. I know how much he meant to you . . ." I didn't know what to say. I had spent a few hours sitting with Melissa and her husband, and I sort of got to know him, too.

"Yeah. And the kicker is that he has the kids. Full custody." Another silence filled the line.

"Oh . . ." It seemed like all I could say was, "oh."

"I don't know what happened after we worked together on your project. One thing led to another. The police got involved. Arrests. Nasty hearings in a courtroom. Now . . ." The silence returned.

"Now?"

"I can only see my kids under certain conditions. We can't seem to work these things out."

"Oh . . . oh . . . I know how much your little ones mean to you . . ." I struggled to find words.

"Do you realize that you say, 'oh,' a lot?" I heard a chuckle. I smiled, gently. It was the same sort of gentle teasing I remembered from years before.

"I guess I do. Maybe it's because I'm not sure what to say. I feel bad . . ."

"No reason for you to feel bad, Ed. You've always been there to listen. That means a lot to me. You told my story. Maybe it can help someone else."

"I remember you telling me that was why you wanted to participate. If we could turn this pain into a positive to help someone else, then we've salvaged something." I replied.

"Exactly. I want to find some sort of good come from this . . . even if it's not much."

"I think it will do a lot of good, Melissa. It will help someone, somewhere."

"Thanks . . ." The silence returned.

"So, tell me. Are you teaching again?"

"Oh, no. I can't. There's no way I can be in a classroom again. It' just too hard. I miss the kids like crazy, but I, well, I just can't."

"I understand . . ."

"I've been taking whatever odd jobs I can get. Now I have something steady, for the first time, over the last year or two."

"What are you doing?"

"I work in a warehouse, moving boxes, basically."

"That's different . . ."

"I actually like it. Things move quickly, and I think using my muscles, you know, burning energy, helps a lot. The pay's not bad, either."

"Well, that's good!"

"I have a boyfriend now, too. And he's patient with me. A kind man."

"That's good, too . . ."

"And some new friends, who weren't around when, well, you know, that happened."

"All positive . . ."

"Talking to Janice the other day gave me a smile. So, in a way, you helped me!"

"A side-benefit, I suppose!" I smiled again. There was, once more, an uncomfortable silence.

"I miss seeing my kids," Melissa said in a whisper.

"I can imagine. Are you still working on that?"

"Yeah, but progress is slow. My counselor is helping a lot."

"Glad to hear you're still talking about these things to a counselor.'

"It's the same one I had back then. I get a long-term value pack discount on the pricing!" Melissa teased. She was like her old self. She always liked to inject teasing, or an aside, when things got a bit tense.

"That helps, I'm sure!"

"Yeah ..." Again, uncomfortable silence filled the air.

"So, did you want to ask about anything else?" Melissa asked.

"I think you answered a lot of what I wanted to know about. I had two things in mind for our talk. One was to just catch up and see how you're doing, and another was to see if we could get together again – and I could do another interview."

"What do you mean?"

"From my research, the effects of witnessing a school shooting don't just disappear a few months later . . ."

"You aren't kidding! Tell me about it!" Melissa interrupted.

"Oh, yeah! But now that it has been over a decade, I'd like to ask you the same types of questions just to gauge how things have changed for you since then. Sort of a follow-up study. We sort of did a measure of things a couple of years after the incident. I wonder how you'd answer those questions now . . ."

"I never thought about that. That would be interesting. Sure, ask the questions!" Melissa replied.

"Oh, now would not be good. I was thinking of setting up a meeting, and doing it close to how we chatted back then. Similar conditions. It wouldn't work as well over the phone, right now."

"I understand. Sure, we can set up a meeting like we did years ago. How soon do you want to do it?"

"I was thinking of doing it while I'm traveling to see my grandchildren in Southern California. We really need to get down there and see them, especially one of our grandsons," I responded.

"In Southern California? Did you move?"

"Yes, I guess I didn't tell you. We moved to Colorado three years ago."

"But your phone number . . . the area code?" Melissa asked.

"I kept my cell number, from where I used to live. I've kept the same number for a couple of decades now."

"Okay, now it makes sense. So, why do you need to see your grandson? Do you mind if I ask?"

"I don't mind. Sadly, it's for a reason you are too familiar with."

"Oh, no . . ."

"Our grandson, Adam, was at Saugus High School last November . . ." I started.

"Oh, my God! There was a school shooting there! I remember it!"

"Right . . .." I started.

"Was he . . . oh, my . . . no . . ."

"No, he wasn't hurt, but it has been hard on him, and on everyone at the school. We worry about his mother, our daughter, too. Been hard on her."

"Believe me, I understand," Melissa responded.

"If anyone can understand, you can."

"Every time I read or hear about a school shooting, I get angry."

"I can imagine why!"

"I just feel for those people who had to be there. For the kids, the teachers, everyone."

"How about you?"

"Me?"

"How does it make you feel? Does it bring some pain back?"

"It's not as raw as it used to be, but, yeah, it brings back some tough emotions. The anger comes from why we're not doing more to stop this insanity. Why can't we get to the bottom of it and figure this out?"

"Excellent question, Melissa. Sometimes I wonder, if when a shooting disappears from the news, we'd rather forget about it rather than dig in and find solutions. Searching for solutions would bring up a lot of pain. A guess."

"More pain than what those people in Saugus will have to live with for the rest of their lives?" Melissa asked.

"Oh, no," I replied in a quiet voice.

"No . . ."

"Melissa, I have another question."

"Okay, what?"

"What would you tell the people of Saugus High School, if you had a chance? You know, from your own experiences?"

"Oh, wow, that's a tall order . . ."

"I can imagine. Just give it a shot . . ."

"I'd tell them to support the people who were there. Don't blame them – they didn't do anything but react. Don't argue about how they feel – whatever they feel is real. Give them chances to express how they feel. Give them space to heal."

"Good words."

"That brought something to mind – do you remember how I asked you to go with me to visit the shooter from my school, in prison?"

"Oh, yes. We dropped that ball, it seems."

"Along with a lot of other things. My life sort of fell apart. I had to push that aside."

"I can see why now. You were just getting by yourself . . . just trying to make it from day to day," I responded. There was quiet on the line for a moment.

"Yeah," Melissa replied. An uncomfortable silence filled the air.

"Yeah . . ." I just repeated her word.

"Hey, didn't you use another teacher in your study? Mark or something?"

"Michael, yes. I focused on you and him, but I did talk to others. Why?"

"How has he been doing?" Melissa asked.

"He walked a different path from you. He was able to retire, as he had planned. He did have some family issues, but he has been able to work through them."

"Why did we have such different results? I know, I should read your paper . . ."

"That's okay. Yeah, I discussed that in my chapter five. It's more like a formula, not a one-switch type of situation. It involved your background, his background, and how the community dealt with the shooting, among other things."

"The community?" Melissa asked.

"Yeah. I noticed you got very little support from your district. They wouldn't make changes, or help you psychologically. One thing that has stayed with me through the years is how they cleaned the carpet in the classroom but wouldn't replace it, or move you to another room . . ."

"Among other things . . ." Melissa interjected.

"Right. But Michael's school district and community labeled him as a hero, and sent people over to check on him. They gave him time off when he needed. He even told me the superintendent would come over to his school, get a sub for an hour, and just take a walk with Michael. He felt cared about."

"Yeah, that was a big difference . . ." Melissa sighed.

"I wish you could have been cared for at that moment . . ."

"I wonder how different things would have been if my school, my district, you know, all of those people, had just seen me as being someone who got hurt, like in a car accident or some other terrible event."

"I agree. Like a veteran returning from a war. It's not so different. In a way, you were treated like how I saw Vietnam veterans treated after that war. Sad how they were blamed. Thankfully, we see them differently now, for the most part."

"So, it's the same kind of psychology?"

"Absolutely. Part of what you're dealing with is post-traumatic stress disorder . . ."

"That's what my counselor tells me . . ." Melissa added.

"He's right. If there is one thing that I want people to walk away with after reading my study, it's the idea that people who witness school shootings are not much different from war veterans. We need to care for school shooting survivors, too."

"Thank you for putting that out there . . ."

"I wish I could do more," I said softly.

"What else could you do?" Melissa asked.

"One of the teachers who witnessed a school shooting that I interviewed, and I talked to more than a dozen, used the phrase 'echoes of gunfire' coming down the hallway, and that he said he sometimes could still hear it."

"I understand that."

"I wish I could take away the 'echoes of gunfire' from the ears of each of you . . ." A long pause followed.

"Me, too . . ."

"Melissa?" I asked.

"Yeah?"

"I know it may not mean much, but I care. I know what you've gone through is a lot for one person."

"It does mean something. More than you know. It makes me a little less alone. Thank you."

"Alone. That is the hardest way to go through trauma, so, if I helped a little there, then all of this was worth it."

"You did. And you're still helping. We'll do another interview!"

"Yes! And I'll be calling back soon to set that up." I felt myself smiling a bit. Just hearing her say my study helped made it all worthwhile.

"But I have one request." I heard Melissa chuckle a bit.

"Okay, what is it?"

"Do you remember one of the interviews, the one where we had pie?"

"Oh, yes I do. Hard for me to forget pie.

"And . . .?" Melissa stopped.

"Huh? Oh, wait – I remember. You ordered two pieces of pie – one from two different types of pie!"

"That's right! That's the favor! Two pieces of pie!"

"You got it!" I smiled.

"Ed?"

"Yeah, Melissa?"

"Thanks for caring. That's the best medicine for someone like me."

The End

SUGGESTED READING

Agaibi, C., & Wilson, J. (2005, July). Trauma, PTSD, and resilience: A review of the literature. *Trauma Violence Abuse, 6,* 195–216. doi:10.1177/1524838005277438

Alinsky, S. (1971). *Rules for radicals: A pragmatic primer for realistic radicals.* New York: Random House.

Andrews, M., Squire, C., & Tamboukou, M. (Eds.) (2009). *Doing narrative research in the social sciences.* London: Sage.

Ardis, C. (2004). School violence from the classroom teacher's perspective. In W. L. Turk (Ed.), *School crime and policing* (pp. 131–150). Upper Saddle River, NJ: Pearson Education.

Beach City (CA) - Demographics. (2010). Retrieved from http://www.city-data.com/

Bekhtin, M. (1981). *The dialogic imagination: Four essays. (C. Emerson, M. Holquist, Translators).* Austin: University of Texas Press.

Belmont Report. (1979). *The Belmont Report: Ethical principles and guidelines for the protection of human subjects of research.* Retrieved from hhs.gov/ohrp/humansubjects/guidance/belmont.html

Berger, J. (1972). *Ways of seeing.* London: Penguin Books.

Blasé, J., & Blasé, J. (2001). *Empowering teachers: What successful principals do* (2nd ed.). Thousand Oaks, CA: Corwin Press.

Boje, D. M. (2001). *Narrative methods for organizational and communication research.* London: Sage.

Borum, R., Cornell, D., Modzeleski, W., & Jimerson, S. (2010). What can be done about school Shootings? A review of the evidence. *Educational Researcher, 39*(1), 27–37. doi:10.3102/0013189X09357620

Boydston, J. (Ed.) (1991). *The collected works of John Dewey*. Carbondale, IL: Southern Illinois University Press.

Burke, K. (1952). *Rhetoric of motives*. New York: Prentice Hall.

Burke, W. W. (2010). *Organization change: Theory and practice* (3rd ed.). Thousand Oaks, CA: Sage.

Butin, D. (2010). *The education dissertation: A guide for practitioner scholars*. Thousand Oaks, CA: Corwin.

Chase, S. E. (2005). Narrative inquiry: Multiple lenses, approaches, voices. In N. K. Denzin & Y. S. Lincoln (Eds.), *Handbook of qualitative research* (pp. 651–679). Thousand Oaks: Sage Publications.

Coffey, A., & Atkinson, P. (1996). *Making sense of qualitative data analysis: Complementary strategies*. Thousand Oaks CA: Sage Publications.

Coles, R. (1967). *Children of crisis*. Boston: Little, Brown.

Coles, R. (2000). *Lives of moral leadership*. New York: Random House.

Creswell, J. (2012). *Qualitative inquiry and research design: Choosing among the five approaches* (3rd ed.). Thousand Oaks, CA: Sage Publications.

Daniels, J. A., & Bradley, M. C. (2011). *Preventing lethal school violence, advancing responsible adolescent development*. New York: Springer.

Daniels, J., Bradley, M., & Hays, M. (2007, December). The impact of school violence on school personnel: Implications for psychologists. *Professional Psychology: Research and Practice, 38*(6), 652–659.

Devereux, G. (1967). *From anxiety to method in behavioral sciences*. The Hague: The Netherlands Mouton.

Dr. Martin Luther King Quotes. (2012). Retrieved from http://www.drmartinlutherking.net/martin-luther-king-quotes.php

Dye, J., Schatz, I., Rosenberg, B., & Coleman, S. (2000, January). Constant comparison method: A kaleidoscope of data. *The Qualitative Report, 4*(1). Retrieved from http://www.nova.edu/ssss/QR/QR3-4/dye.html

Elliot, D., Hamburg, B., & Williams, K. (1998). *Violence in American schools: A new perspective*. Cambridge: Cambridge University Press.

Fox, S., & Stallworth, L. (2010, March 2). The battered apple: An application of stressor-emotion-control/support theory to teachers' experience of violence and bullying. *Human Relations, 63*(927). doi:10.1177/0018726709349518

Freire, P. (2000). *The pedagogy of the oppressed*. New York: Continuum International Publishing.

Glaser, B. G. (1978). *Theoretical sensitivity*. Mill Valley, CA: Sociology Press.

Goffman, E. (1969). *The presentation of self in everyday life*. New York: Penguin.

Goffman, E. (1974). *Frame analysis: An essay on the organization of experience*. Cambridge, MA: Harvard University Press.

Gold, L. H., & Simon, R. I. (2016). *Gun violence and mental illness*. Arlington, VA: American Psychiatric Association Publishing.

Hansen, D. T. (Ed.) (2007). *Ethical visions of education: Philosophies in practice*. New York City: Teachers College Press.

Harris, W. T. (1958). *Public schools and moral education: The influence of Horace Mann*. New York, NY: Columbia University Press.

Hartman, R. J. (2011). *The twelve steps to the formation of PTSD*. Retrieved from http://aaph.org/rjhartman/articles/twelve_steps_to_PTSD

Heath, S. B. (1983). *Ways with words: Language, life and work in communities and classrooms.* New York: Cambridge University Press.

Herman, D., Jahn, M., & Ryan, M. (Eds.) (2005). *Routledge encyclopedia of narrative theory.* London & New York: Routledge.

Hymes, D. (1974). *Foundations in sociolinguistics: An ethnographic approach.* Philadelphia: University of Pennsylvania Press.

Jordan, K. (2003). A trauma and recovery model for victims and their families after a catastrophic school shooting: Focusing on behavioral, cognitive, and psychological effects and needs. *Brief Treatment and Crisis Intervention, 3*(4), 397–411. https://doi.org/10.1093/brief-treatment/mhg031.

Kazdin, A. (Ed.) (2000). *Encyclopedia of psychology*. New York: Oxford University Press (USA).

Kohler-Riessman, C. (2008). *Narrative methods for the human sciences* (2nd ed.). Thousand Oaks: Sage Publications.

Kondrasuk, J. N., Greene, T., Waggoner, J., Edwards, K., & Nayak-Rhodes, A. (2005). Violence affecting school employees. *Education, 125*, 638–647.

Lama, D. (1999). *Ethics for the new millennium*. New York City: Riverhead Books.

Lauterbach, D., & Vrana, S. (2001, January). The relationship among personality variables, exposure to traumatic events, and severity of posttraumatic stress symptoms. *Journal of Traumatic Stress, 14*(1), 29–45.

Lawrence, J., & Fauerbach, J. (2003, January/February). Personality, coping, chronic stress, social support and PTSD symptoms among adult burn survivors: A path analysis. *Journal of Burn Care & Rehabilitation, 24*(1), 63–72.

Maginnis, R. L. (2000). *Violence in the schoolhouse: A ten year update*. Retrieved from http://www.frc.org/insight/ is94e5cr.html

Mann, H. (1855). *Lectures on education*. Boston: L.N. Ide.

Mills, C. W. (1959). *The sociological imagination*. New York: Oxford University Press.

Mitchell, J., & Everly, G. (2001). *Critical incident stress management: Basic group crisis interventions*. Ellicott City, MD: International Critical Incident Stress Foundation.

Newman, K., Fox, C., Roth, W., & Mehta, J. (2004). *Rampage: The social roots of school shootings*. New York, NY: Basic Books.

Primer on Critical Incident Stress Management (CISM). (1997). Retrieved from http://www.icisf.org/

Robers, S., Zhang, J., & Truman, J. (2012). *Indicators of school crime and safety: 2011* (NCES 2012-002/NCJ 236021). Washington, DC: Government Printing Office.

Roberts, A. R. (2007). *Crisis intervention handbook: Assessment, treatment and research* (2nd ed.). New York: Oxford University Press.

Saldana, J. (2009). *The coding manual for qualitative researchers*. Thousand Oaks, CA: Sage Publications.

Scollon, R., & Scollon, S. B. (1981). *Narrative, literacy, and face in interethnic communication.* Norwood, NJ: Ablex.

Seligman, M. (1972). *Helplessness: On depression, development and death.* San Francisco: Freeman and Company.

Spence, D. F. (1982). *Narrative truth and historical truth: Meaning and interpretation in psychoanalysis.* New York & London: Norton.

Steinberg, A., Brymer, M., Decker, K., & Pynoos, R. (2004). The University of California at Los Angeles post-traumatic stress disorder reaction index. *Current Psychiatry Reports, 6,* 96–100.

Strauss, A. (1987). *Qualitative analysis for social scientists.* New York, NY: Cambridge University Press.

Suter, W. (2012). *Introduction to educational research: A critical thinking approach* (2nd ed.). Thousand Oaks, CA: Sage Publications.

Szabla, D. (2006). *A multidimensional view of resistance: Exploring cognitive, emotional, and intentional responses to planned organizational change across different perceived change strategies.* (Doctoral dissertation, George Washington University).

The National Commission on Teaching and America's Future. (2002, August 20–22). Unraveling the "Teacher Shortage" problem: Teacher retention is the key. *NCTAF Symposium* (pp. 1–16). Washington, D.C.: The National Commission on Teaching and America's Future.

Van der Kolk, B. (1993). Biological considerations about emotions, trauma, memory and the brain. In S. Ablon, D. Brown, & J. Mack (Eds.), *Human feelings: Explorations in affect development and meaning.* New York: Routledge.

Watson, R. J., & Watson, R. S. (2002). *School as a safe haven.* Westport, CT: Greenwood Press.

White, H. (1981). The value of narrativity in the representation of reality. In M. J. Mitchell (Ed.), *On narrative* (pp. 1–23). Chicago: University of Chicago Press.

INDEX

www.ingramcontent.com/pod-product-compliance
Lightning Source LLC
Chambersburg PA
CBHW050415280326
41932CB00013BA/1864